IMAGES
of America

AROUND SOUTHWICK

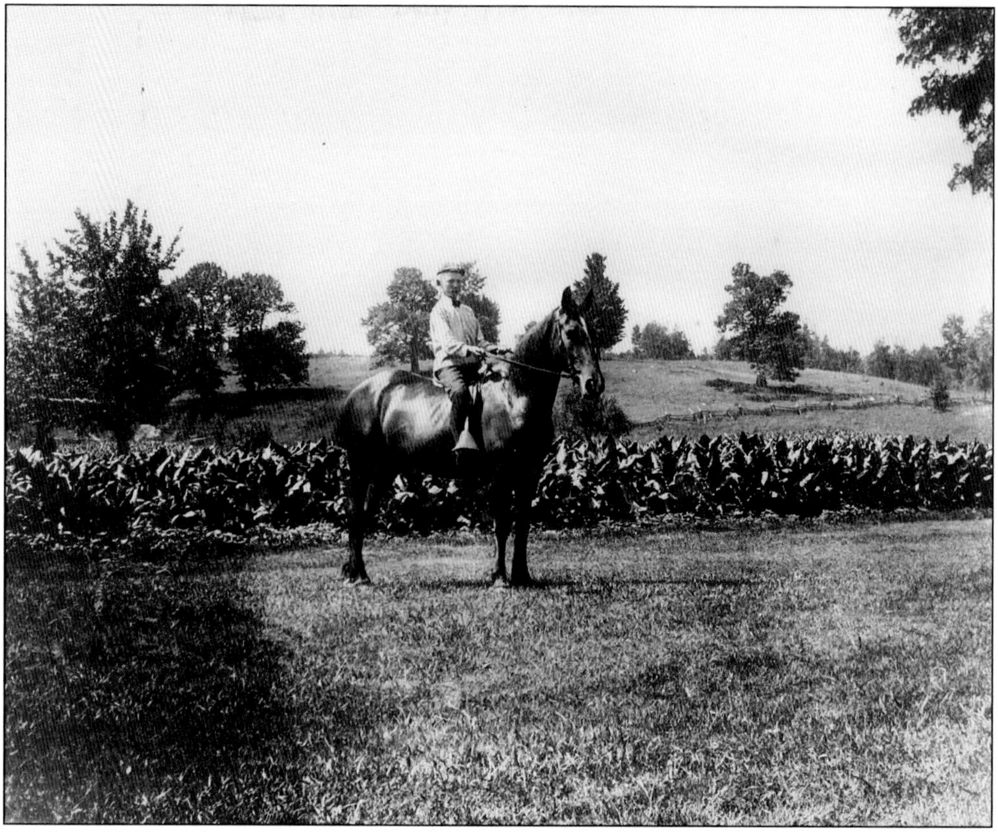

Southwick's First Paper Boy. The second son of Harry and Nellie (Tupper), Harold Hudson, astride his horse "Daisy," delivered newspapers in Southwick between 1904 and 1908. The Hudson family lived at 217 Sheep Pasture Road, where the Robert Davis family now resides. The Davises call the farm "Blossoming Acres."

IMAGES
of America

AROUND SOUTHWICK

The Southwick Historical Society, Inc.

ARCADIA
PUBLISHING

ISBN 978-0-7385-6424-1

Published by Arcadia Publishing
Charleston, South Carolina

Printed in the United States of America

Library of Congress Control Number: 2009921949

For all general information contact Arcadia Publishing at:
Telephone 843-853-2070
Fax 843-853-0044
E-mail sales@arcadiapublishing.com
For customer service and orders:
Toll-Free 1-888-313-2665

Visit us on the Internet at www.arcadiapublishing.com

Dedicated to Lee David Hamberg
for his vision, skills,
and his thousands of hours of labor
utilized in preserving the 1751 Moore House
and other aspects of Southwick history

Front Cover: Ice House Workers in Summer. Workers who had harvested ice during the winter months were also needed in the summer months to transfer the ice blocks from the five large ice houses to waiting railroad cars.

Contents

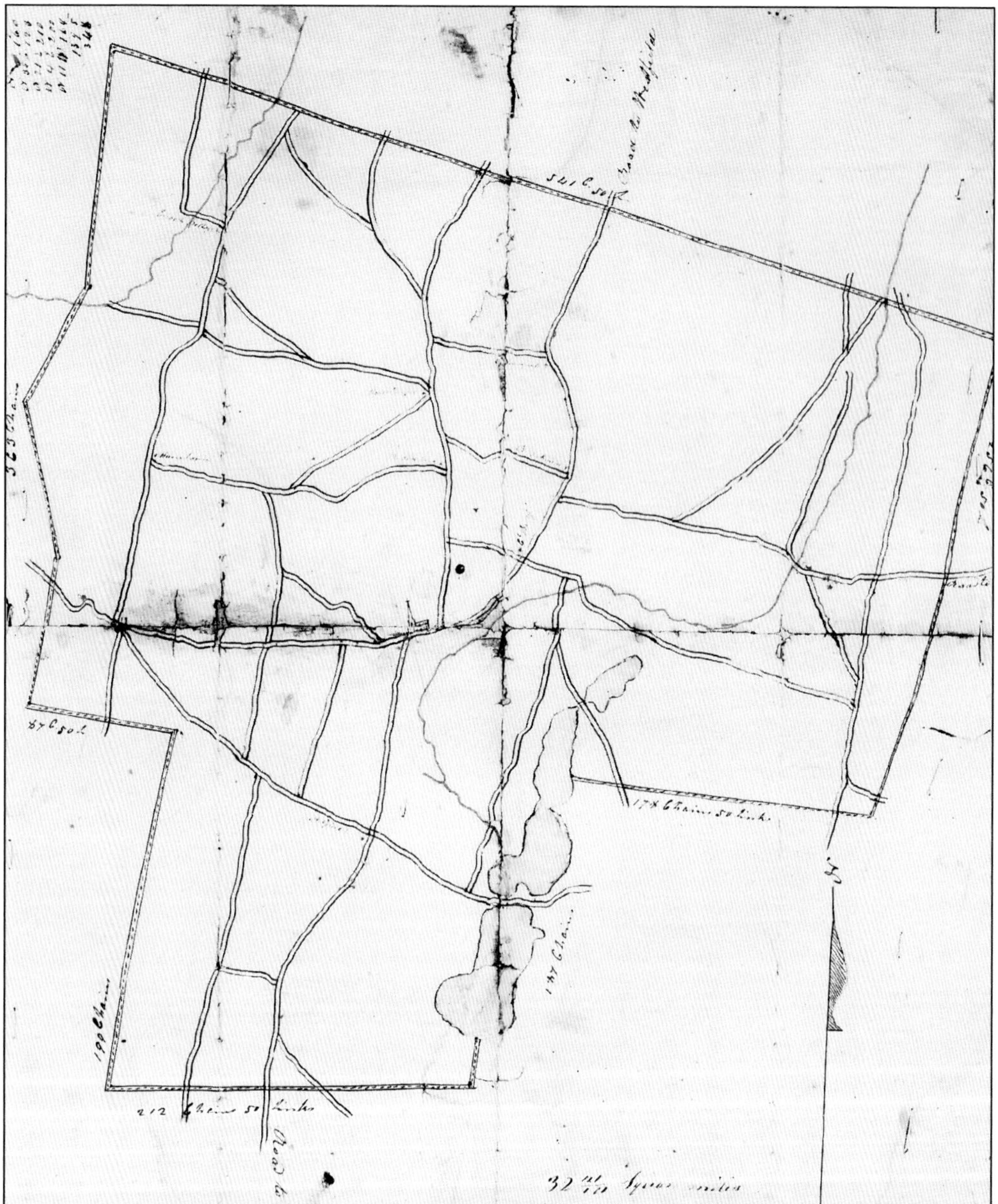

A pre-1823 Map of Southwick. Because it shows the Congregational Meeting House which burned in August 1823, this earliest map of Southwick can be dated. Notice the three main north-south arteries of modern-day Southwick: Loomis Street on the left, College Highway in the center (the "Road to Westfield" and the "Road to Simsbury"), and Longyard Road on the right. A close examination shows how Sheep Pasture Road got its name; the sheep could be enclosed in a large pasture bounded by the western shores of Middle and North Lakes and the banks of Great Brook. The short distance between North Pond and the brook was fenced. During the 1955 flood, North Pond flowed over its banks and into Great Brook at that spot, destroying the Bernard Drummond house and the old canal lockhouse owned by Frank and Rose (Amard) Jarry.

Introduction

The old adage "Times change" is just as true in the Town of Southwick, Massachusetts, as in any other small community in the United States. Who could have predicted that the demand for ice to keep food in "iceboxes" cold, which caused the building of five large ice houses on the western shores of the Congamond Lakes, would disappear when electric refrigerators became widely available? If someone asked Henry R. Barnes, a Southwick wagon and carriage manufacturer, how his business was in 1890, he would have replied "Great!" Yet, within a few decades, his business was finished, and a new shop, called a "garage," which serviced automobiles, was located on the site where his factory had been. Southwick's peak of population in the nineteenth century was in 1830, when 1,355 people were counted by the census taker. In 1840, out of 379 people whose occupations were listed, 352 were in agriculture. Even as recently as 1900, more than two-thirds of Southwick's population of about 1,100 described themselves as farmers or farm laborers. In 1850, almost every farm household had at least one horse, several "milch" cows, a pair of working oxen, and swine. Many also had sheep and other cattle. Farms produced large quantities of butter and some cheese, beeswax, honey, and "orchard products." A majority planted buckwheat, rye, Irish potatoes, Indian corn, and oats; a few raised tobacco or wheat. Farm acreages were usually no less than 30 with several over 300.

Try to imagine the feelings of a second-grader who had been attending, with his brothers and sisters, the one-room schoolhouse in the neighborhood, being told that on a certain Monday in May 1929, his school would close and he would be attending the big school, the Southwick Consolidated School. His family and most of his other former schoolmates would not be in the same room with him in the new school. Ten of the eleven buildings closed on May 10, 1929, the largest consolidation of schools in the Commonwealth of Massachusetts to that date. Schools named for the roads they were on, Hillside, Vining Hill, Congamond, Point Grove, North Longyard, and South Longyard, closed. Schools near College Highway, Poverty (north), Center, and Mooretown (south) closed, along with the Loomis Street school on North Loomis and the Root District school on what is now Klaus Anderson Road. Eldon Johnson recalled his experience on that day. Because he was attending Center Primary School, he and his schoolmates went to the old school on that Monday, cleaned out their desks, and marched carrying their papers, books, and pencils the short distance to the "new school." Thus, the eleventh school closed on May 13. (The Dickinson Grammar School also closed.)

From Southwick's settlement in 1732 as the south village or "wick" of Westfield, throughout all of that century and most of the nineteenth, there are no photographs to document the lives of the people of this town. The early inhabitants, with surnames like Campbell, Forward, Fowler, Gillett, Granger, Holcomb, Kellogg, Kent, Laflin, Loomis, Moore, Noble, Palmer, Rising, Root, and Stiles, created the institutions and ways of life here and then moved on. Although very few of those names appear in our current street directories, their influence lives on.

In the past one hundred years, many immigrant families from England, France, Italy, Ireland, Russia, Poland, Bohemia, Sweden, Canada, Germany, Hungary, Austria, Denmark, Finland, and Slovakia have come to Southwick and settled here. The decennial censuses from 1790 through 1910, which the Southwick Historical Society, Inc., has published, also show that Southwick has from the early days been a racially mixed population. Mr. "Ocro (Negro)" and his family lived here in 1790, and several black people appeared in each census through 1900. In 1910, there were no persons listed as black but twenty-nine people were listed as mulatto, including the Phillips, Leonesio, Williams, Smith, and Pierce families.

Now for a few details. In all group photographs, names are listed from left to right, moving from the back row to the front, unless numbers have been assigned to each person. We apologize for any misspelling of names; many were copied from captions which came to us with the original photographs. All the dwellings we have included are more than one hundred years old; the current owner or occupant is listed as a thank-you for enduring such things as odd-sized windows and drafts while living in these historic buildings. Because the purpose of the Images of America series is to preserve and share images of a bygone era, our focus has been on the Southwick which existed before World War II. Two exceptions were made, however. After an October 1942 photograph of the fifth grade class of the Southwick Consolidated School was published in the August 1996 issue of *Southwoods, A Journal For Country Living*, a booklet of photographs of all the classes at the school, taken on that same day, was offered to us by Philip Mason, whose photograph appeared in the published article. Although attempting to match a name to each face entailed many hours of work, the opportunity to share this portrait of the entire grammar school population of Southwick was well worth the effort. In order to include all places of worship connected directly with Southwick, the second exception was made in the case of the two newer churches, the Our Lady of the Lake Church and the Christ Lutheran Church.

It is by the *written* word, passed from one person to another, that civilization has progressed. Southwick is very fortunate that a native, Maud Etta Gillett Davis, took the time and effort to gather information about Southwick's history to 1950 and produce a book. It is our fervent hope that some other native will continue the written story of Southwick for the five decades since then, for the events of today are tomorrow's "history."

Since the invention of the camera in the nineteenth century, people have been given another tool for recording history. Images of places and people long buried in our memories can evoke intense emotion. We hope that the images of Southwick's past which we have been able to obtain and share will give you pleasure.

The Southwick Historical Society, Inc.
Southwick, Massachusetts
October 1996

Chapter One

The Town Center

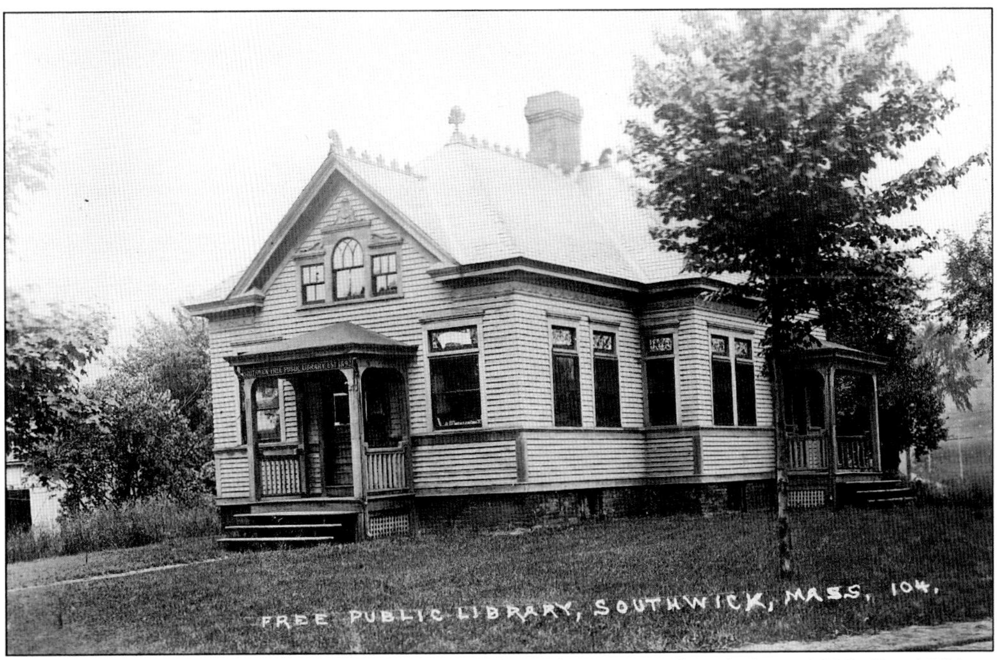

The Southwick Library. The Southwick Public Library was founded in 1892. By 1894, a building to house its growing collection had been built, complete with stained-glass windows and decorative touches, at the southwest corner of Granville Road and College Highway. More than one hundred years later, this library building is still being used, pending completion of a new library at the southeast corner of Feeding Hills Road and Rebecca Lobo Way.

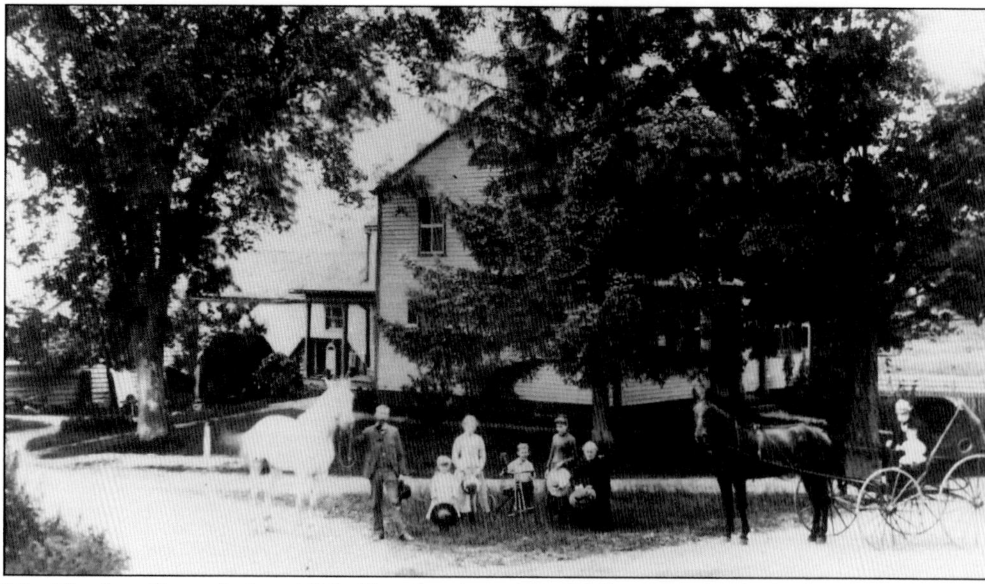

The Fletcher House before 1893. Shortly after 1821, William Fowler built this dwelling at 17 Depot Street. Elizabeth (Mills) Rockwell, the wife of Dr. Joseph Rockwell, inherited the home from her uncle William. The Rockwell family lived in the house for at least forty years, from 1854 to 1894. Shown are William Fletcher; his daughter Grace; Flora Hosmer; William's son William Jr.; William (Sr.)'s wife, Ada (Mills) Fletcher; Ada's aunt, Elizabeth (Mills) Rockwell; Dr. Joseph Rockwell in the carriage holding William and Ada's second son Raymond. (Patricia Beavis, 1995).

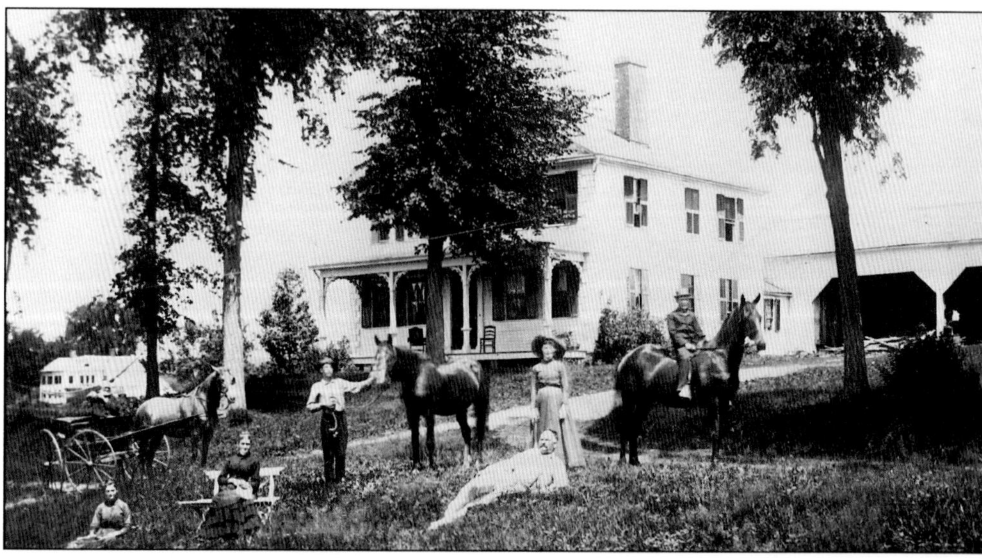

The William Phelps House before August 1893. The family of William W. and Jane (Boyle) Phelps pose in front of their home at 20 Depot Street. Jane is seated on the bench, William is reclining, and their children—Mary, George, Frances, and Charles—are seen left to right. The man in the buggy may be John Boyle, Jane's father. Notice the "Field House" in the left background behind the buggy and the hammock. Mary later married Calvin West; Frances later became Mrs. John Struthers. The owners in 1854 and 1870 were Heman Laflin and Marcus Phelps. (Reginald and Julia Phelps, 1995).

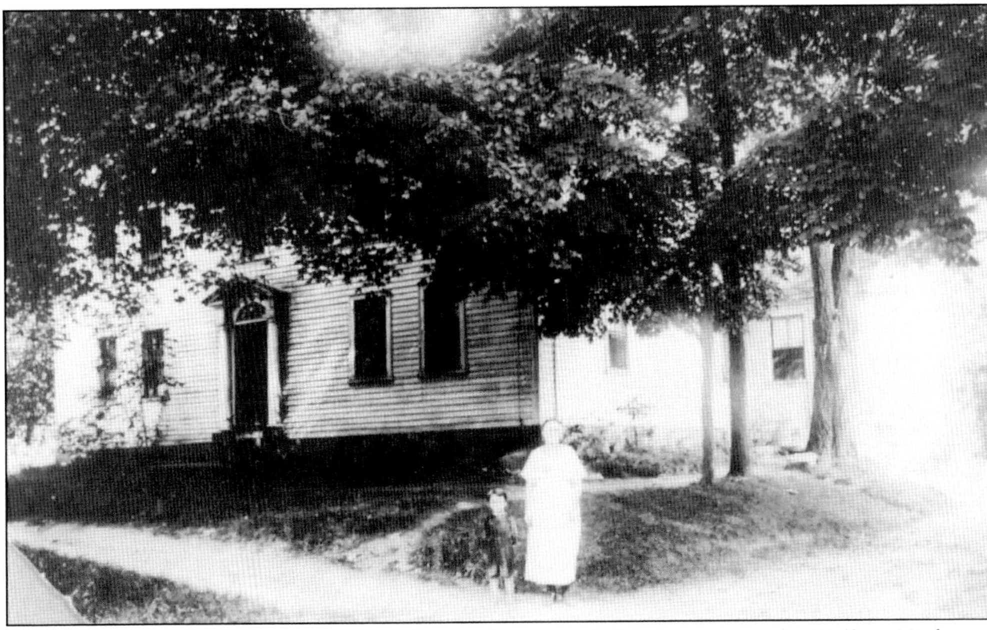

The Doane Tavern. Henry R. Barnes, who made wagons in his shop across the College Highway, owned the former Doane Tavern, which he left to his nephew, Arthur Merton Goddard. Mrs. Goddard and her five-year-old grandson, Robert Lee Silvernail, are shown here in August 1925. Notice the unusual doorway. Robert was killed in action during World War II.

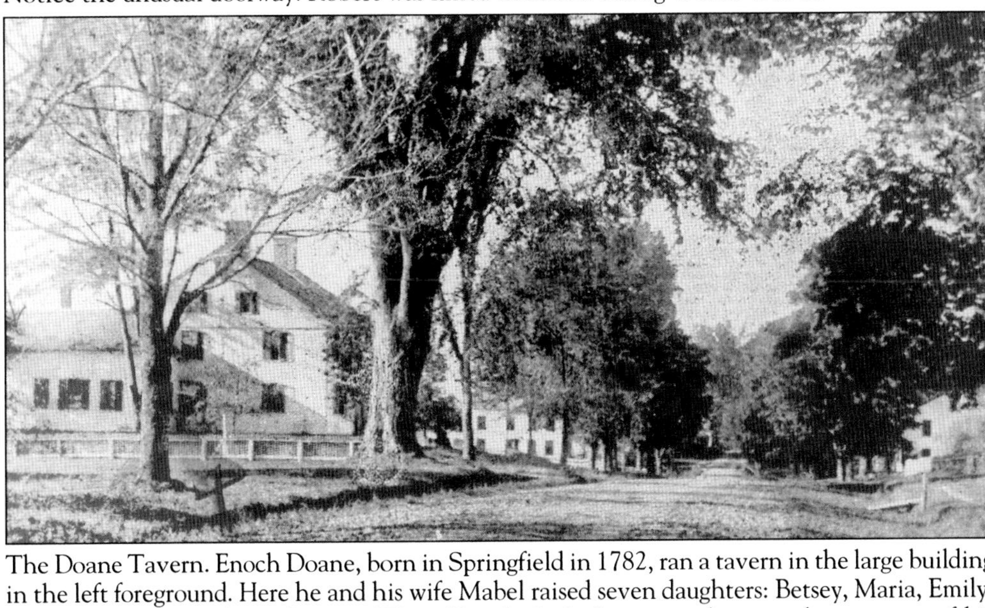

The Doane Tavern. Enoch Doane, born in Springfield in 1782, ran a tavern in the large building in the left foreground. Here he and his wife Mabel raised seven daughters: Betsey, Maria, Emily, Mabel, Julia, Amanda, and Mary. When Enoch died, the tavern became the property of his daughter Mabel and her husband, Theron Rockwell. The dwelling was taken down and rebuilt in Washington, Connecticut, before 1928, when the Southwick Consolidated School, which stands there now, was built. The house in the left background is #448 College Highway, which is shown in closeup on p. 122. Richard G. Loomis owned #449 College Highway, to the right, in 1854; it was owned by his widow Harriet in 1870, and by Henry Barnes in 1894.

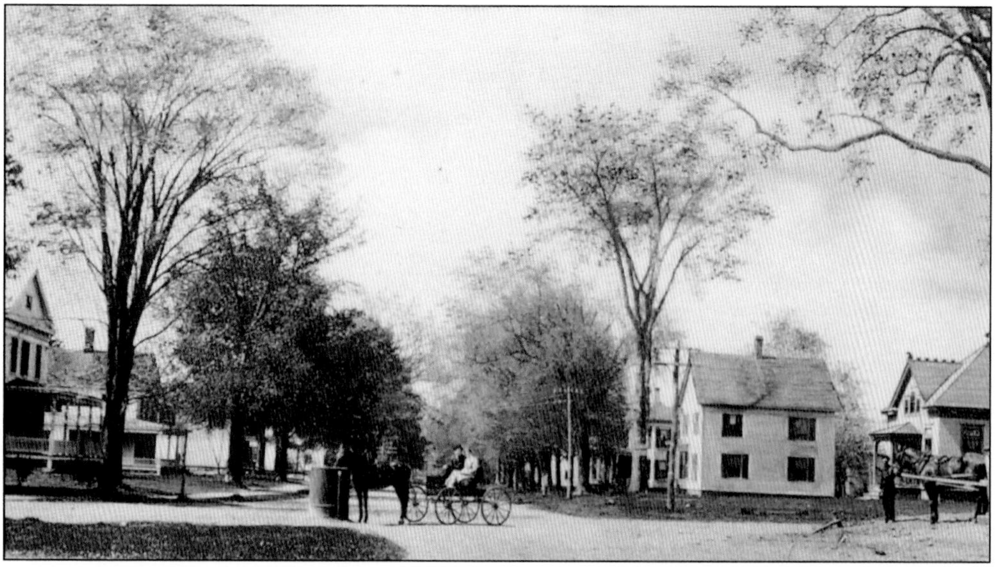

Broad Street Looking South. Gladys Reed's horse is drinking from the watering trough at the intersection of what is now College Highway and Depot Street (left), and Granville Road (right), where another horse waits its turn. The houses which later belonged to Cooley Griffin and his son Raymond are visible on the left. The Southwick Public Library, the Baptist Church parsonage, and the Edward Gillett house are visible on the right.

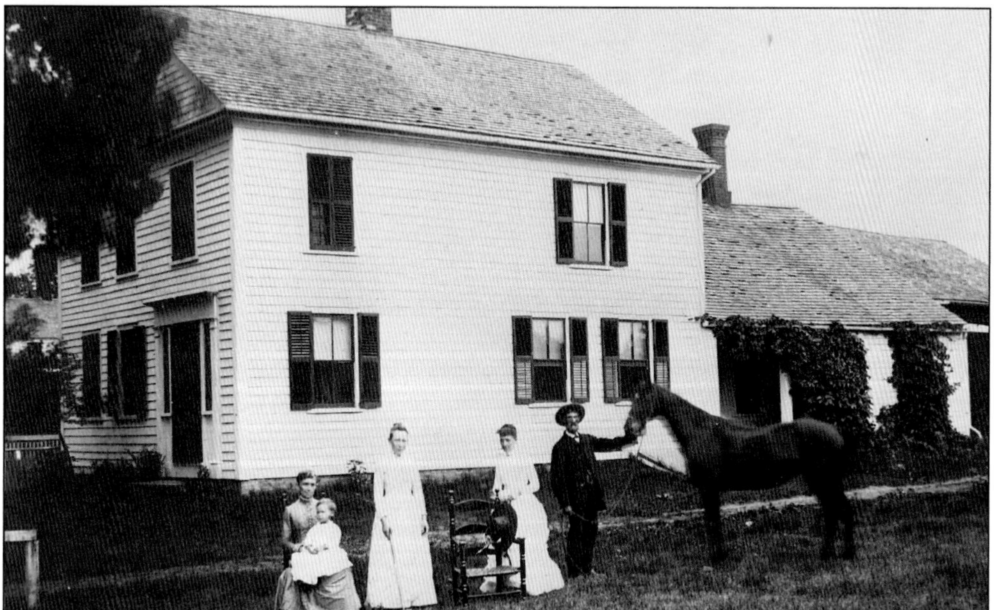

The Loomis J. Sackett House, *c.* 1895. Mr. Sackett holds his horse, while his wife Martha (nee Tupper) holds baby Clarence Hudson. Martha's sister, Nellie (nee Tupper) Hudson, Clarence's mother, is holding the croquet mallet, with Emma Eddy beside her. In the twentieth century, this home was owned by Raymond Griffin, right next door to his parents Cooley and Effie. The residence was torn down after October 1942; the site is now the parking lot for the Southwick Package Store.

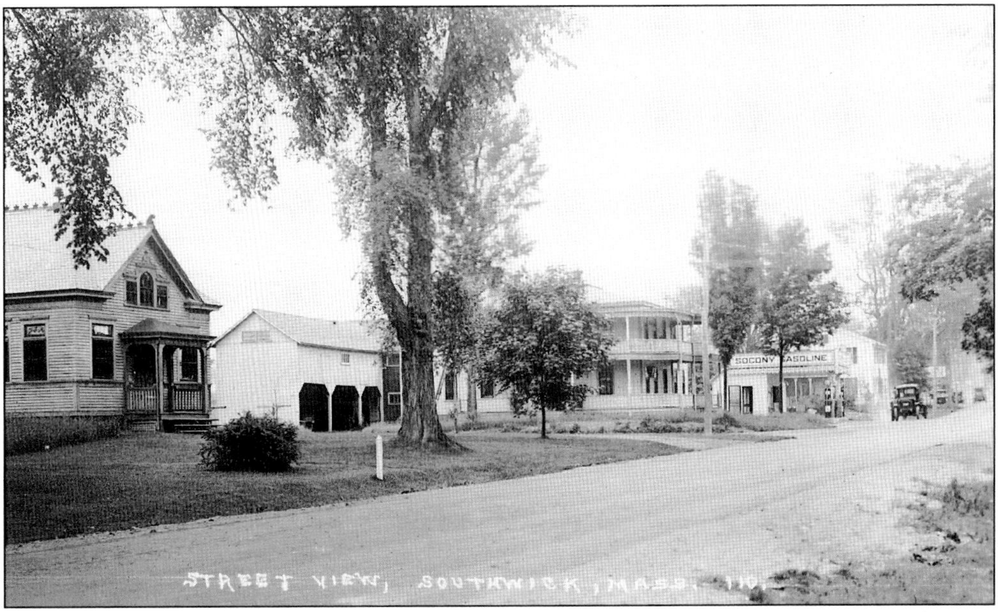

A Street View after 1905. Looking northwest on what is now College Highway, one can see the Southwick Public Library, the Southwick Hotel and its vehicle stalls, the Socony gasoline station, and the Joseph Forward home (later occupied by the Bernadara family).

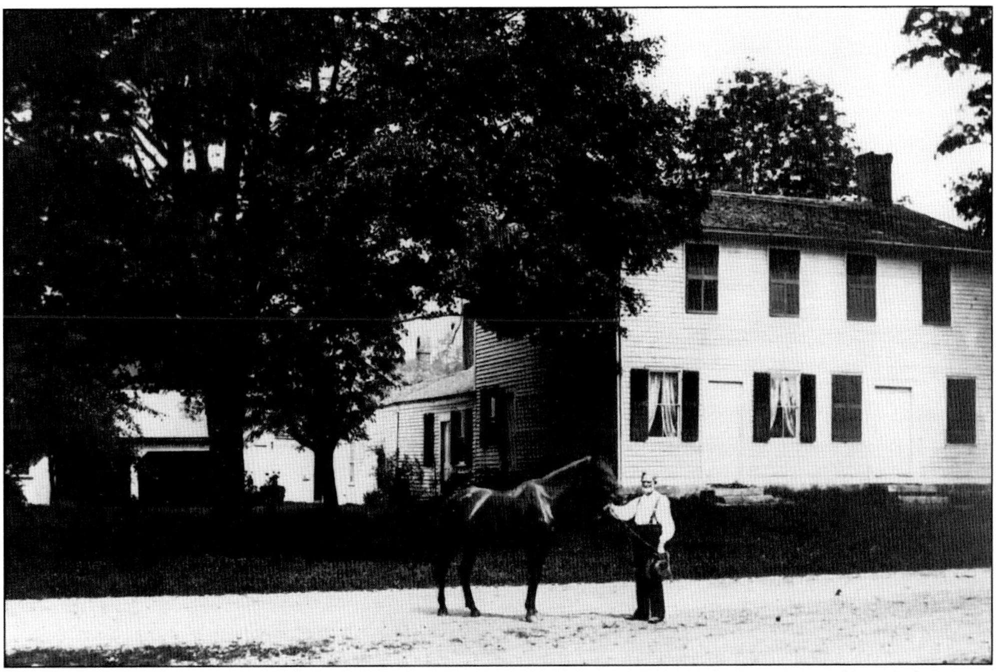

The Forward House. In about 1821, Joseph Forward, a prominent man in Southwick history, built this house. Two bachelors, Andrew Jackson Forward and Joseph Morton Forward, lived in this house for a long period. Andrew (shown here) and Joseph were the sons of Joseph and Fanny (Moore) Forward and the grandsons of Revolutionary War veteran Joseph Forward and his wife, Mary Owen. Augustino Bernadara was the last owner before the house was taken down piece by piece, stored, and later reassembled on a new site.

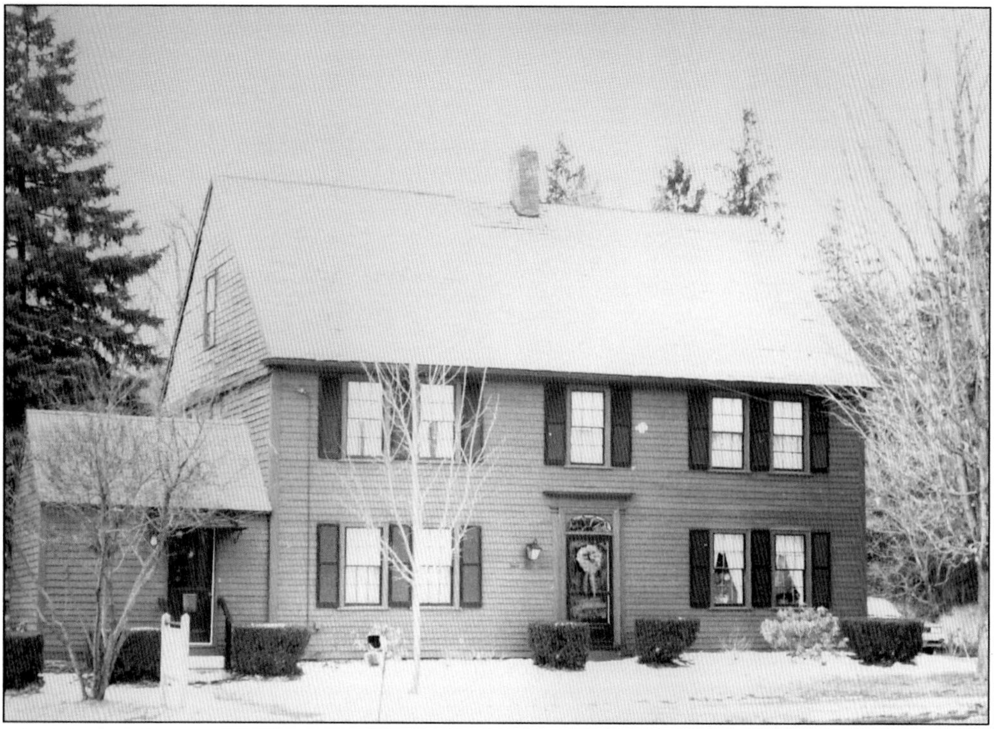

The Keenan House. Based on a title search conducted by Rose (Jarry) Keenan, this house at 457 College Highway was built by a Mr. Graves some time before 1762. In 1870 it was owned by G. Palmer; the current owner is Rose and Daniel's daughter, Attorney Mary Keenan.

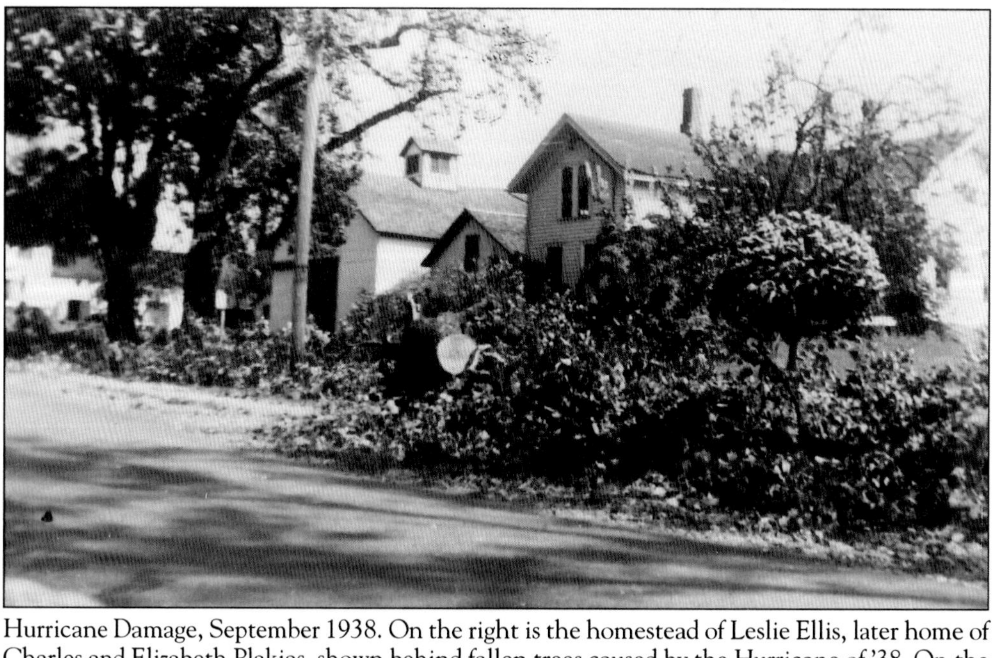

Hurricane Damage, September 1938. On the right is the homestead of Leslie Ellis, later home of Charles and Elizabeth Plakias, shown behind fallen trees caused by the Hurricane of '38. On the left is the house of Joseph and Ann Galpin, which was later owned by Howard Dewhurst. On p. 38 is a sketch of that home when John Boyle owned it.

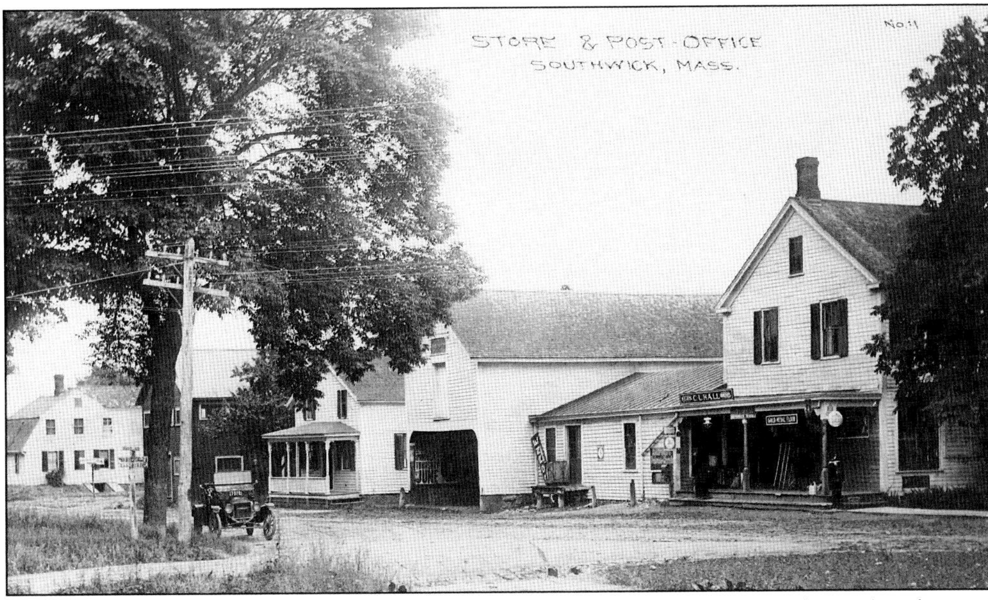

The L.C. Hall Store. In 1916, Leslie C. Hall sold "groceries, meats, general merchandise and agricultural implements" from his store on what is now the corner of Depot Street and College Highway. Charles Reed ran a store there before Mr. Hall, and Raymond Balch ran one there after Mr. Hall. Notice the LeBlanc house which burned in 1927. The house farthest to the left still stands and the neighboring barn has been moved to the back of its lot. Both are the property of Marion Cutter.

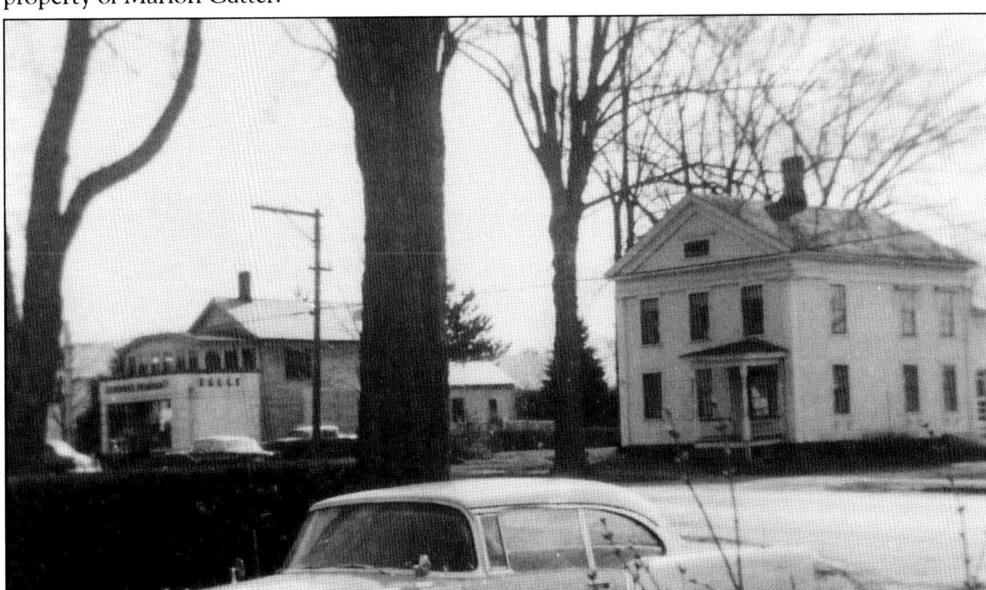

The Holcomb House, 1950s. When Westfield Savings Bank sought a site for its Southwick branch, the bank opted to locate in an existing structure, to help ensure its preservation. They chose the Holcomb House (to the right, at 462 College Highway), which was built about 1841 by Carmi Shurtleff next door to the parents of his new bride, Amanda Doane. More recently it was the home of G. Newton III and Virginia Holcomb, who operated Holcomb's Nursery here for many years. The Southwick Pharmacy building is on the left.

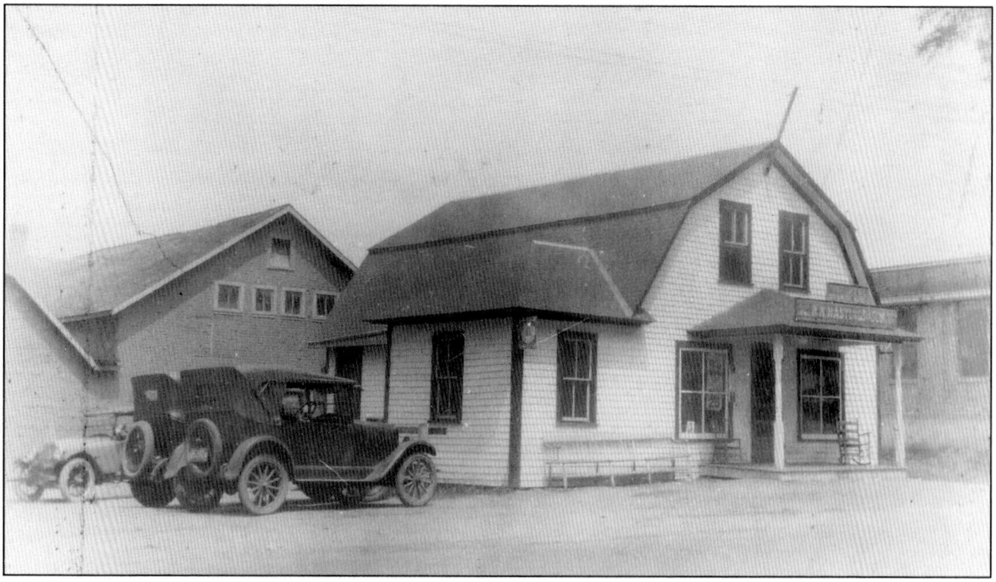

Benjamin Hastings Store, 1920s. Benjamin M. Hastings ran a grocery store, where the post office was also located, from around 1900 until his death in 1934. He was active in town affairs, particularly as a school committeeman and fire chief for many years. Notice the Johnson tobacco warehouse to the left behind the store.

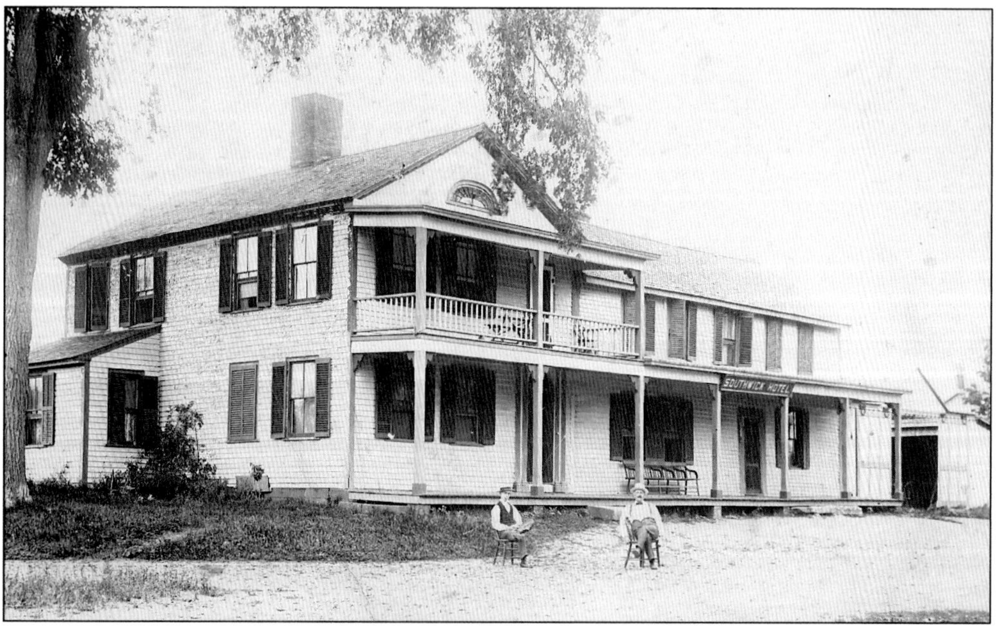

The Southwick Hotel. There has been an hostelry at this crossroad for many generations. The Southwick Hotel, in 1885, had a large wing on the right side. After the hotel burned in 1905, the Southwick Inn replaced it. The inn had porches on two sides, with small buildings situated where the hotel's wing had been.

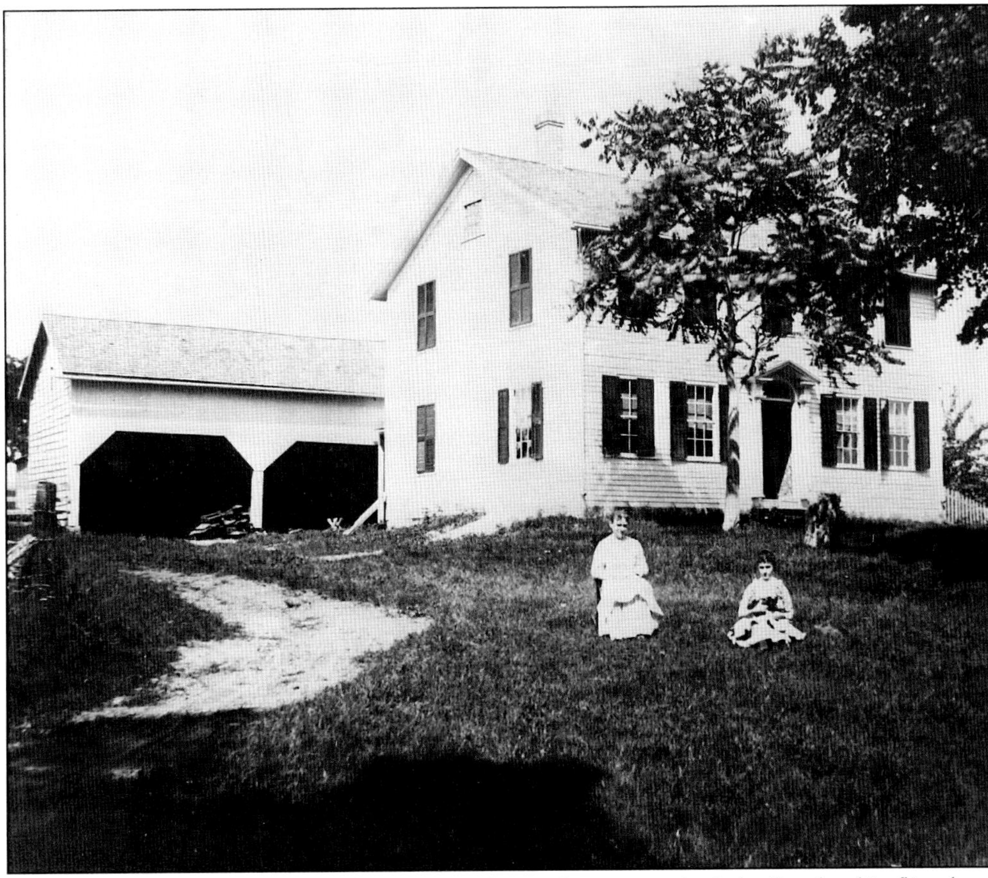

The George Phelps House. This house, at 28 Depot Street, was built by Rowland Laflin about 1820, and Rowland was the owner in 1854. Several generations of the Laflin family manufactured gunpowder along Great Brook in mills whose remains could still be seen along Powder Mill Road in 1903. Chauncey M., Rowland Laflin's son, and his wife Mary L. (nee Scantlin) lived at this location until his death in 1879. James W. Phelps, a selectman for many years, resides here with his sister Helen.

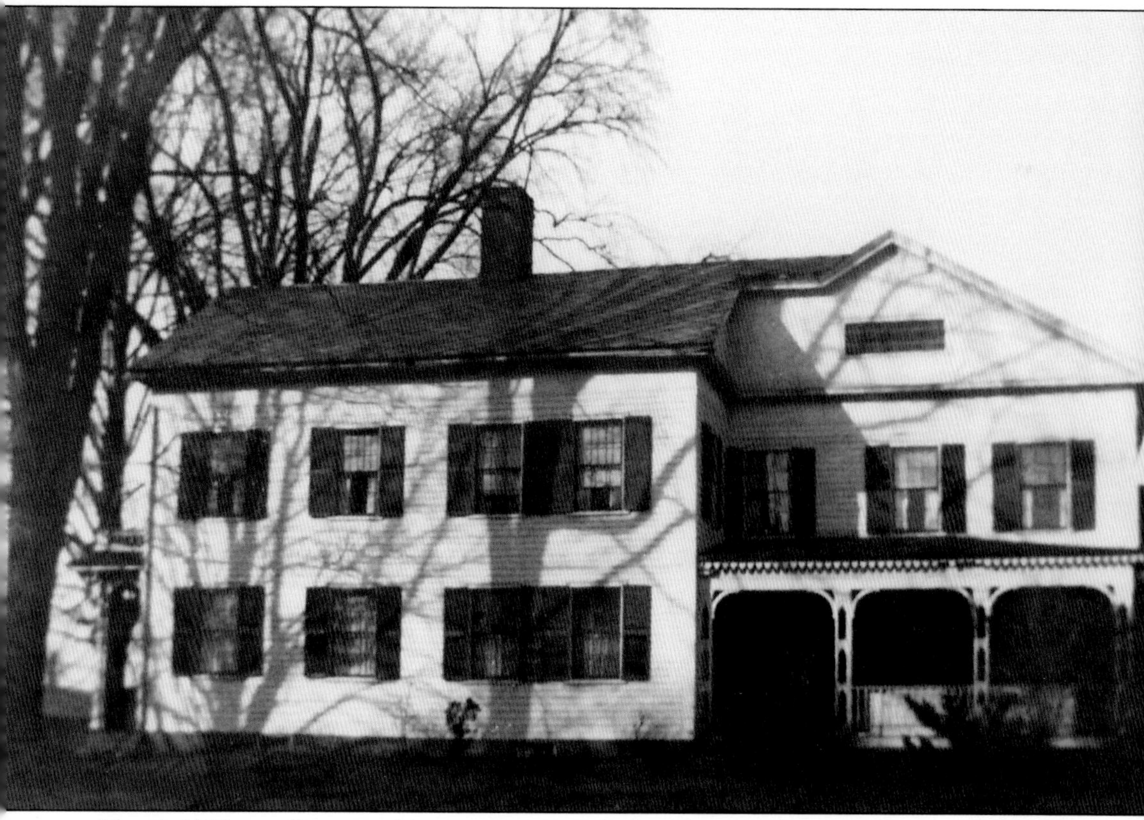

The Field House. Because of its association with the illustrious family of Reverend David D. Field, D.D., of Stockbridge, Massachusetts, this house has always been referred to as the Field House. Built in 1803 for Enos Foote, who became a colonel in the War of 1812, the home was later owned by Heman Laflin, who bequeathed it to his daughter Clarissa, the wife of Matthew Dickinson Field. It is said that Matthew, a civil engineer, was often visited by his brothers Stephen (a lawyer), Cyrus (a merchant), and Henry (who preached for a time in West Springfield). Stephen became a justice of the United States Supreme Court. Cyrus W. Field achieved international renown as the entrepreneur who first succeeded in linking North America to Europe by telegraph using a cable laid in the Atlantic Ocean. His story is a stirring example of American ingenuity and the ability to bounce back after adversity. Matthew and Clarissa had several children. Their granddaughter, Rachel Field, was an author, whose *All This And Heaven, Too,* a true love story, has many reminiscences of Southwick.

The Lowell Mason Grocery Store. Southwick-born Lowell G. Mason, the eldest son of John and Emma (Tryon) Mason, married Ella Ripley of Granville in 1907 and farmed. By 1916, he was a meat peddler, delivering his product in Southwick and neighboring towns. By 1920, Lowell was operating this store, which he built next to his house. When his business closed, Lowell put a second story on the store and established his residence there.

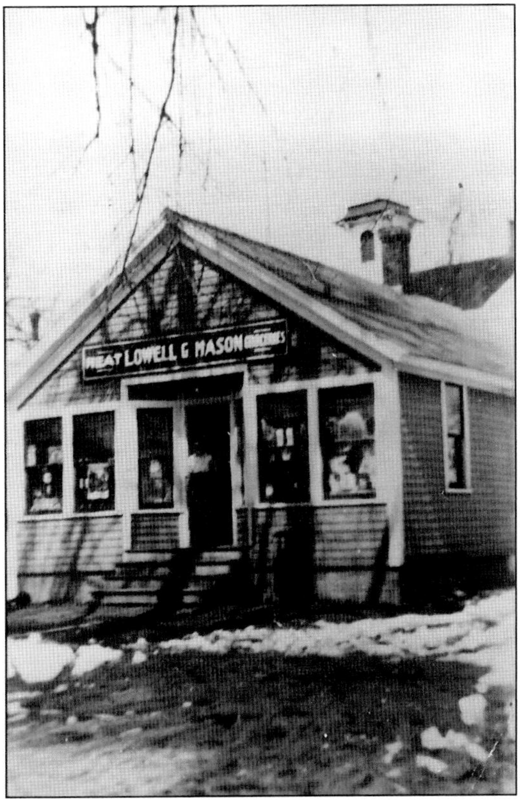

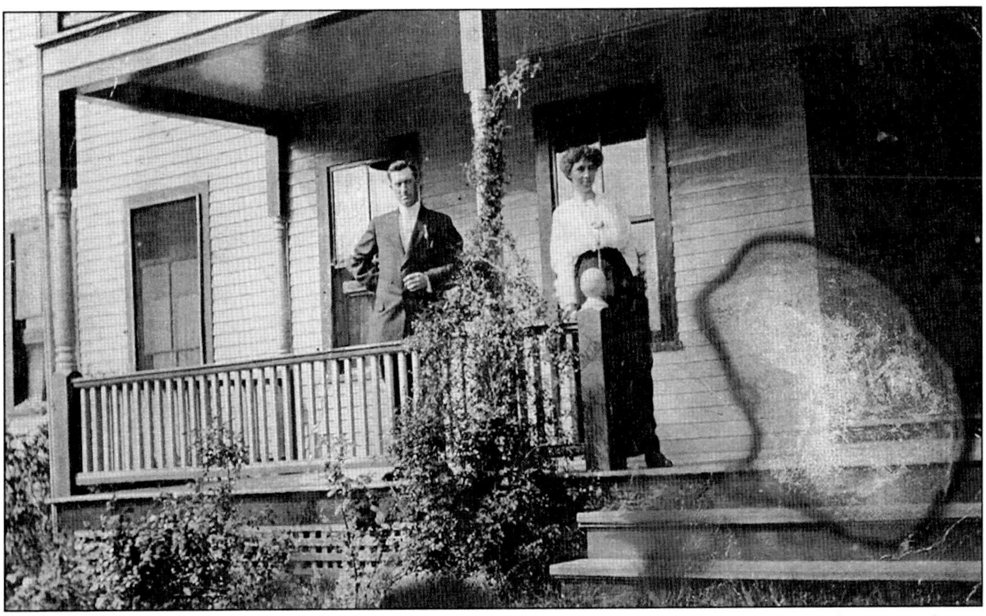

The Southwick Inn, c. 1915–1920. George Malone and his wife, Alice Houghton Malone, stand on the porch of the Southwick Inn. George managed the inn for several years, at first with his uncle, John T. O'Neil, and later on his own.

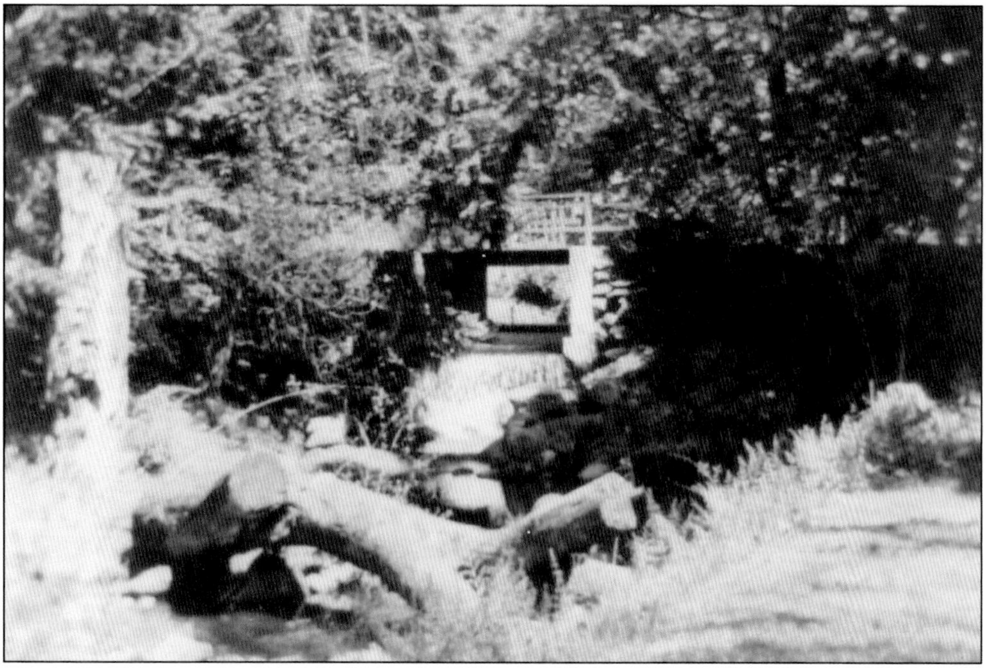

The Bridge behind the Southwick Public Library. This bridge and its falling waters often provided a natural setting for aquatic plants displayed in the catalogs of Edward Gillett and his son Kenneth. The business ended when Kenneth and his son Thornton both died in the 1940s.

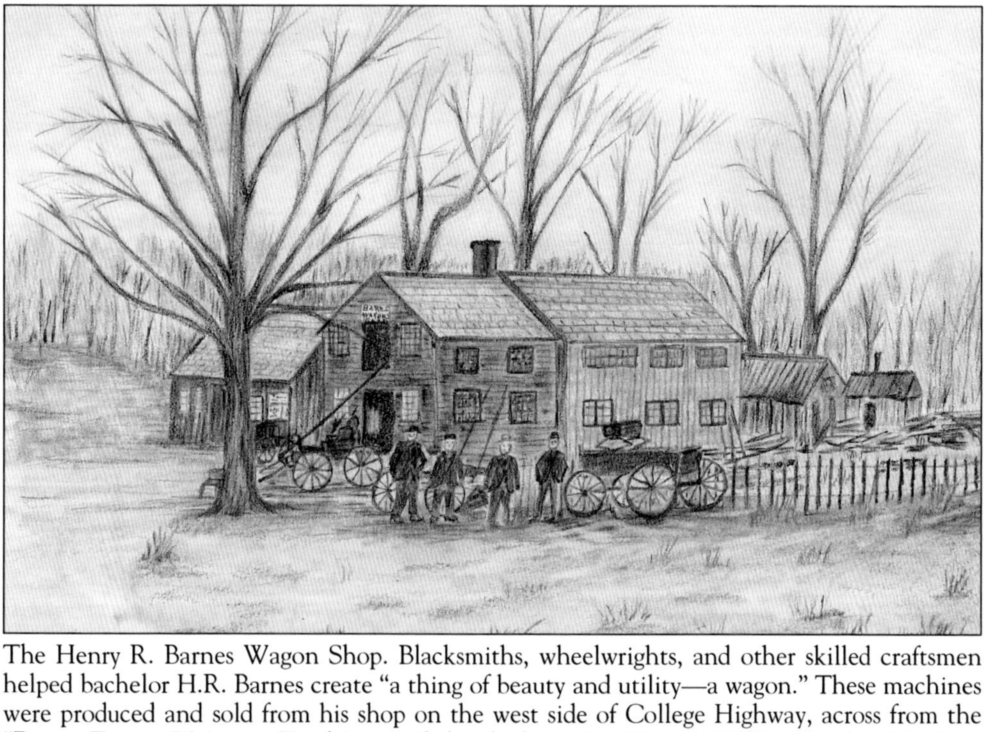

The Henry R. Barnes Wagon Shop. Blacksmiths, wheelwrights, and other skilled craftsmen helped bachelor H.R. Barnes create "a thing of beauty and utility—a wagon." These machines were produced and sold from his shop on the west side of College Highway, across from the "Doane Tavern." Merwin Tuttle's pencil sketch shows Mr. Barnes, William Taylor, Matthew Malone, and LaFayette Carlton in 1885.

Chapter Two

Businesses

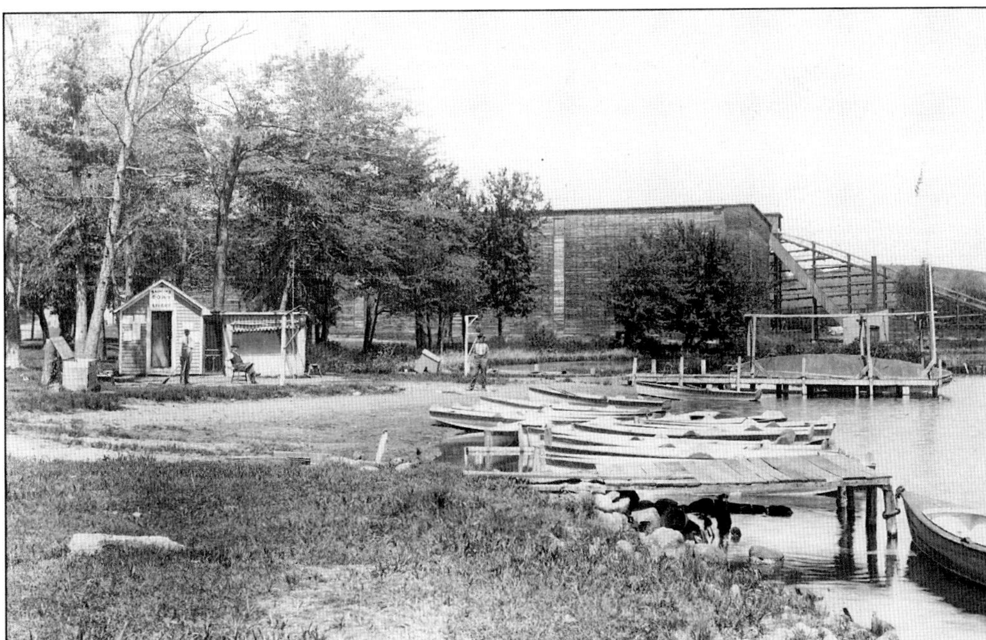

The Saunders Boat Livery. The oldest family-operated business in town, Saunders Boat Livery was established by William Saunders in 1843. The Saunders' original business, renting rowboats and tackle to fishermen and pleasure-seekers, has been augmented by the addition of a boat-repair shop, a restaurant, and, in 1955, a package store. Notice the Crystal Ice House in the background.

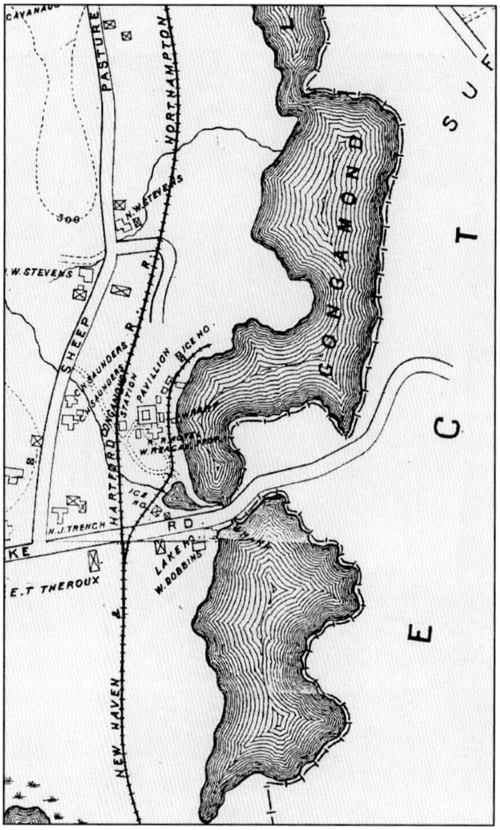

A Detail of the L.J. Richards Map of 1894. This section of the 1894 map shows the area near the lakes. Notice that Berkshire Avenue does not exist; access to the Pavilion, Congamond Station, the Railroad Hotel, and the Crystal Ice House was by a private road off Sheep Pasture Road. The railroad spur, which served the Railroad and Crystal Ice Houses, is clear.

The Railroad Ice House. One of four ice houses situated on the west side of Middle Congamond Lake, the Railroad Ice House was one of the first built. A railroad spur allowed the great blocks of ice to be loaded from the ice house directly onto railroad cars for shipment.

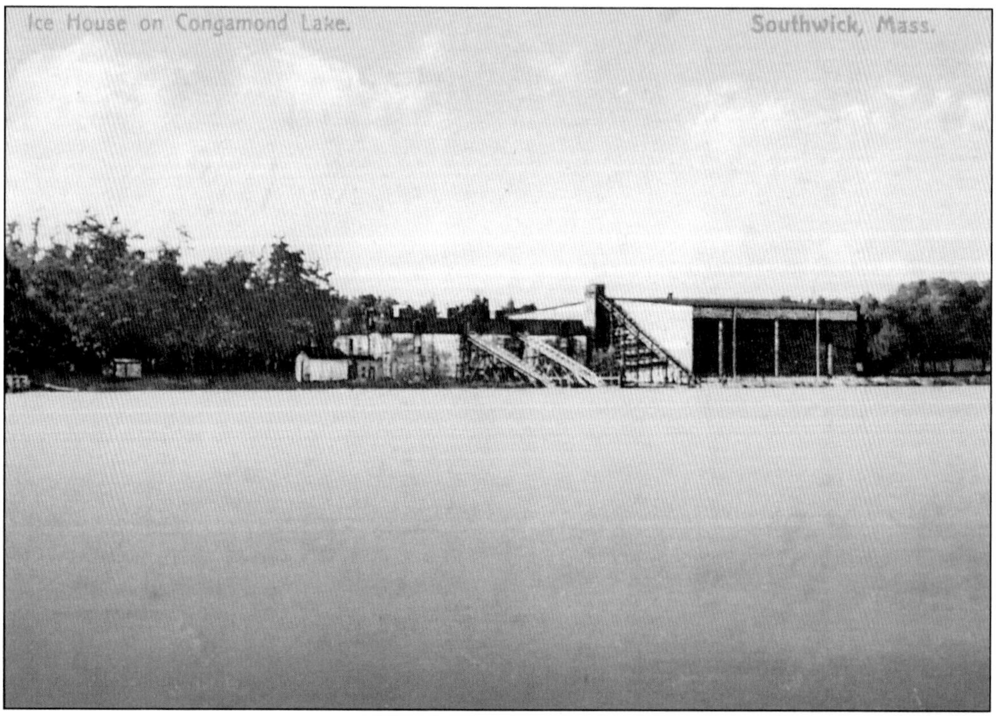

A Detail of the Richards Map of 1912. A section of Southwick similar to the one on the facing page shows how much development occurred in the area, including the three new ice houses which were built. Notice also that there are no roads on the south side of Lake Road, now Congamond Road.

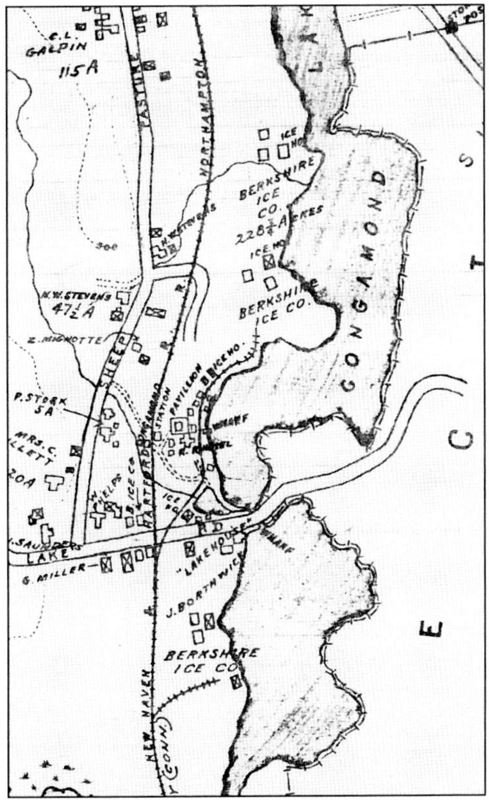

The Berkshire Ice House. The only ice house located on South Congamond Lake, the Berkshire Ice House was built between 1894 and 1912. Notice the long conveyors which carried the ice blocks from the lake surface to the top floor of the ice house.

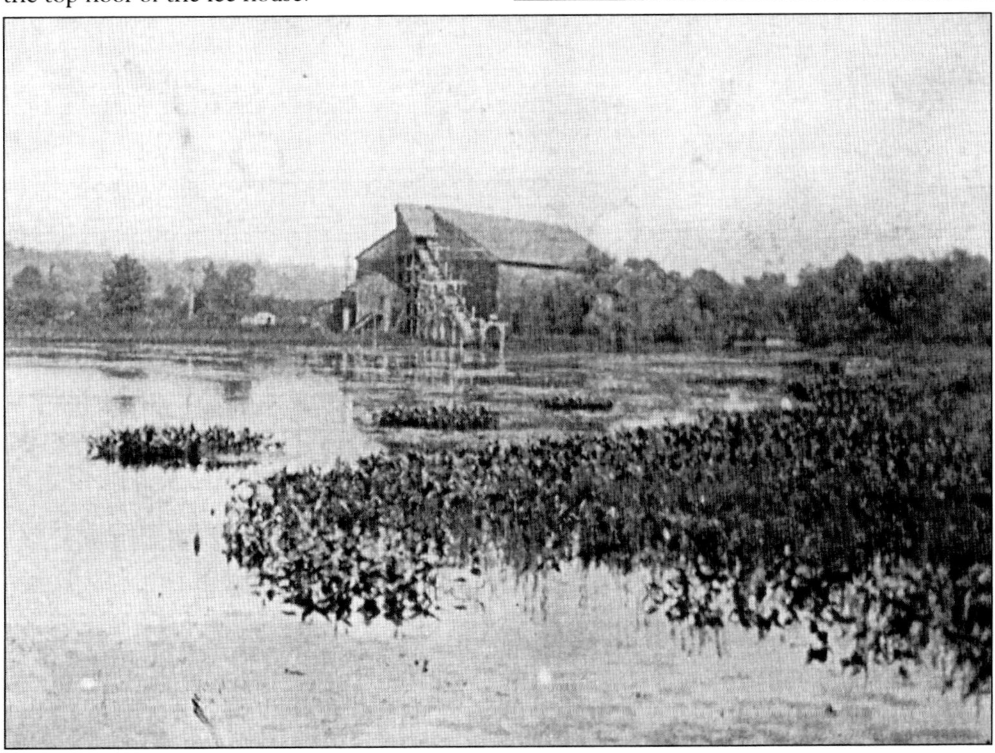

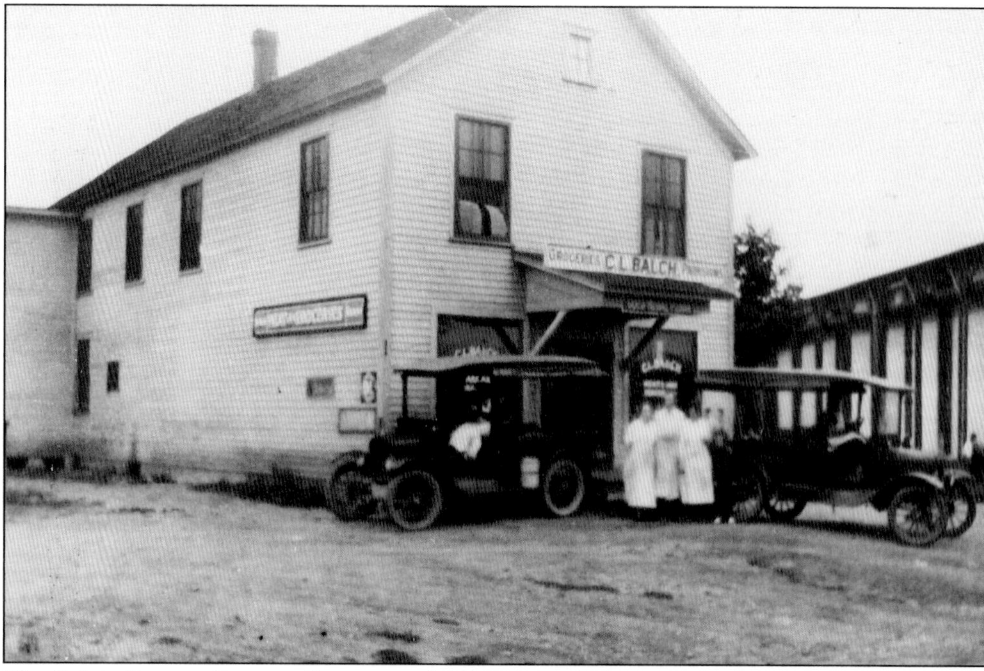

The Balch Grocery Store at Congamond. The store of Clayton L. Balch, opened about 1920, was located very near the Crystal Ice House, which can be seen on the right.

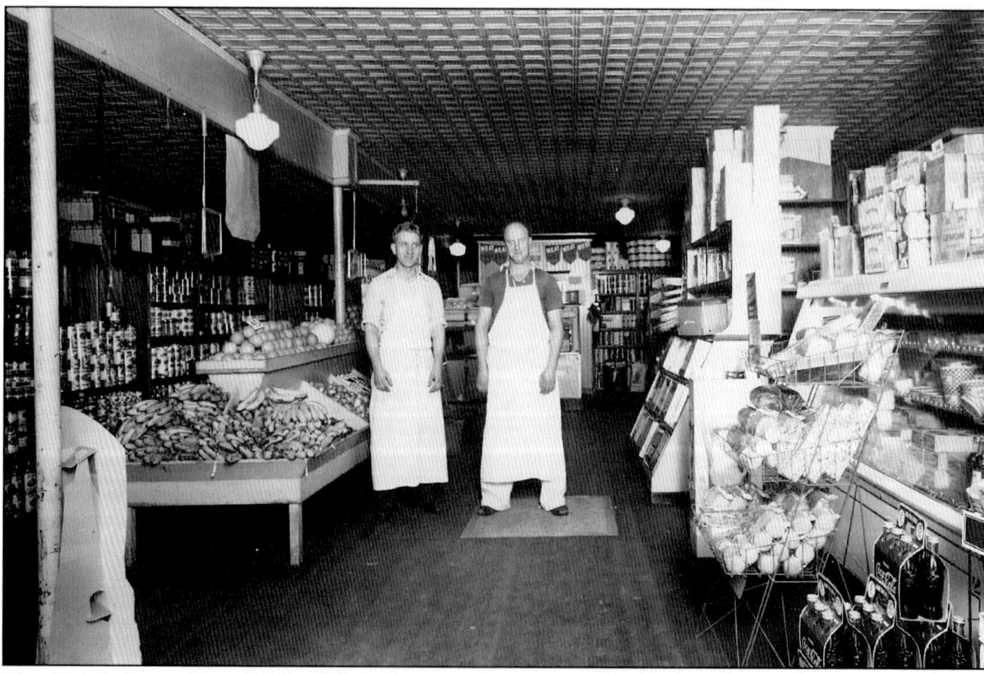

The Balch Store, late 1930s. Bill Jackson and Lawrence Lemon worked under store manager A.H. Phillip for Raymond Balch, one of two brothers who began this business on Congamond Road and then moved to the town center, where this photograph was taken. Notice the fresh produce and party supplies. Bill, who later worked for Stanley Home Products, had a keen appreciation of the natural world.

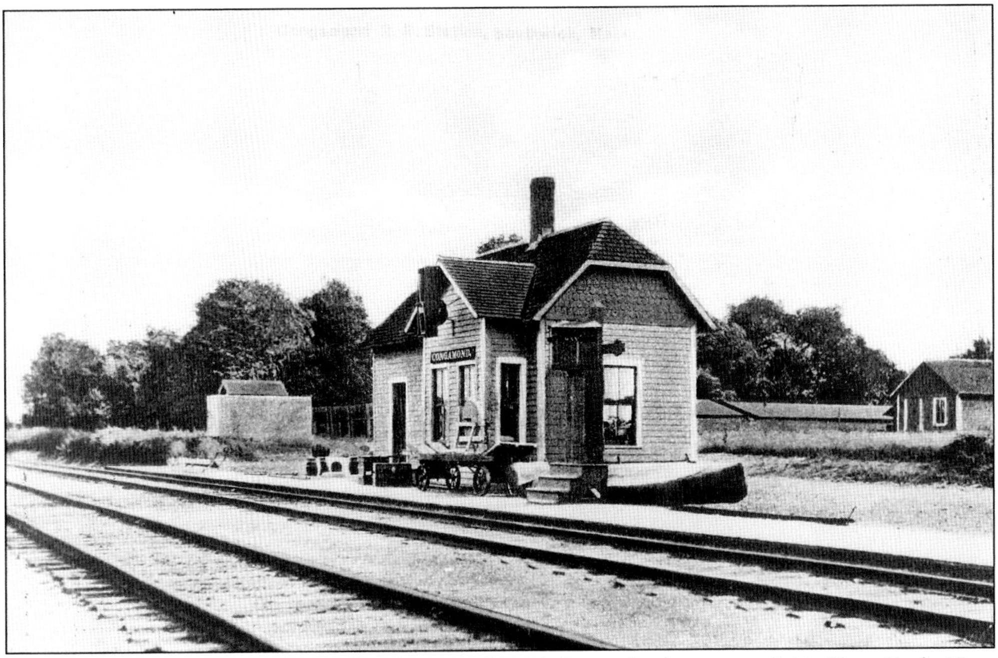

The Congamond Depot. The Richards map of 1894 shows the location of this New York, New Haven & Hartford Railroad station, which served the needs of both business and pleasure in the Congamond area of Southwick. The barns in the right background were used as winter stables for the horses that worked on the ice.

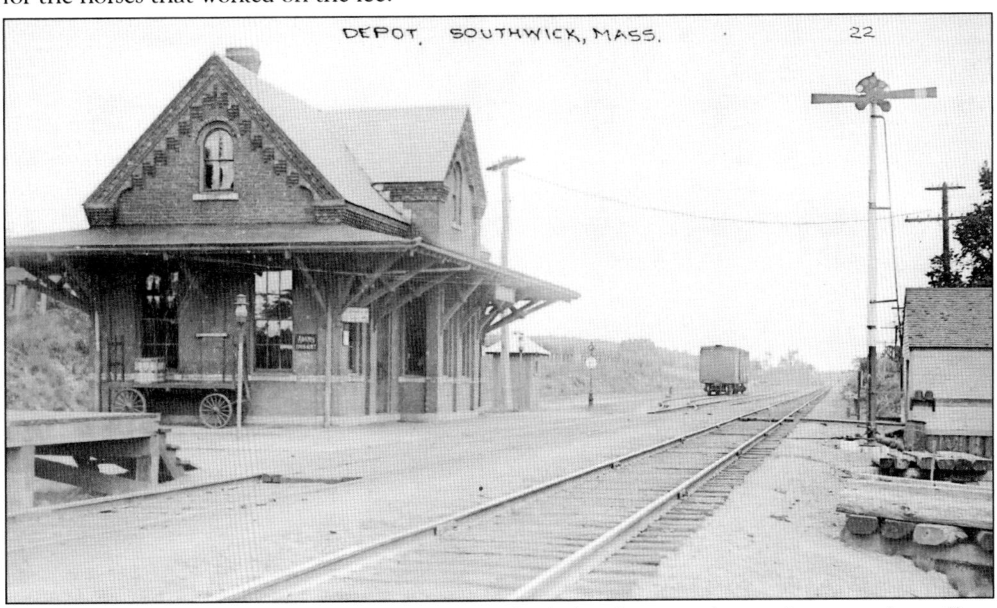

The Southwick Depot. The Southwick Depot, which faced, across the tracks, a powder mill on the west side of what is now Powder Mill Road, also faced several powder mill buildings on the east side of that road in 1894. The railroad brought thousands of people to visit Southwick and carried thousands of tons of freight from the ice houses, farms, and mills of Southwick to distant destinations. Although the bridge that had carried the tracks over Depot Street was taken down many years ago, the concrete bridge abutments remained in existence until the 1980s.

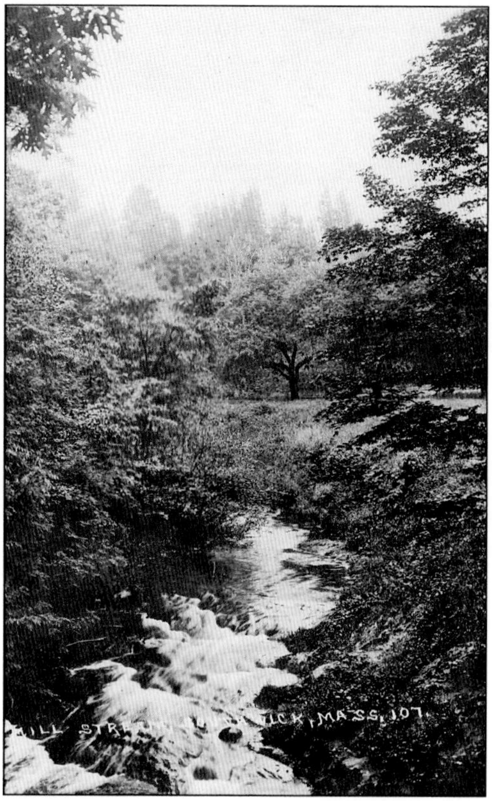

Great Brook. Water from Great Brook supplied power for the gristmill and gunpowder mills that were situated between what is now Powder Mill Road and the brook.

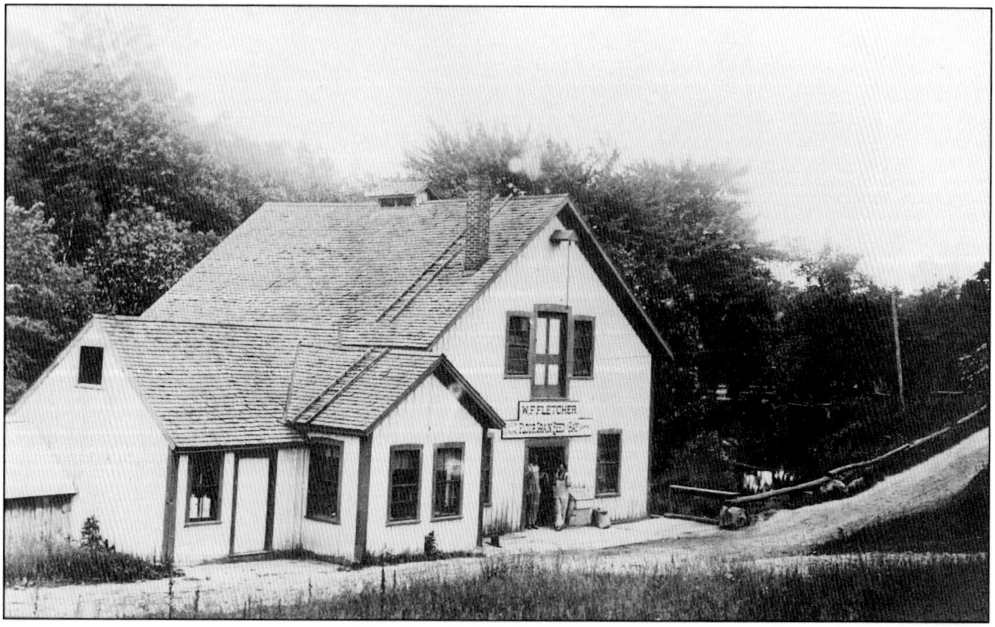

The William F. Fletcher Mill. Beginning in 1875, William Fletcher processed grain into flour at this gristmill for the firm of Boyle & Gilbert. Fletcher later purchased the business, which he ran until after his 84th birthday in 1935. Notice the canal which diverted water from Great Brook for operating the waterwheel.

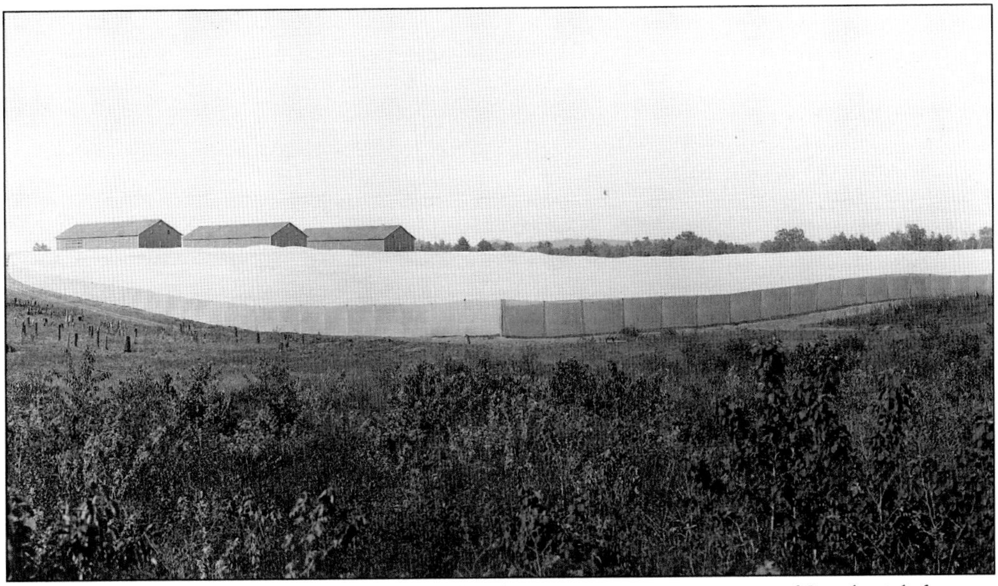

A Tobacco Field, 1915. Raising tobacco and making cigars was an activity of Southwick farmers at least as early as 1850. When the plants were placed under tents in 1902, the resulting product was called shade-grown tobacco. Because some of the many leaves could be used for cigar wrappers, the crop fetched a higher price than field tobacco.

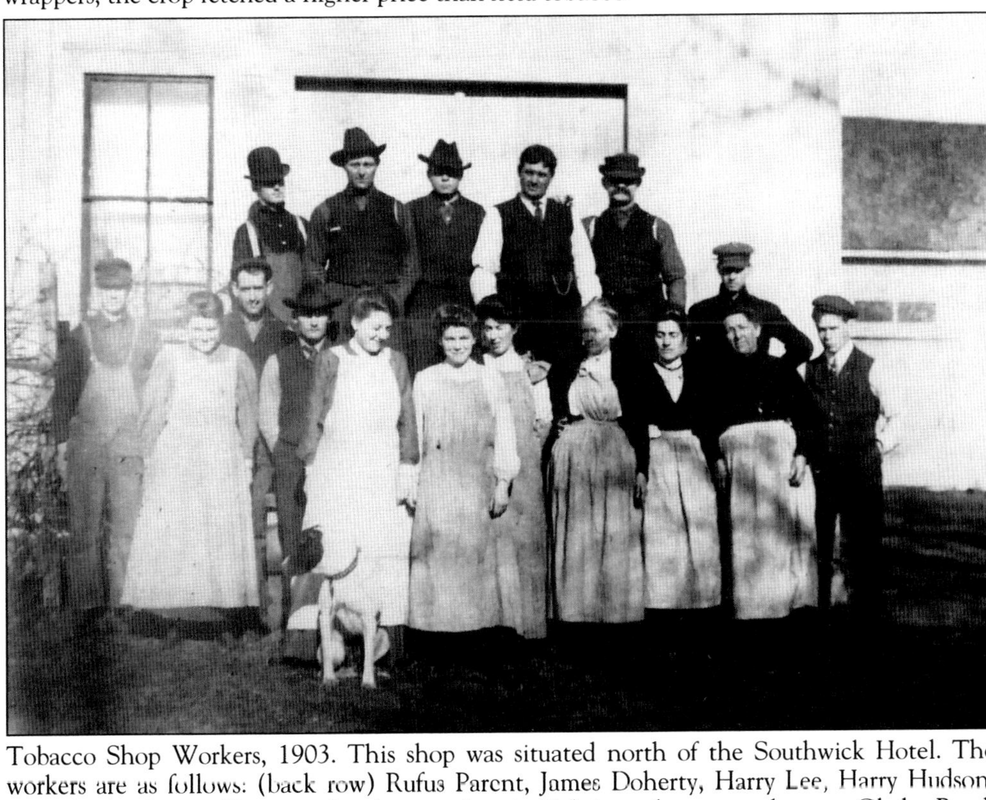

Tobacco Shop Workers, 1903. This shop was situated north of the Southwick Hotel. The workers are as follows: (back row) Rufus Parent, James Doherty, Harry Lee, Harry Hudson, and Charles Stone; (front row) unknown, Jennie Galpin, unknown, unknown, Gladys Reed, unknown, Jennie Malone, Mrs. Parent, Jennie Lee, Nellie Doherty, and unknown.

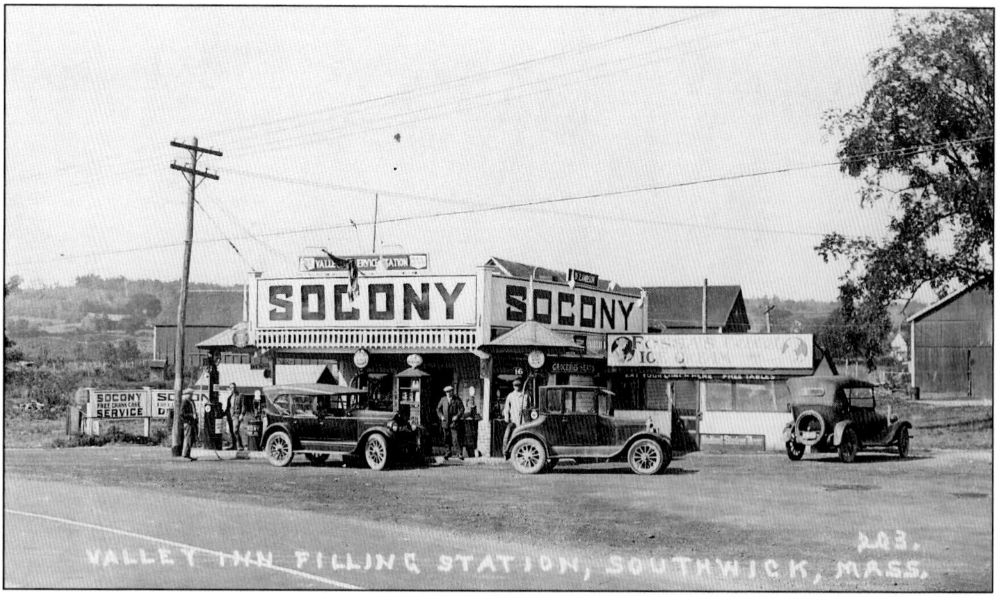

The Valley Inn Filling Station. Proprietor Frank D. Lambson, who offered Socony gasoline, free crankcase service, and other automotive services, evidently also sold groceries, meats, and Fossa's Velvet Ice Cream at this location. The station was later owned by Earl Davis, whose son George was in the second grade in October 1942. This site, at 365 College Highway, across from the Old Southwick Cemetery, is presently occupied by Cusson Power Equipment.

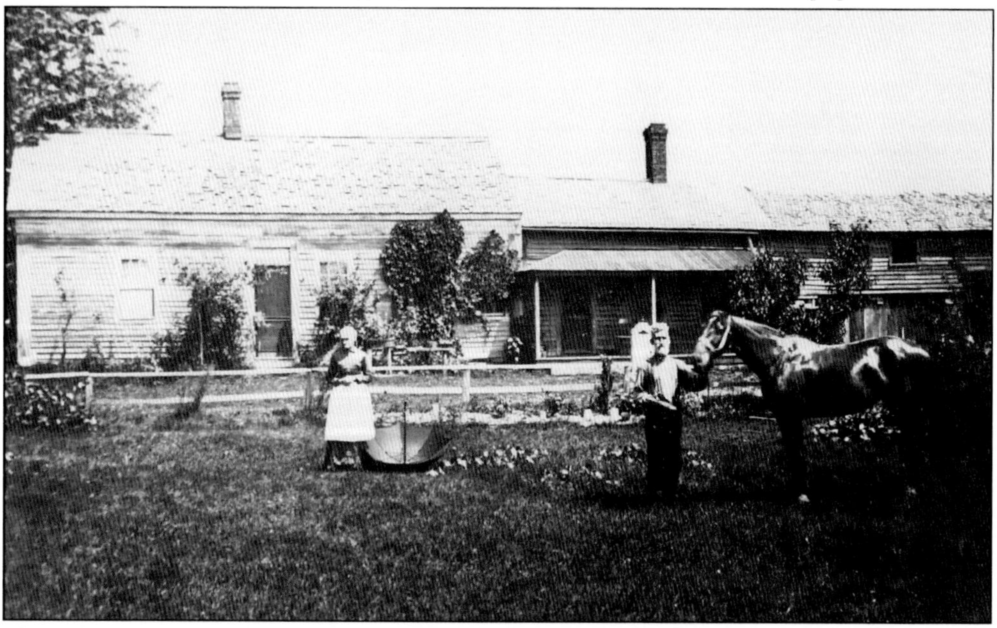

The Luke J. Hitchcock House before 1900. Hitchcock, a blacksmith and carriage-maker, had a shop that also housed equipment for shoeing oxen. It was located on Granville Road between the Southwick Public Library and the little brook. Luke's home at 636 College Highway was owned by S. Boynton on the 1854 map. Boyington and Byington, surnames that appear on many gravestones in the Old Southwick Cemetery, are merely variant spellings of the original Boynton name. (Southwick Florist, 1995).

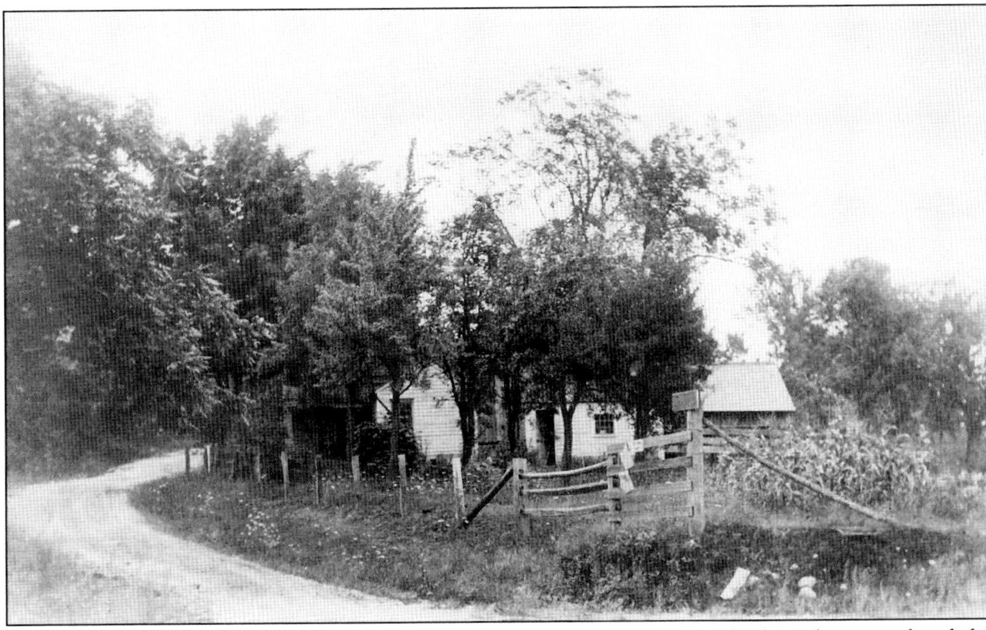

The Humphrey Campbell House. In 1901, Delbert M. Coarser took this photograph of the Humphrey Campbell house on the east side of Sheep Pasture Road. The 1854 map of Southwick shows Sylvanus Talmadge living here. Sylvanus died in 1854; in 1857, his widow Huldah married Humphrey Campbell, who worked as a yeast peddler. The family of Nelson Stevens owned this house for a time. It was abandoned for many years and then torn down in the 1930s.

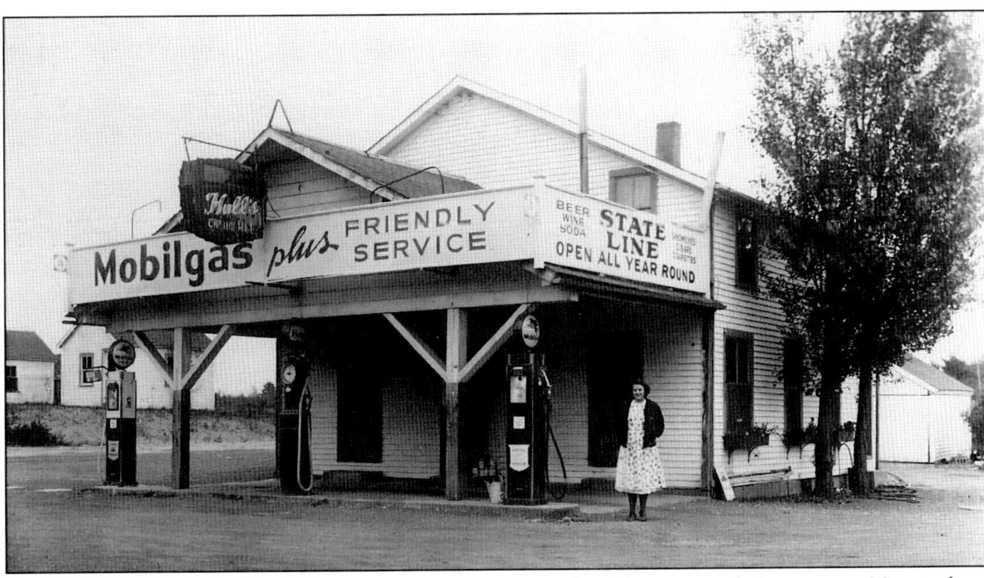

State Line Station, Inc., 1935. Established in 1934 by Thomas and Domenica Nascimbeni Battistoni, this business has been operating for sixty-two years. After Thom died, his wife and his nineteen-year-old daughter Norma continued. Norma's husband, John Henry Yourous, joined the business when Mrs. Battistoni retired, and their children continue to help. Norma Yourous, a Girl Scout leader for forty years, was presented the Grange Community Citizen's Award in 1995.

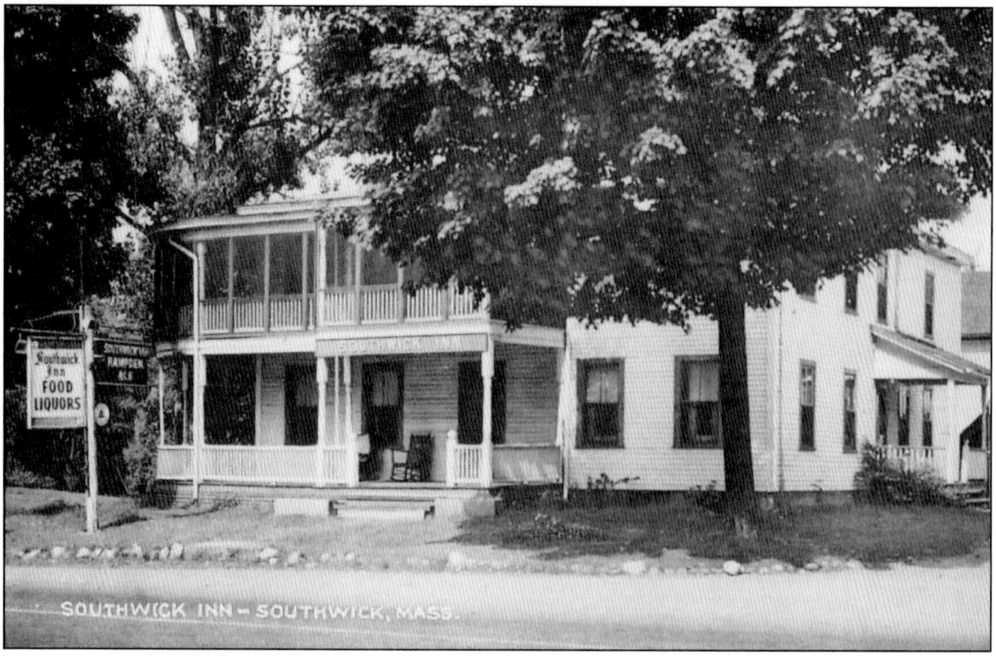

The Southwick Inn. A 1930s postcard shows the Southwick Inn with its upper porch screened for summer use. Signs advertise "Food, Liquors and Hampden Ale" as well as a public telephone.

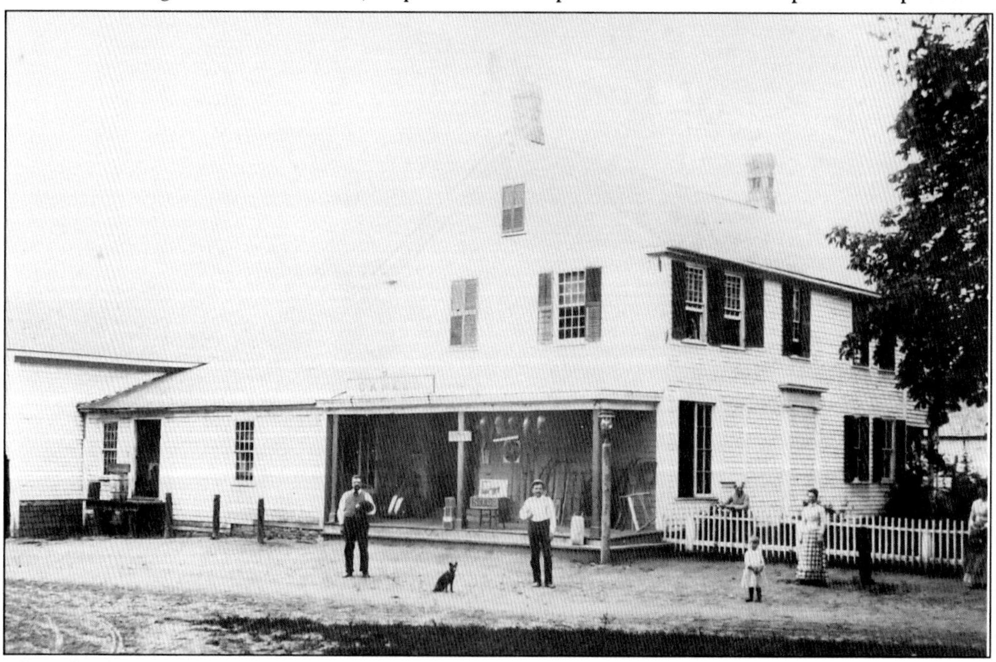

The Charles A. Reed Store. The Reed store, shown here between 1890 and 1900, was a private home in 1854 owned by lawyer John Mills and his wife Emily, the daughter of Colonel Enos Foote. The little girl is Gladys Reed, the daughter of Charles and Etta (Hollister) Reed. The others are Charles Reed, Goodman Palmer, Louisa B. Reed (mother to Charles), Etta Reed, and one of Goodman Palmer's two sisters, either Laura or Dora. Notice the many farm tools and the cured hams hanging from the porch rafters.

Chapter Three

"Castles"

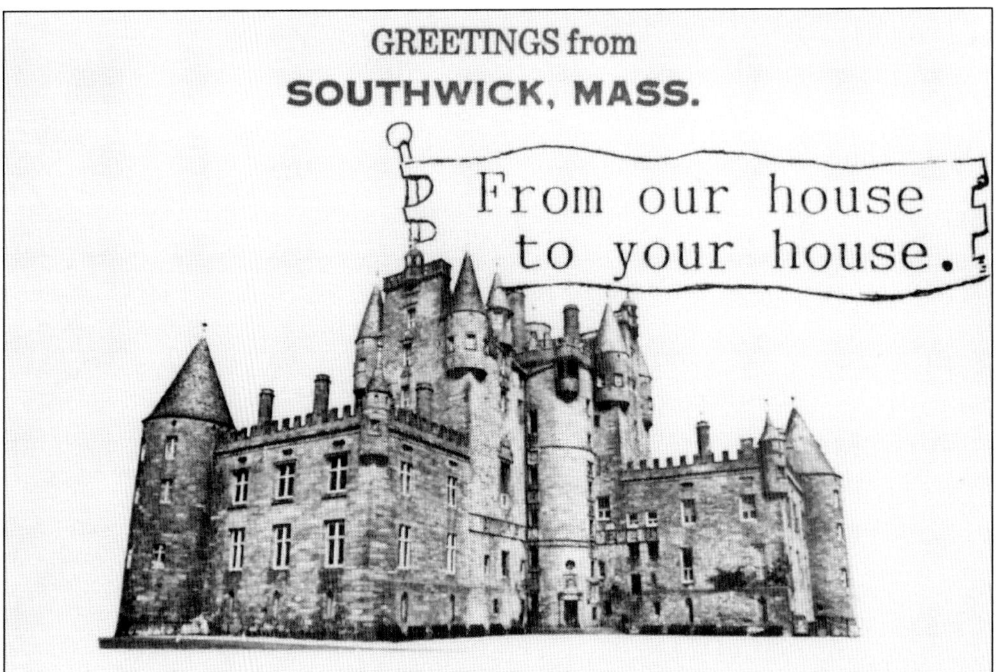

A Castle Postcard. The "castles" of Southwick are the substantial, usually wood-frame, houses of prominent citizens of the town throughout its history, from the first settlement in 1732 to the present.

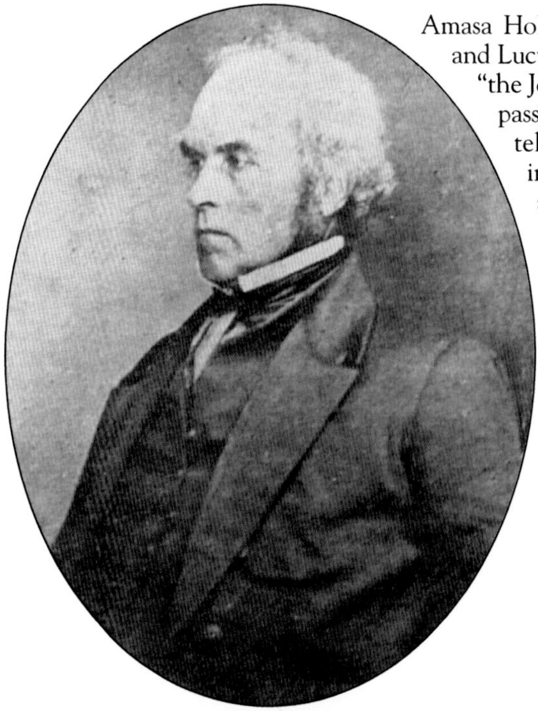

Amasa Holcomb (1787–1875). The son of Elijah Jr. and Lucy (Holcomb) Holcomb, Amasa was born in "the Jog." His autobiography describes his lifelong passion for learning, from surveying to making telescopes, and his ability to share his faith in preaching and his knowledge in teaching apprentices. His home is shown below.

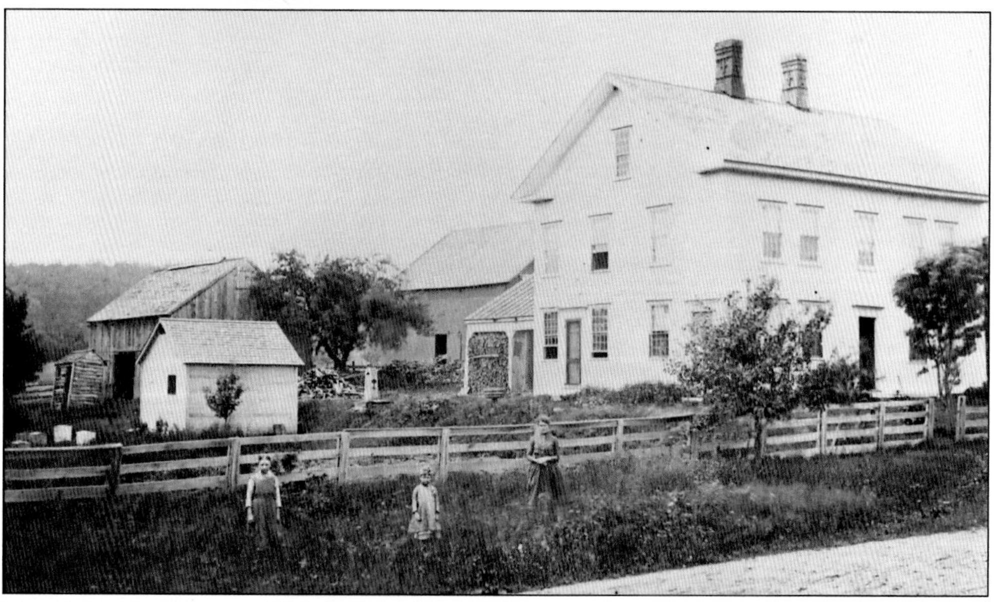

The Holcomb House, *c.* 1895. Built by Hiram Vining in the early 1800s, this dwelling, located at 249 College Highway, was home to Amasa Holcomb's son Henry in 1894. Henry Holcomb's granddaughters, Grace and Eva, are shown here with Julia (Lyons) Holcomb, the second wife of Henry's son Amasa. Grace married Whitney Steere in 1897, and Eva married William Storey in 1902. Notice the coffin door on the southeast corner of the house, nearly hidden by the small tree in the right foreground outside the fence. The beehives and pump are also worthy of notice. James and Frances Putnam have owned this farm since Jim returned from service in World War II, and one of their sons continues to run the Putnam Farms Store, which they established.

George M. Steere. George, who lived all but the last six of his ninety-eight years in Southwick, was the grandson of Marcus M. and Elmina (Campbell) Steere, and was the son of Everett and Alice (Peck) Steere. He attended Christ Church United Methodist and was an active charter member in the Southwick Grange and the Southwick Historical Society, Inc. He bequeathed to the society a substantial donation in his will, which has been used for structural work on the Moore House.

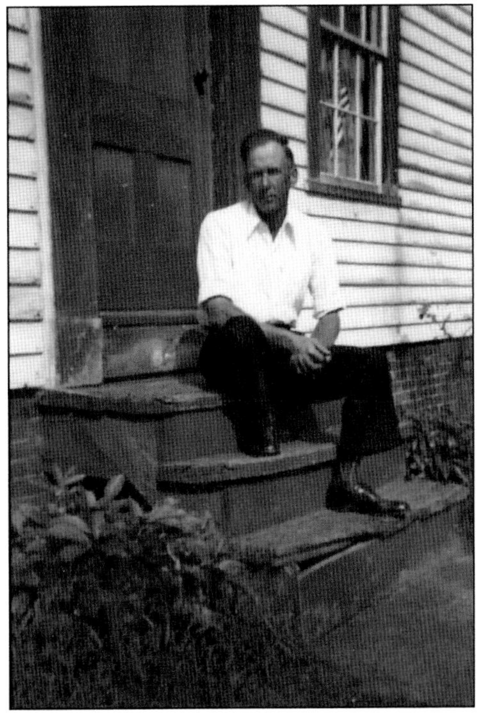

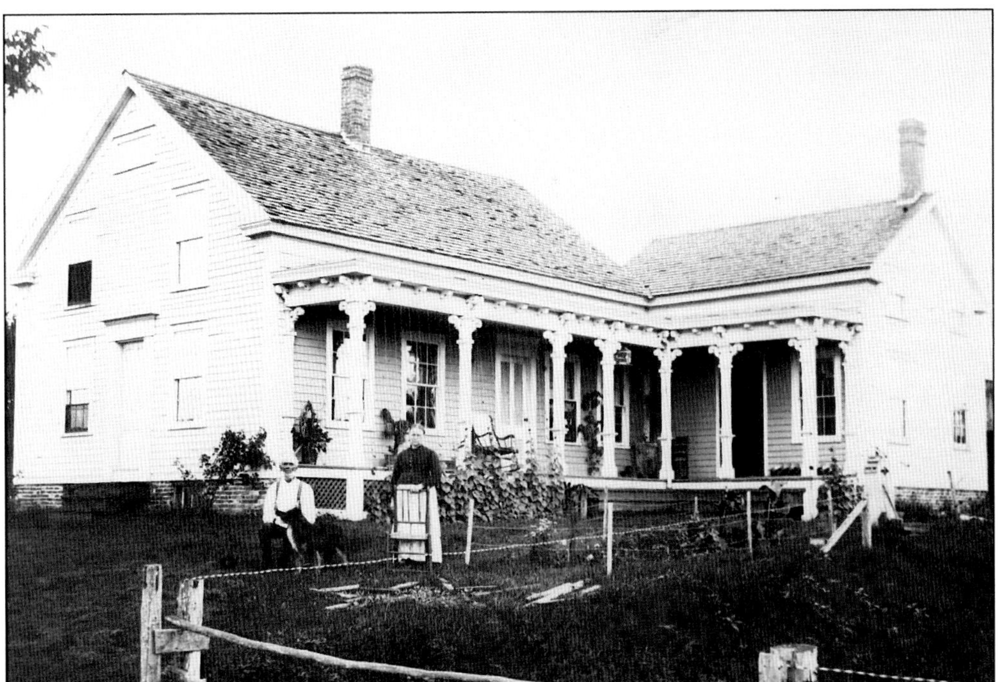

The Steere House. Taken before July 25, 1895, this photograph shows Marcus M. Steere and his wife Elmina at their home at 18 Vining Hill Road. This property was listed as being owned by Elisha Steere, the father of Marcus, in 1854 and 1870; until recently, it was owned by George, the grandson of Marcus and Elmina. (Edward and Karen Roberts, 1995).

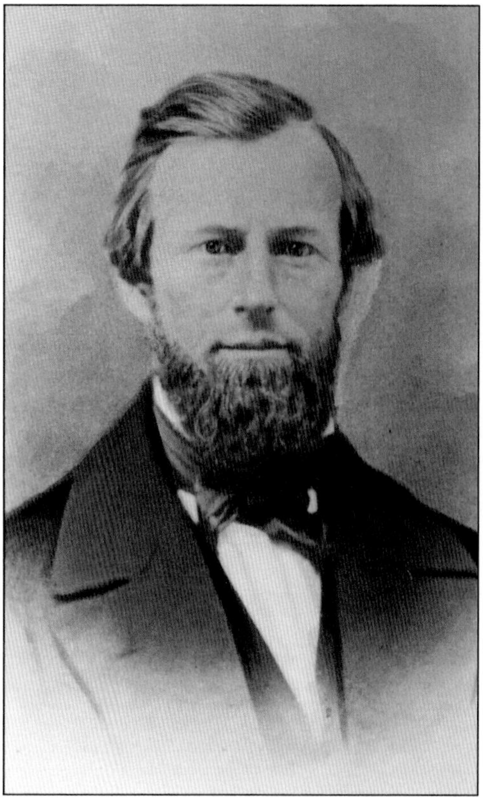

Burrage Yale Butler (1818–1867). A seventh-generation descendant of Richard, Burrage Yale was the son of Divan and Mary Butler. He and his wife Maria had two daughters and a son named Charles, who married Helen Chapman. Their granddaughter, Edith Louise (Collins) Avery, has donated much valuable primary source material and several family treasures to the Southwick Historical Society, Inc.

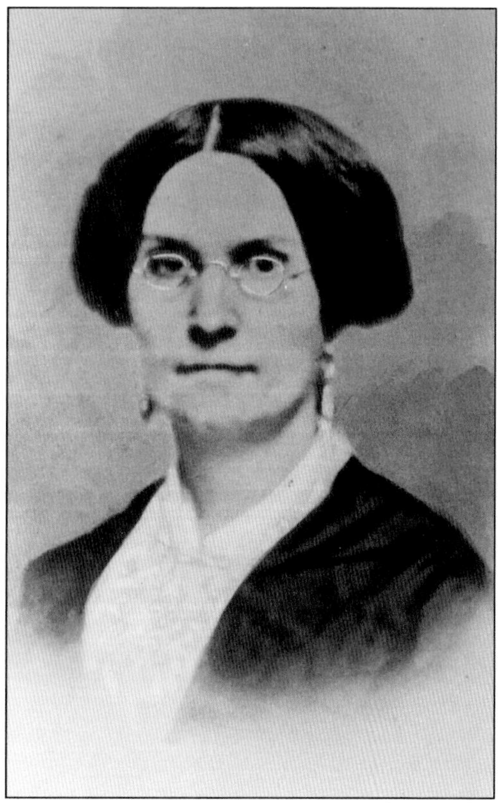

Maria Louisa Butler. The daughter of General Joseph M. and Fanny (Moore) Forward, Maria was the great-granddaughter of Joseph Moore, who served in the American Revolution as a lieutenant of the 18th Regiment of Connecticut militia and was taken prisoner by British forces at the Battle of Kip's Bay. Maria's daughter, Ellen-Louisa, married Southwick native Wallace Holcomb, the son of Milton and Elvira (Gillett) Holcomb.

The Moore House Sign. The Southwick Historical Society, Inc. is restoring the home built in 1751 by Joseph Moore. (The right ell was added in the 1840s.) Joseph and his wife, Mary (Stevens) Moore, had eleven children, four of whom did not survive until their twenty-first birthdays. Roger Moore (1752–1838), their fifth son, lived in the dwelling shown below his entire life. Due to boundary changes, however, he is considered to have lived in both Westfield and Southwick, MA; in both Simsbury and Granby, CT; and in three counties—Hampshire and Hampden in Massachusetts and Hartford in Connecticut.

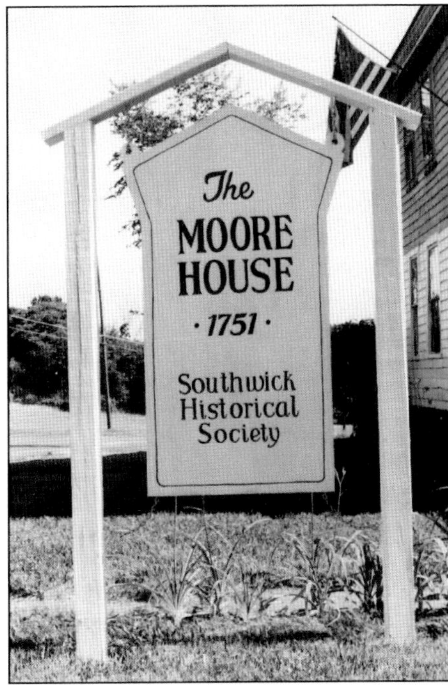

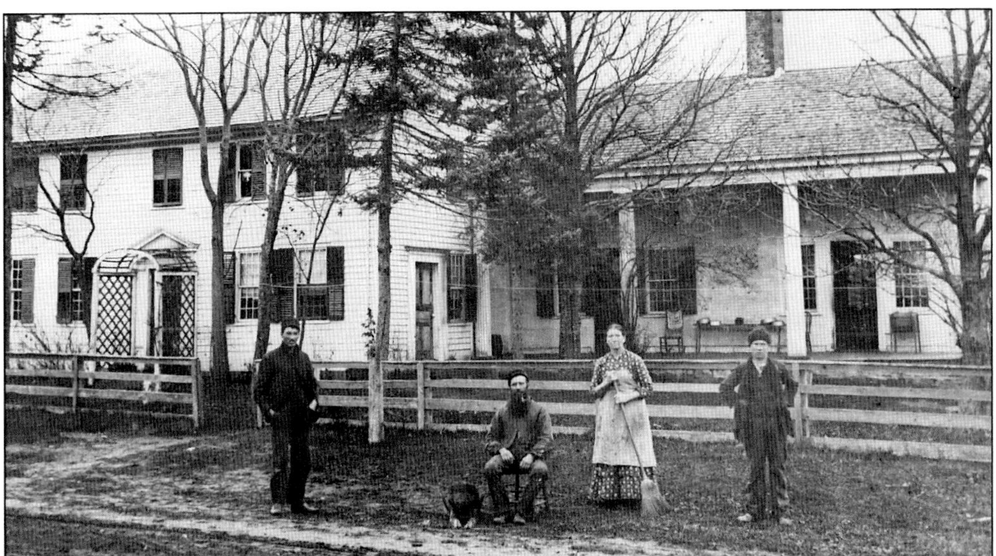

The Nicholson House. The oldest home located in "the Jog," an unusual geographical oddity which interrupts the fairly smooth Massachusetts-Connecticut boundary, this property is located at 86 College Highway. In 1990, the Southwick Historical Society, Inc. purchased the land on which this dwelling stands when Richard and Ruth Waterman donated the building to the society. Among many wonderful architectural features are a coffin door and a Connecticut Valley doorway. When Roger Moore's son, Roger Sherman Moore, moved to Springfield in 1849, the property passed out of the Moore family. The owner in 1854 was Ralph Plympton; in 1870, the owner was C. Eno. By 1894, the family of Robert Nicholson, who came to this country in 1876 from Ireland, was living there. Robert is shown seated; his son William is on his right, and his wife Mary and son John are on his left.

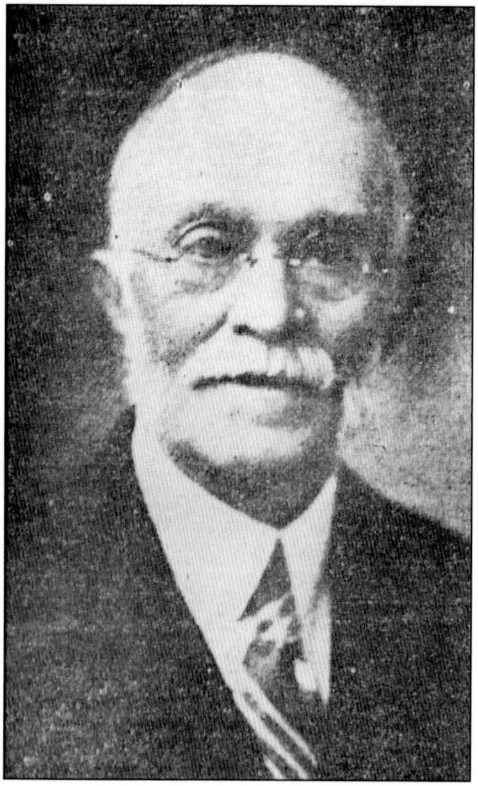

Edward Gillett. Edward Gillett, the brother of Charles J. Gillett, was the proprietor of a wildflower nursery called Gillett's Fern and Flower Farm, located behind his home. He grew plants and shipped the seeds all across the United States and overseas as well.

The Edward Gillett House. Built a little before 1870, this house at 467 College Highway was owned by Milo Spring when the 1870 map was produced. The maple trees in the foreground of this photograph were planted by Edward Gillett shortly after October 10, 1882, when he married Jennie S. Vining, the daughter of Ward and Jane (Reed). Two of Edward and Jennie's three children, Maud and Kenneth, are seated on the steps. Another son, Ward, died before his second birthday. (Jerry and Angela Sambrook, 1995).

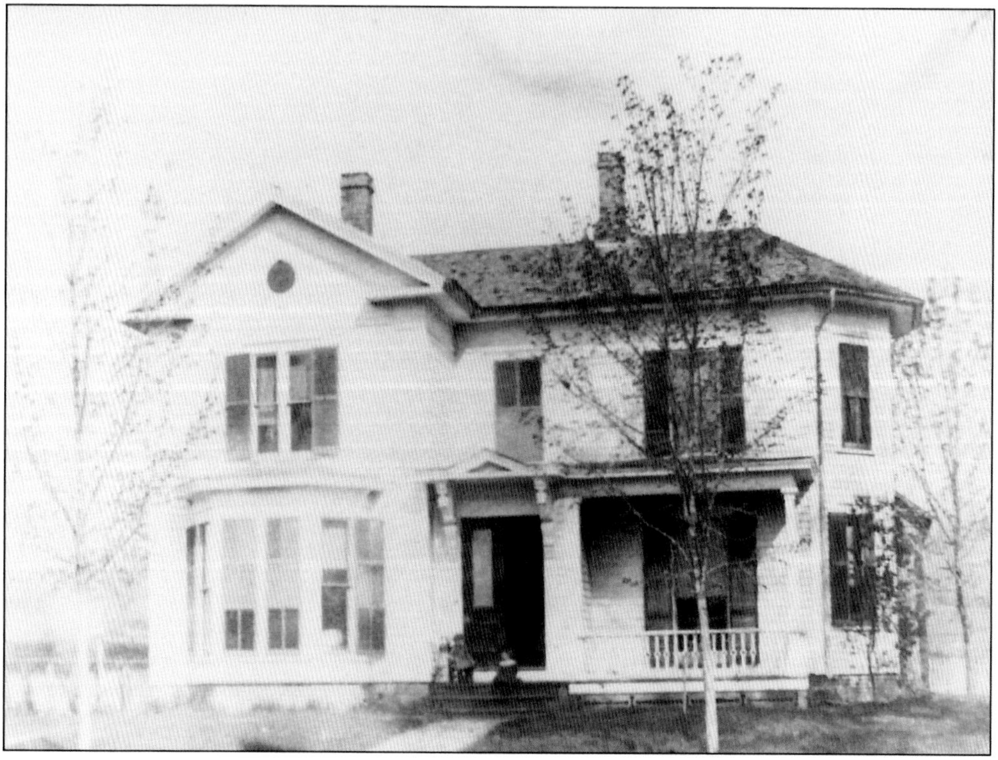

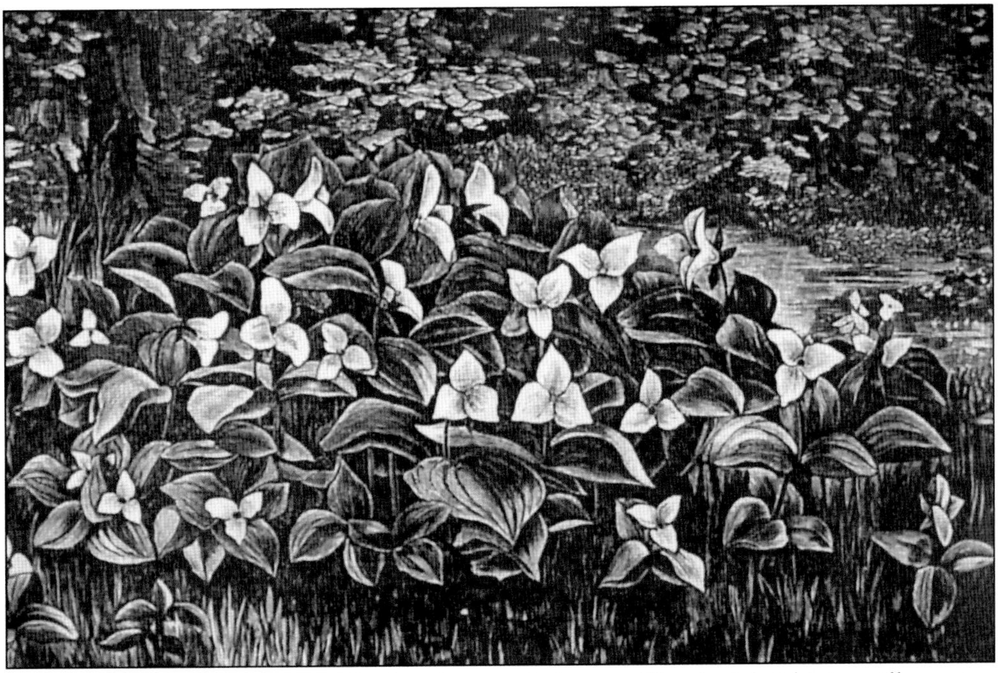

Trillium. Trillium plants can still be found in wooded areas of Southwick. This is an illustration from the catalog of Edward Gillett, who pioneered the use of wild plants in gardens and introduced rhododendrons and azaleas to northern climes.

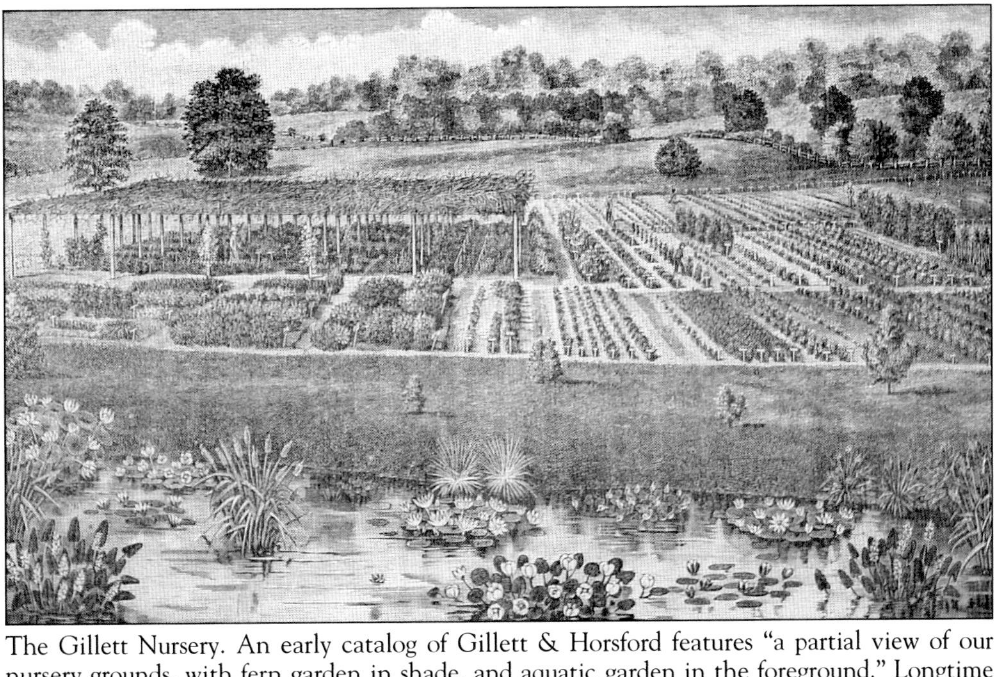

The Gillett Nursery. An early catalog of Gillett & Horsford features "a partial view of our nursery grounds, with fern garden in shade, and aquatic garden in the foreground." Longtime residents recall that the Gilletts utilized land on Feeding Hills Road, across from the present Powder Mill School, for raising plants. Perhaps this is the locality shown. Notice the labels placed on stakes throughout the garden.

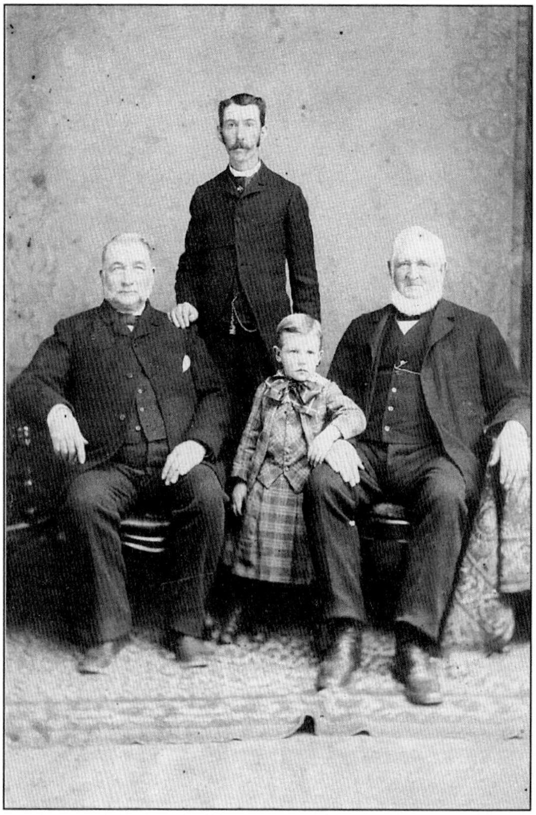

Four Generations of the John Boyle Family. John Boyle (1803–1890) and his son Robert (1830–1893) are seated. Robert's son, John R., is standing with his only son, J. Earl Boyle, standing in front of him. The date, November 23, 1889, was not a birthday for any of them, as their ages in years and months are listed on the reverse.

The John Boyle House. John Boyle (1803–1890) was born in Ireland and came to Southwick via Prince Edward Island. He was a contractor for the Hampshire and Hampden Canal Company, which built and operated the section of the "Farmington Canal" from Northampton to the Connecticut border. He later became a contractor for the railroad, which followed a similar route, and eventually became one of the wealthiest men in Southwick. Notice the carriage in front of this house (at 526 College Highway) and compare it with the one at the William Phelps home on p. 10.

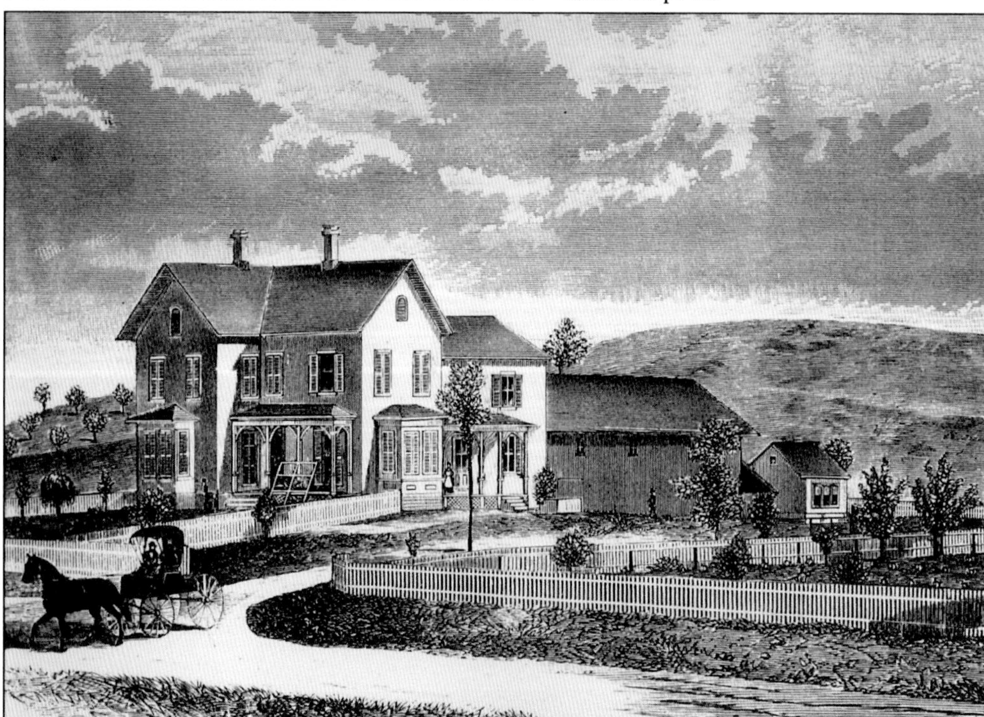

Chapter Four

Farms

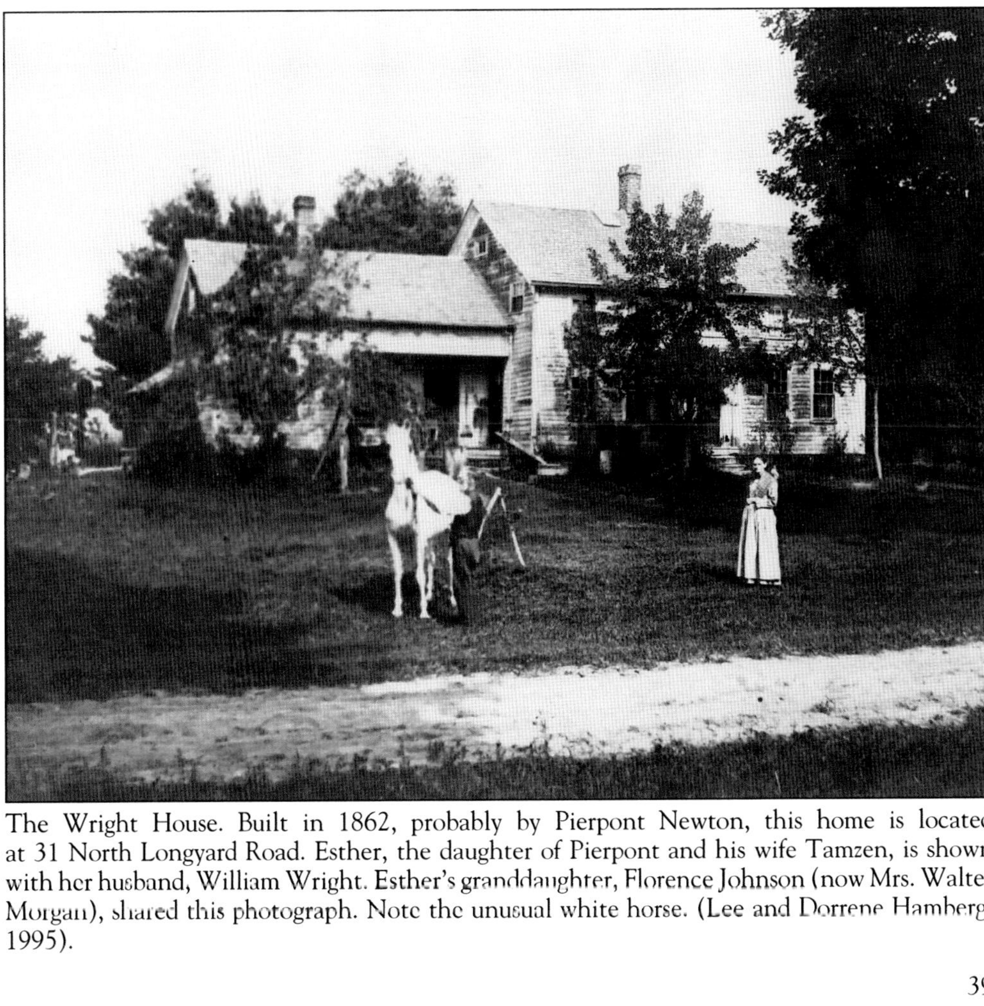

The Wright House. Built in 1862, probably by Pierpont Newton, this home is located at 31 North Longyard Road. Esther, the daughter of Pierpont and his wife Tamzen, is shown with her husband, William Wright. Esther's granddaughter, Florence Johnson (now Mrs. Walter Morgan), shared this photograph. Note the unusual white horse. (Lee and Dorrene Hamberg, 1995).

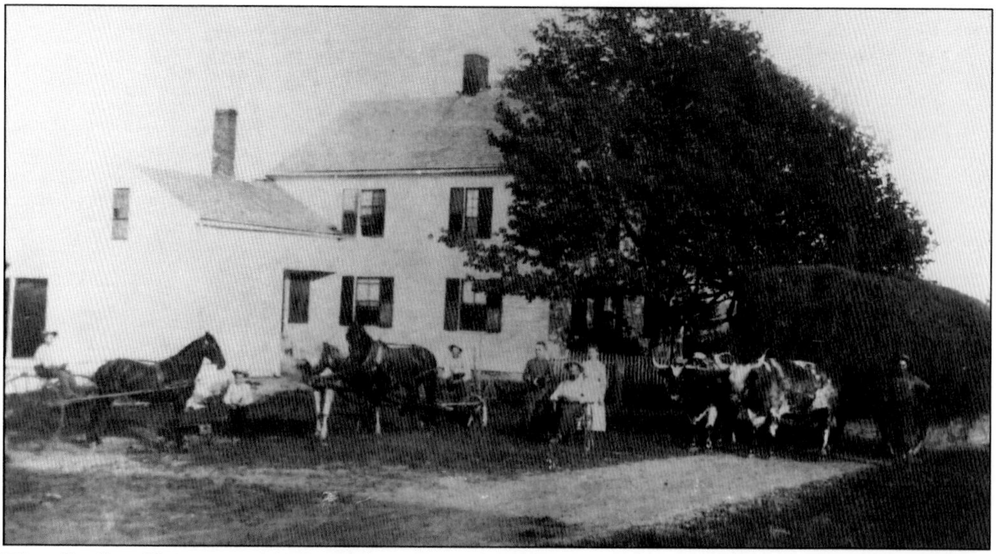

The Griffin House, *c.* 1885. Walter P. and Helen L. "Lena" Griffin lived in this house on 12 Hillside Road with their children: Caroline, Charles, Helen, Vernon, and Cooley. Shown here are Charles (on the rake), Vernie (standing), Cooley (on the mower), Lena (nee Dibble), Walter, Helen, and a hired man. Previous owners of the house were B. Rising in 1854 and E. Johnson in 1870. Notice the two-wheel ox cart loaded with hay. (John and Anna Brzoska, 1995).

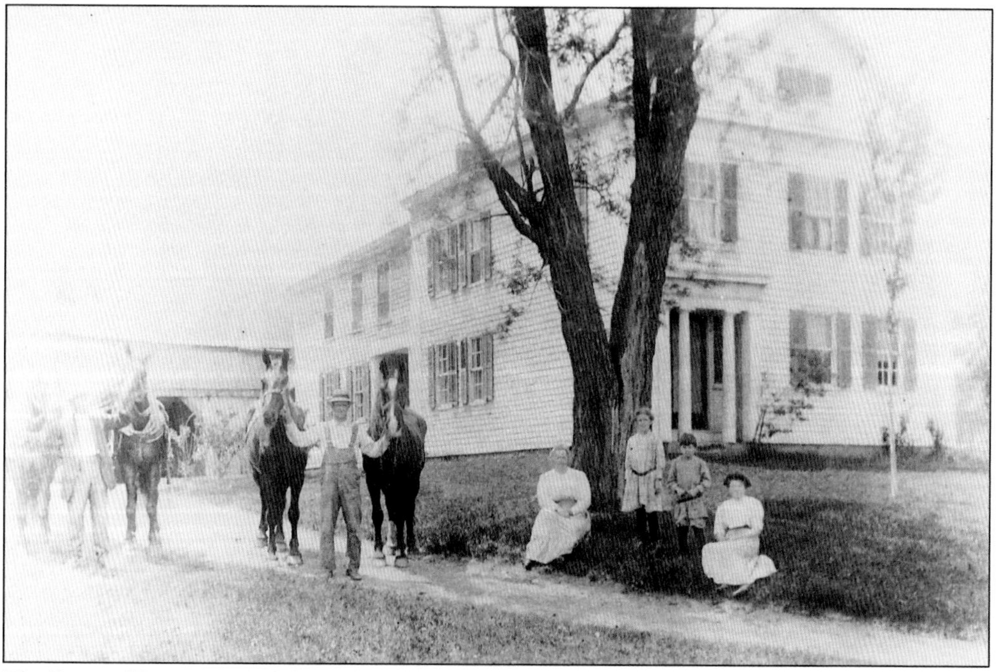

The Barnes House, *c.* 1910. Leon Barnes contributed this photograph of his home, which stood on what is now the parking lot of Chuck's Steak House. Leon's father, William Barnes, is shown; to his right is his hired man, Andrew (?) Antos, and to his left are wife Martha (Dibble) Barnes, daughter Marion, son Harold, and Suzie Chernik. This photograph dates to about 1910. Marion appears also in the 1916 Dickinson Grammar School Graduation photograph.

A Domestic Scene. The owner of the home at 6 Powder Mill Road is shown here in the back yard tending his chickens (the front of the house and yard are shown in the photograph below). Most farmers kept a flock of chickens for their eggs and, after their laying days were over, for meat.

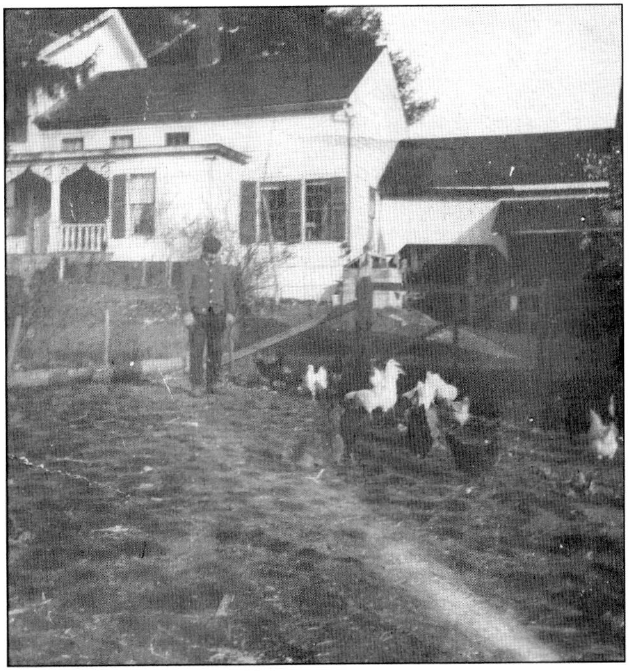

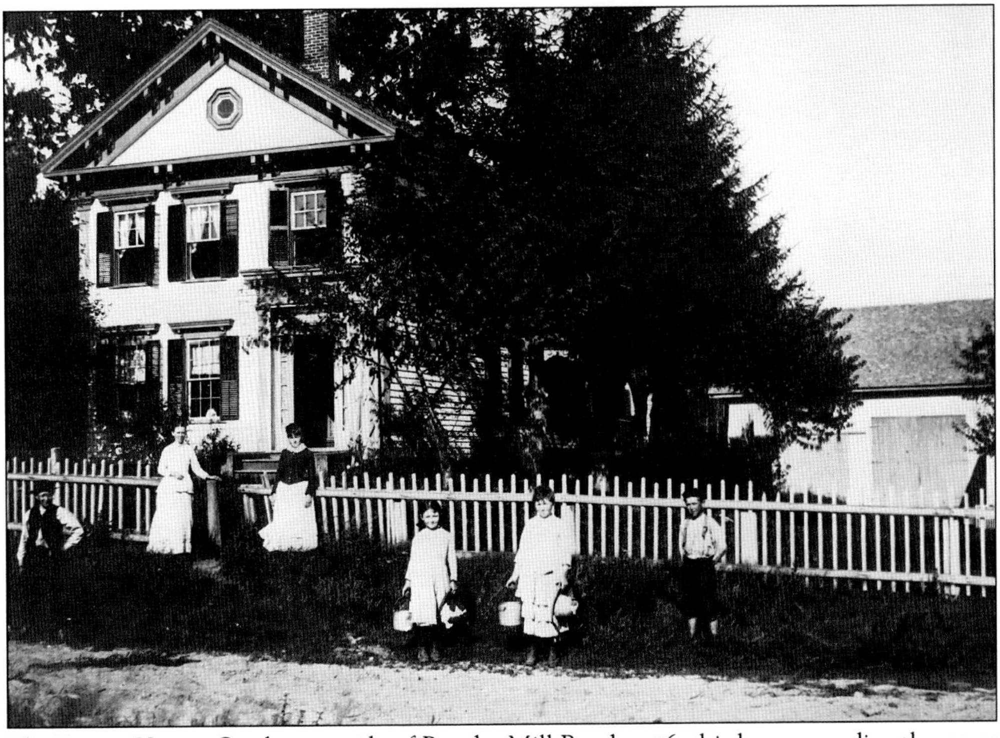

The Legate House. On the east side of Powder Mill Road at #6, this house was directly across the road from the railroad depot, which gave Depot Street its name. Frederick W. Legate owned this home in 1894. If this photograph was taken about 1885, the people would be Mrs. Olivia Legate, in white, with her children: Fred B., Ida, Mattie, Darling, and Henry. Ida Legate was killed parachuting from a trapeze. (Thomas and Rachel Fry, 1995).

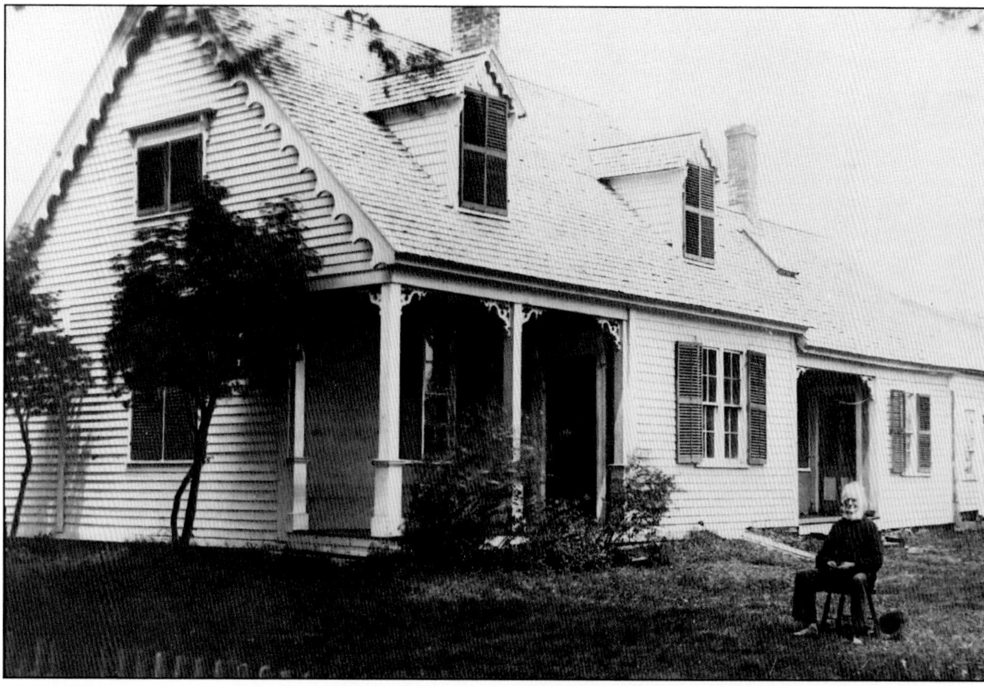

The Tillotson House. The N. Tillotson home at 241 South Longyard Road was moved there from the opposite side of the road. Silence Mathews lived here in this century. The house, which has been extensively remodeled, is now surrounded with brick. (Frank and Mary Bannish, 1995).

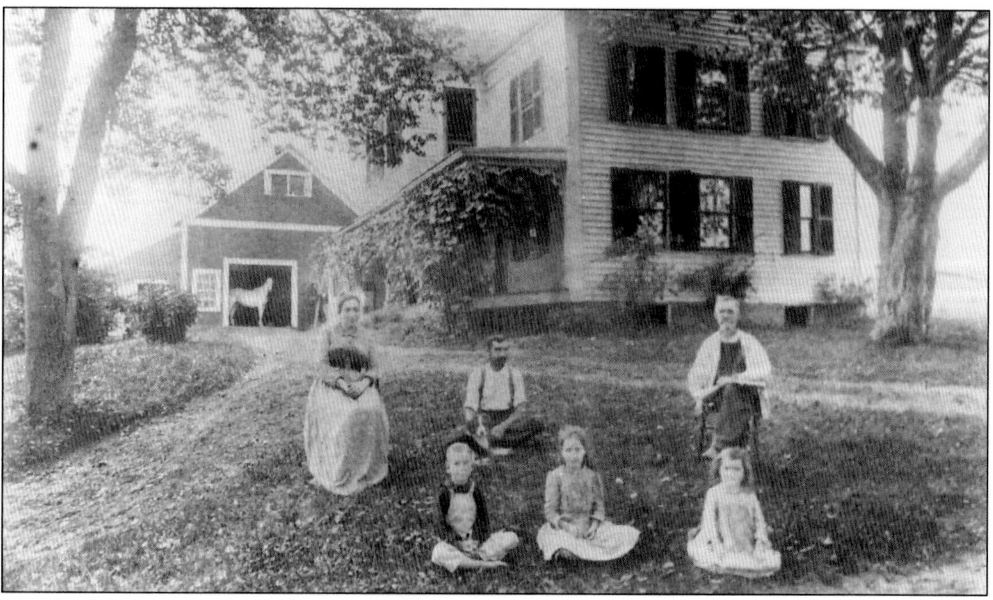

The Fred Jackson House before 1902. Dewey and Adeline Jackson had another son, Fred, who lived on the road which bears his name. Shown are Mrs. Hattie (Palmer) Jackson, Mr. Frederick Jackson, and Dewey L. Jackson. Three of Hattie and Fred's children, Orlo D., Helen E., and Adeline, are seated in the foreground; their fourth child, Graham, would soon be born. This house later burned. Leon Barnes shared this photograph from his collection.

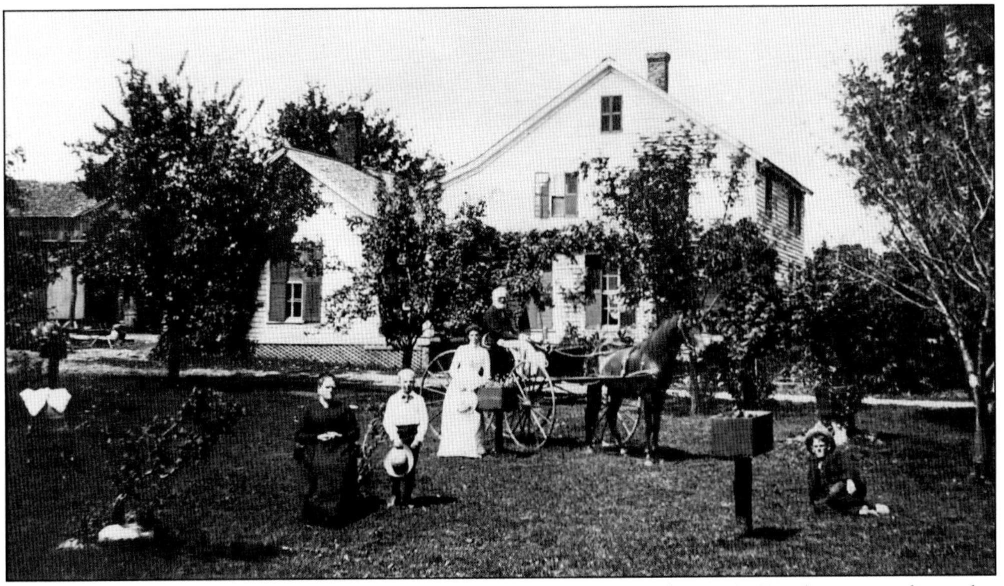

The Hastings House. Virgil Hastings is seated in his wagon; his wife Sarah is seated on the grass. The woman standing may be Virgil and Sarah's daughter Anne (Hastings) Viets, with her husband Charles reclining on the right and their son holding his hat. T. Rising Jr. owned this abode in 1854, Virgil Hastings owned it in 1870, and A.B.M. Hastings owned it in 1894. This house, which was located on the west side of Hastings Road, burned to the ground in 1955.

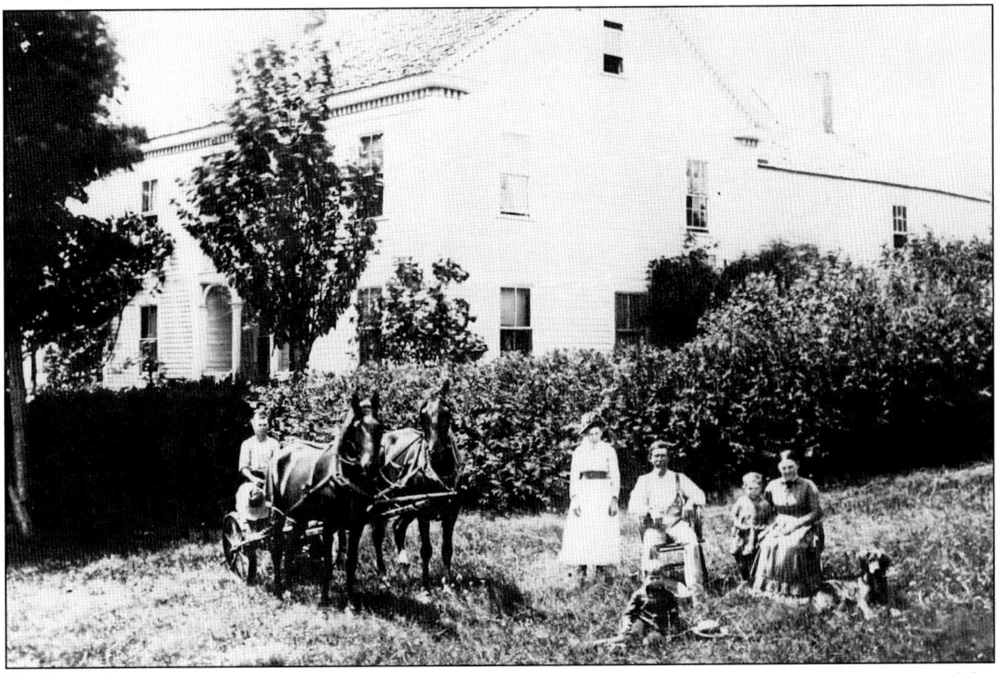

The Julius Hollister House after October 1883. This house at 31 Hillside Road was owned by Hiram Hollister in 1854, and by his son, Julius F. Hollister, in 1870 and 1894. It is probable that Hiram built a new residence at what is now 103 Granville Road before turning his farm over to his eldest son. Julius and his wife, Juliette (Loy) Hollister, are shown seated with four of their seven children: Herbert, Grace, Cyrus, and Edmond. (Frank and Agnes Piekarski, 1995).

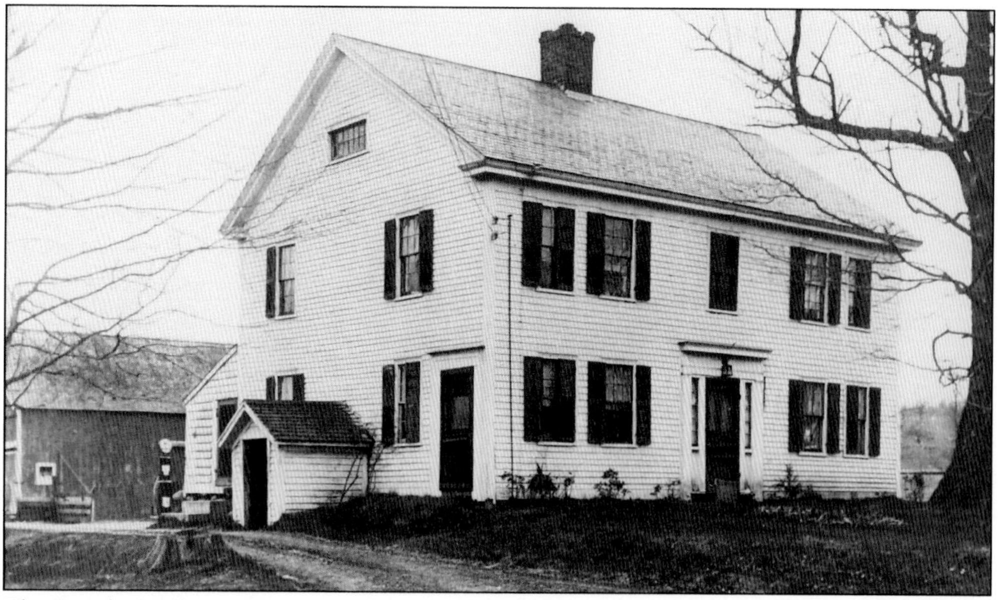

The Dwight Hollister House. Hiram Strong Hollister came to live in Southwick before 1830, the first Hollister to establish a residence here. Although this house at 103 Granville Road was not on the 1854 map, Hiram was living here by 1870. His son, Hiram Dwight (called Dwight), owned the house in 1894, and he and his wife Mary raised six children: Jennie, Albert, Luther, Ernest, Edna, and Eliza. Some descendants of Hiram Strong Hollister still live in Southwick. (Richard and Mary Brown, 1995).

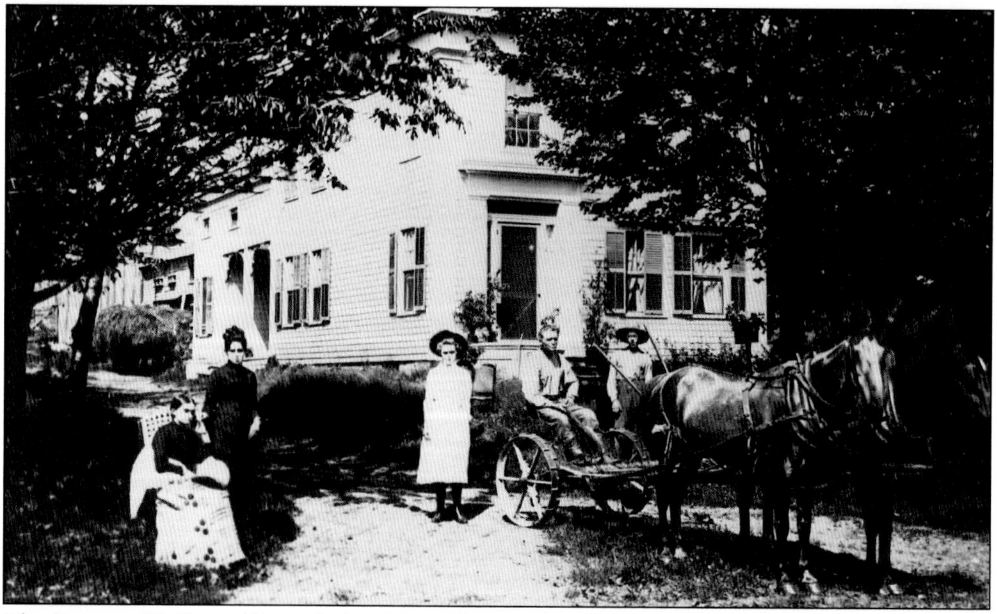

The Bennett Hollister House before December 1896. John Bennett Hollister, the third son of Hiram Strong Hollister, was the owner of this home at 91 Granville Road in 1870 and 1894. The dwelling was built after 1854 for John, who is shown here sitting on the farm equipment near his wife Abilenah (nee Mason) and his daughters Lilla and Lennie. The boy's identity is not known. Lennie Hollister later married Lincoln Bugbee, for whom Bugbee Road is named. (Steven and Kristie Girroir, 1995).

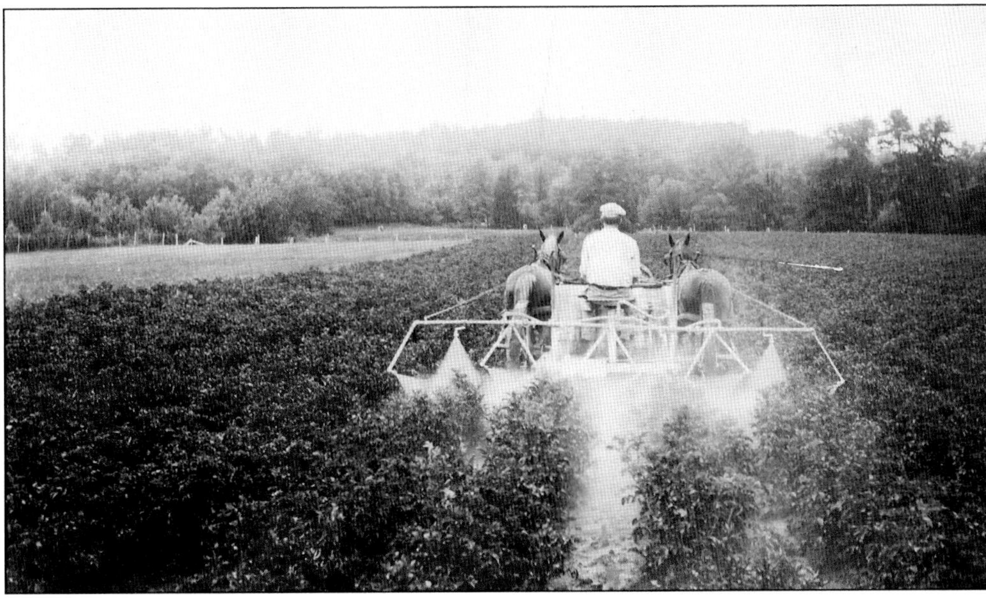

Spraying the Potato Crop. For many years, the threat insects have posed to crops has necessitated spraying. Here a two-horse team pulls the sprayer.

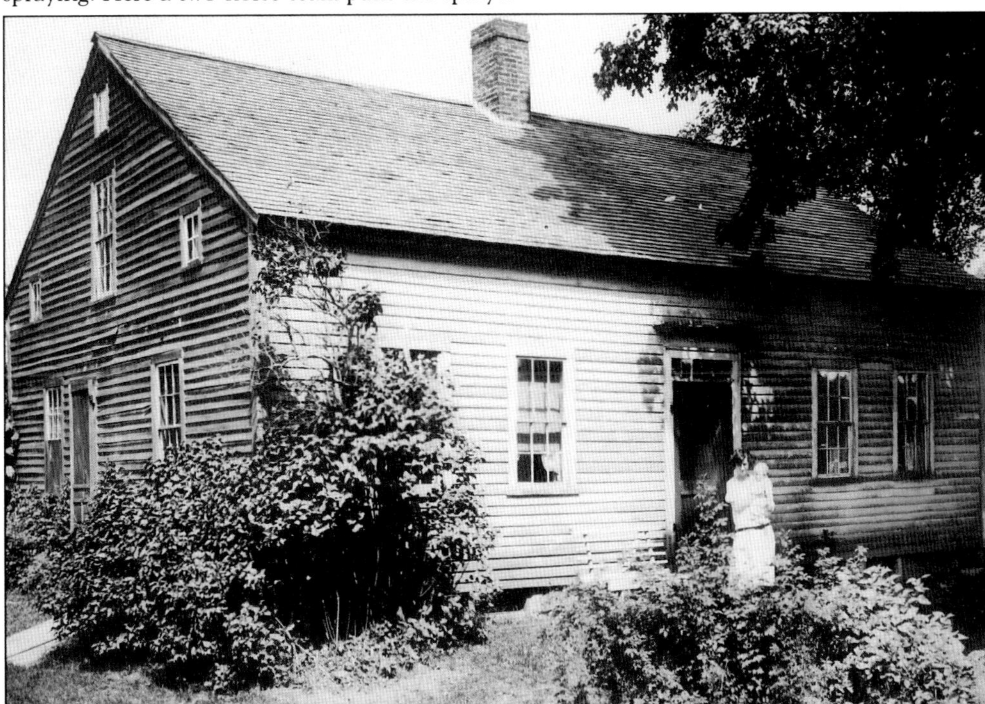

The Seth Gillett House. Very near the road, on the northwest corner of the intersection of Vining Hill Road with College Highway, this house was built by Rodolphus Gillett. His son, Seth Gillett, lived there in 1854, and Seth's son, Charles J., was owner in 1894. This photograph, taken on August 3, 1925, shows Hazel Feldman holding her son, five-month-old Jacob Jr. The house was moved in 1991 and is now located at 73 Vining Hill Road. (James and Lori Reardon, 1995).

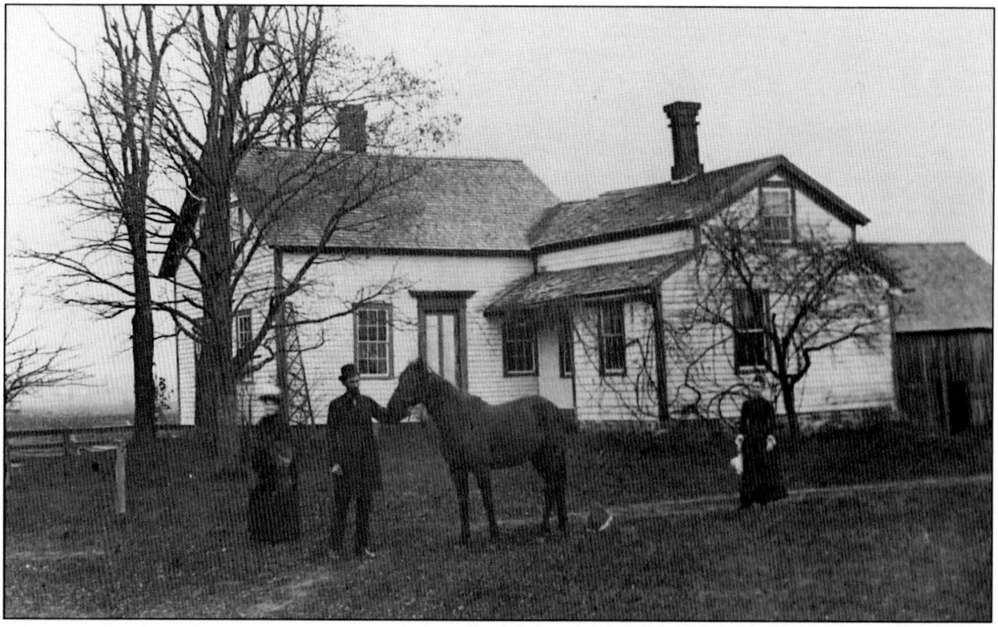

The Hills House. On the east side of College Highway just a short distance from the Connecticut border is the home of Elwin C. Hills. Shown are Mrs. Elwin C. Hills (nee Emily C. Loomis), Elwin, and their daughter Mabel, who became the wife of Whitney J. Root in 1900. This house, at 22 College Highway, was Elwin's first Southwick location; he later built a large Victorian home at 26 College Highway.

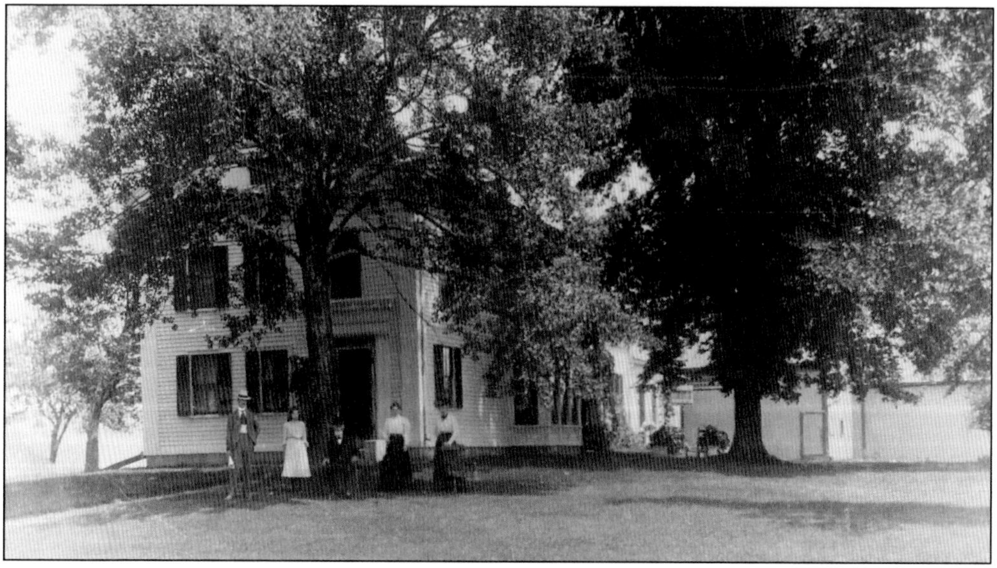

The Miller House. This dwelling, at 264 College Highway, was owned by H. Vining in 1854, and by Calvin S. Miller in both 1870 and 1894. Notice the tree sticking out of the tobacco tent on the left side. Since shade tobacco tents were first used in Massachusetts in 1902 (by the Millers and Arnolds of Southwick), this photograph can be dated as 1902 or later. Three generations of Millers are shown here: Herbert Miller (son of Calvin), Herbert's daughter Agnes, Calvin S. Miller, Herbert's wife Jennie (nee Hollister), and Calvin's wife Melissa T. (Loomis) Miller. (Steven Haas, 1995).

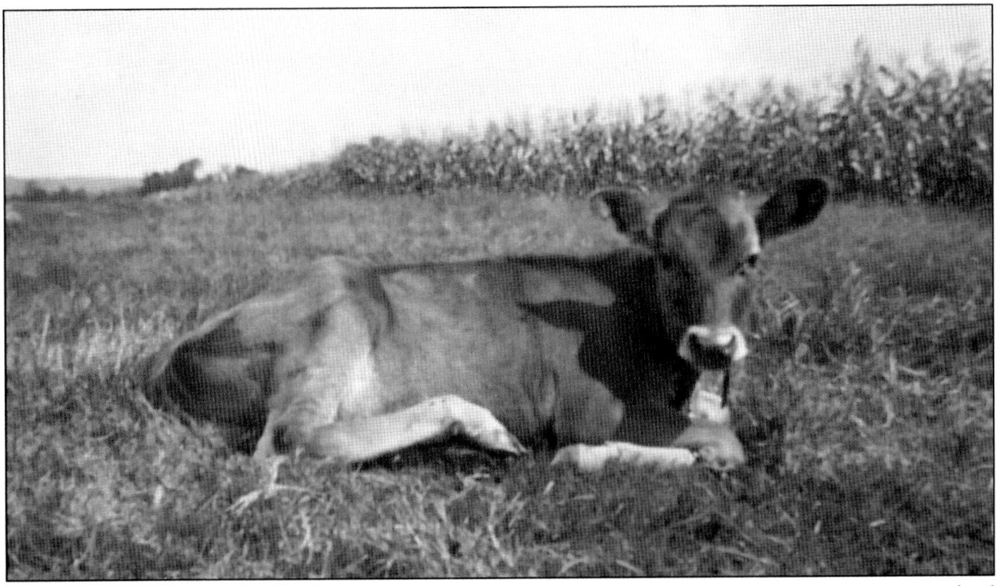

A Dairy Cow. George Steere, in addition to bee-keeping and other farming activities, had a herd of dairy cattle, whose milk he sold to H.P. Hood and later to Pioneer Dairy. This is "Clementine."

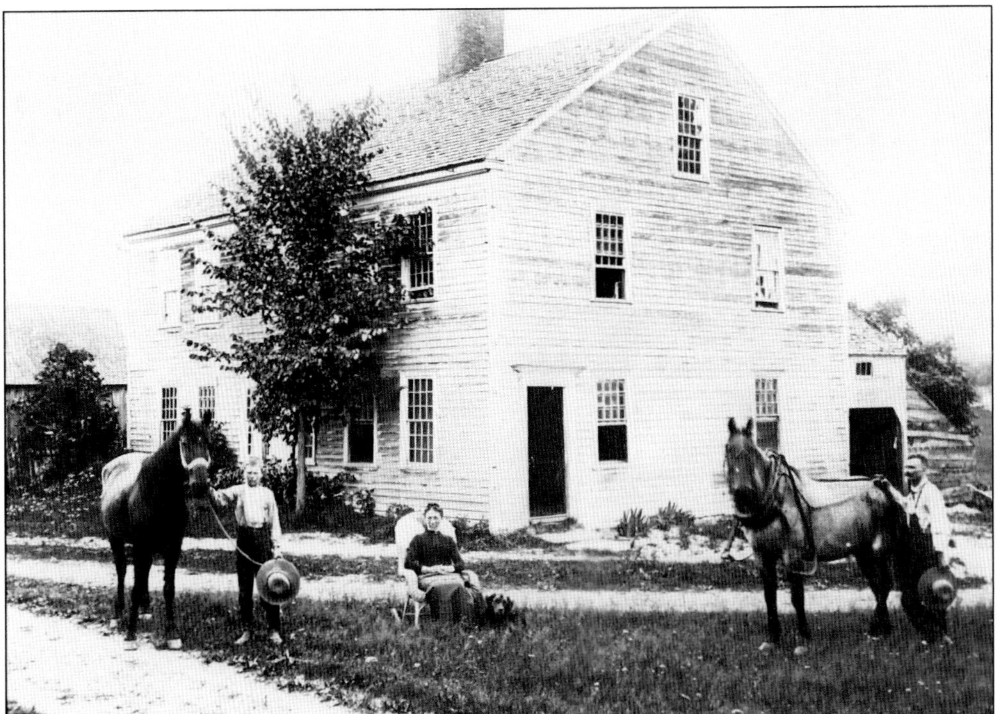

The Doherty House. This house, owned by Ham Loomis, appears on the earliest map we have, dated before 1823. J.W. Loomis was the owner in both 1854 and 1870. Some time later, it was bought by George Doherty, who is shown here in about 1893 with his wife Nellie and his son James. George came to the United States from Ireland in 1868 and became a naturalized citizen.

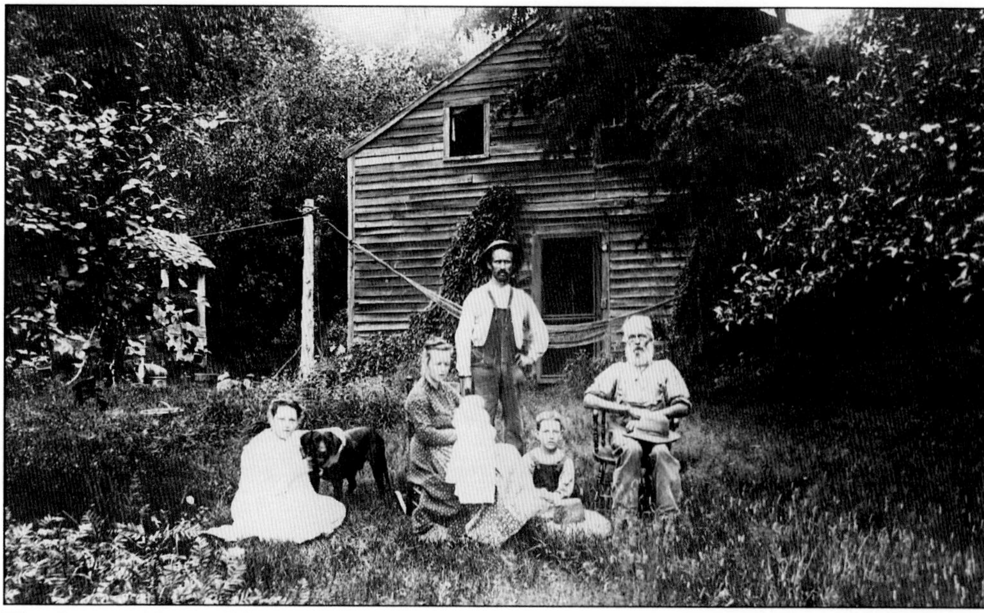

The Stevens House. Edwin Stevens, a veteran of the American Civil War who served in the 27th Massachusetts Infantry (from his hometown of Southwick), is sitting in front of his house, one of the oldest in town. With Edwin are his sons Sumner (standing) and Hubert (sitting on the ground). The others have been tentatively identified: Sumner's wife is holding the baby and Edwin's daughter Minerva has her arm around the dog. Hubert was born in about 1876. (Porter and Avis Stevens, 1995).

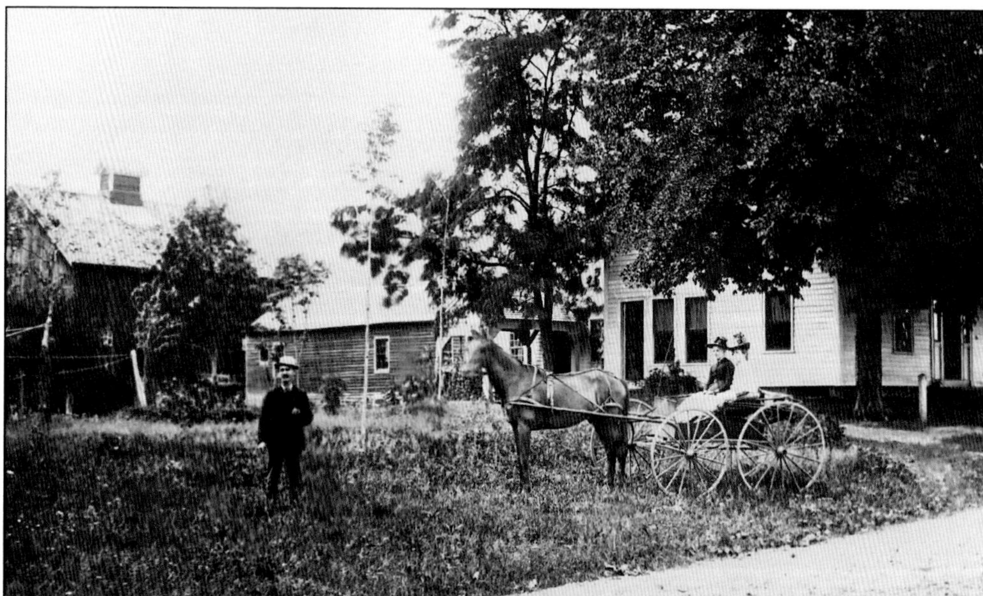

The Marvin Lambson House. Lorenzo A. Lambson owned this home at 261 South Loomis Street in 1870. By 1894, Lorenzo's son, Marvin D., lived here, and in the twentieth century, Marvin's son, Lorenzo D., was the owner. Marvin D. Lambson is shown. The ladies are unidentified, but a family member states that Marvin's wife Cora and his sisters Izetta and Elizabeth are not among them. (Joseph and Judy Radwilowicz, 1995).

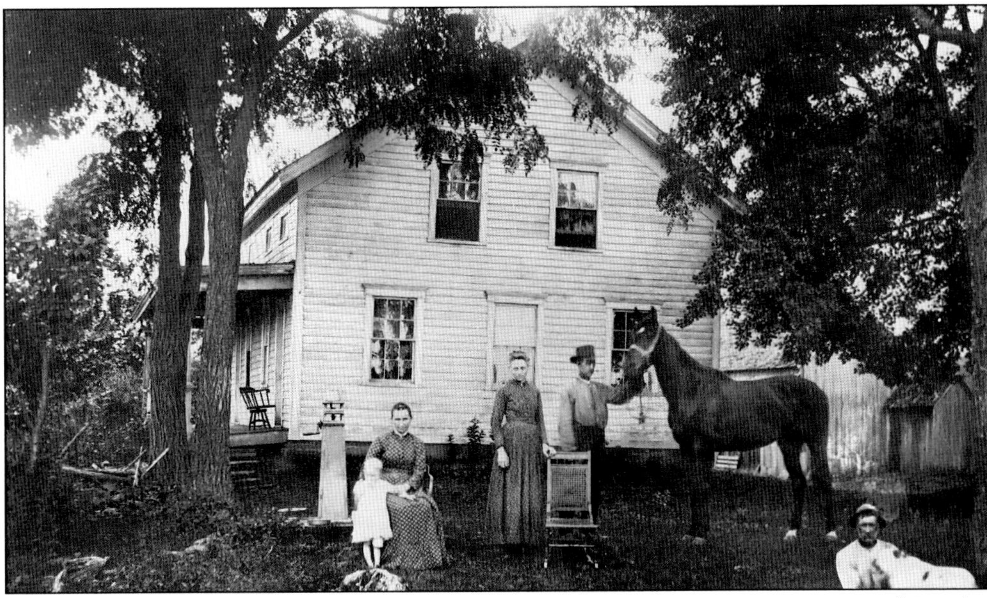

The C.H. Cushman House. Charles H. Cushman owned this house at 139 Vining Hill Road in 1894. G. Vining, probably Gaius Vining, was listed as the owner in 1854 and 1870. Gaius and his wife Martha both lived into their nineties, and are buried in the Old Southwick Cemetery. Eric and Alida Anderson, the parents of Walter S. Anderson, were later owners of this house. The people in the photograph have not been identified. (John and Cindi Francis, 1995).

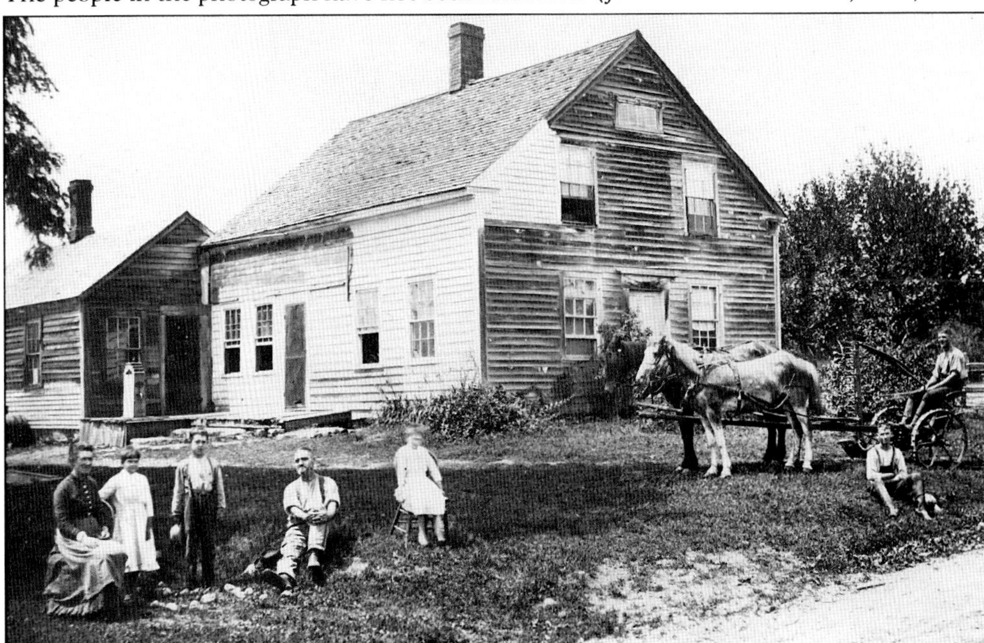

The Skinner House. Elisha H. Skinner served in Company C of the 25th Connecticut Regiment during the American Civil War. He and his wife Julia (Weeks) lived in this house at 115 Mort Vining Road, the second house south of the former Swedish Church parsonage. A. Fowler owned this property in 1854 and 1870, and Enfred Anderson owned it after Elisha Skinner. (Del and Suzanne Bentley, 1995).

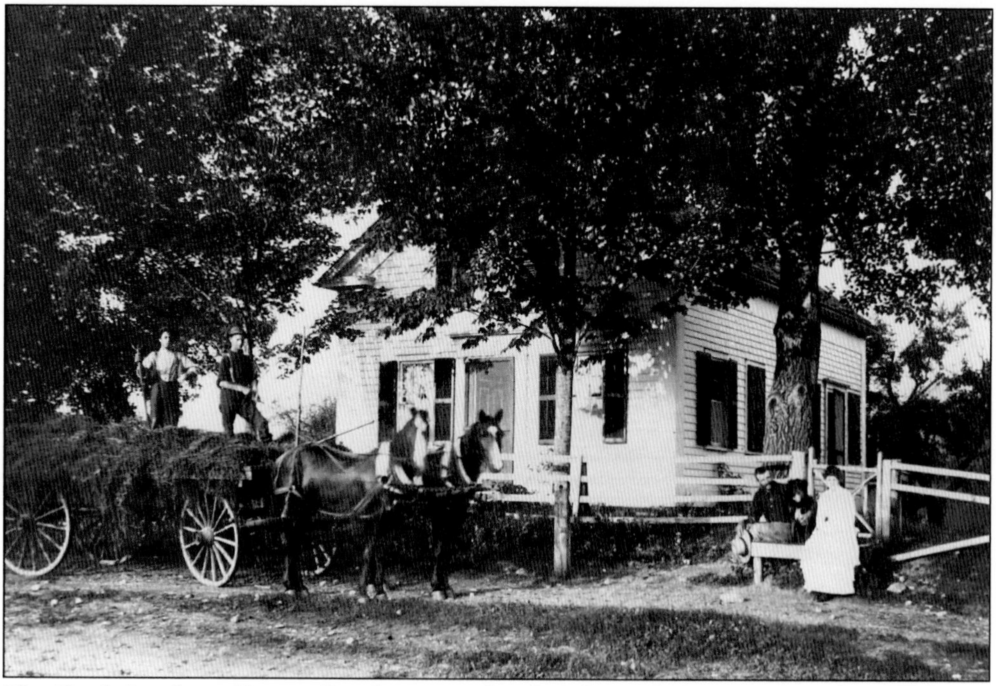

The Frank Lambson House. On the east side of College Highway, just south of the Old Southwick Cemetery, is this dwelling at #356. The house appears on the 1854 map, but the owner is unidentified. In 1870 and 1894, the owners were George Prior and Frank D. Lambson respectively. Shown are Frank D. Lambson and his wife, Fannie E. (Webb) Lambson, who were married in March 1884. The boys on the haywagon have not been identified. (Robert Johnson and Diane Wojcek, 1995).

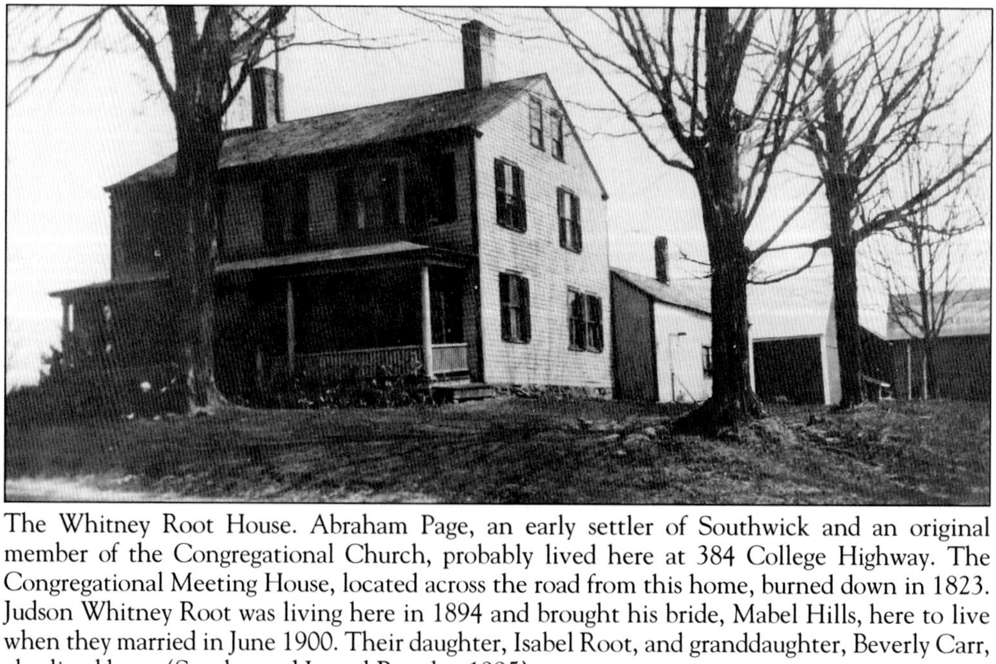

The Whitney Root House. Abraham Page, an early settler of Southwick and an original member of the Congregational Church, probably lived here at 384 College Highway. The Congregational Meeting House, located across the road from this home, burned down in 1823. Judson Whitney Root was living here in 1894 and brought his bride, Mabel Hills, here to live when they married in June 1900. Their daughter, Isabel Root, and granddaughter, Beverly Carr, also lived here. (Stanley and Laurel Brzoska, 1995).

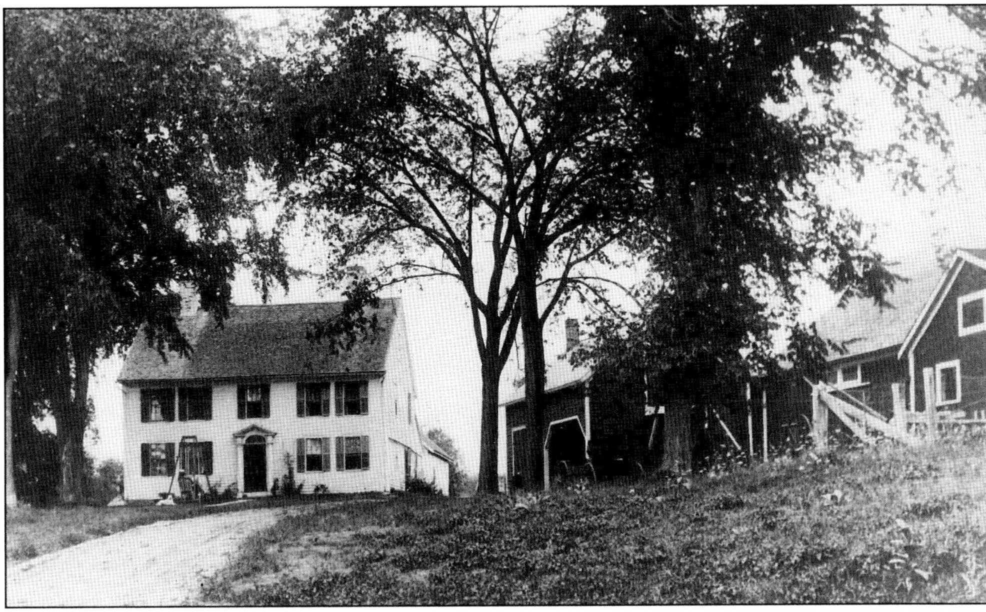

The Webb House. This dwelling was built about 1740, probably by John Root, one of the original settlers of the town. Reuben Clark was an innkeeper in this building shortly after the American Revolution. Captain Clark was killed in a powder mill explosion on October 9, 1813. Owners of this home, at 18 Klaus Anderson Road, have included Amos Webb, his son, Albert F. Webb, and Albert R. Webb, grandson of Amos. The house was a twin to the C.J. Root house, shown below. (Philip and Cornelia Jacquier, 1995.)

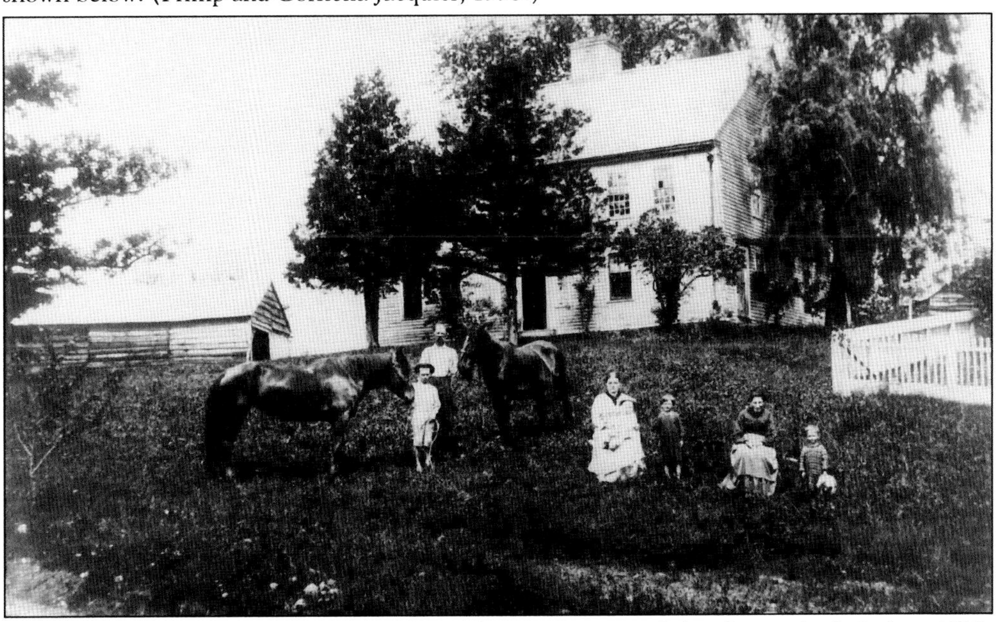

The C.J. Root House. In 1887, Charles Judson Root owned this home, built before 1792, which was located on what is now Klaus Anderson Road. Charles holds his horse, with his son Whitney in front of him. Charles' second wife Emma holds daughter Josephine, with daughter Julia next, then Mariah Root (mother of Charles) and daughter Nellie. The Root home was destroyed by fire on July 5, 1918.

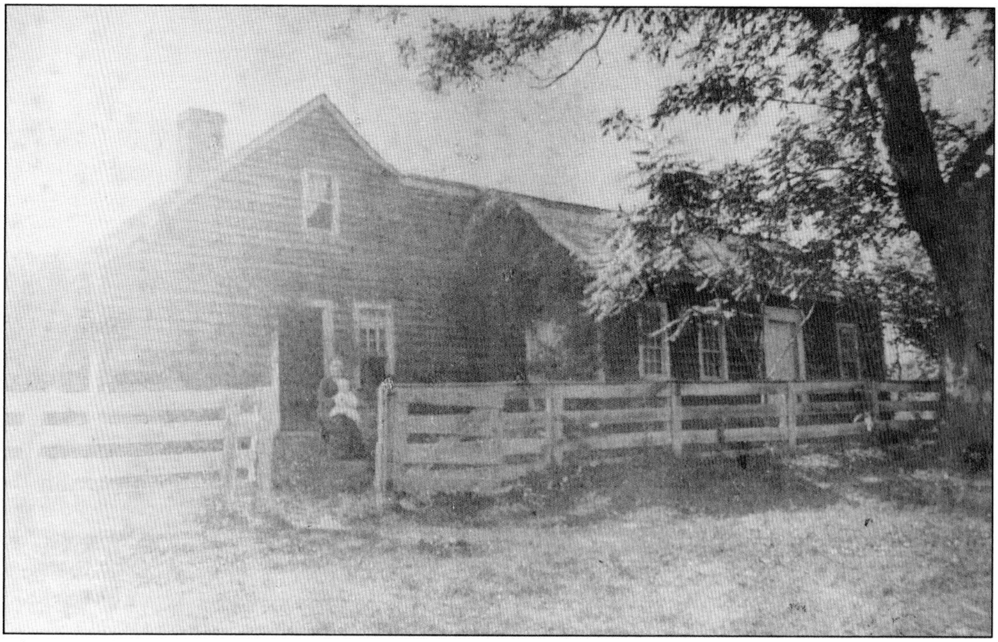

The French House, 1880. Sampson French was probably the original owner of this eighteenth-century dwelling, which was located on the west side of Sheep Pasture Road. A depression between the cutleaf maples between #125 and #117 shows the former location of this house. Mary Ann (Blood) Arnold has her oldest child, Charles M. Arnold, on her lap.

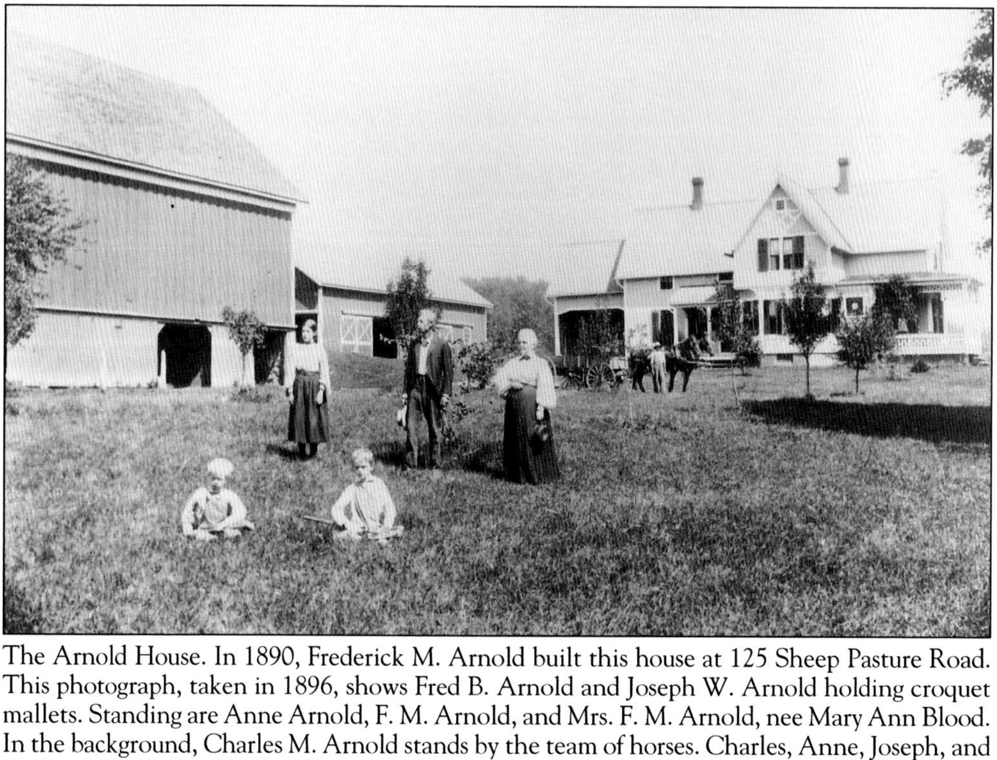

The Arnold House. In 1890, Frederick M. Arnold built this house at 125 Sheep Pasture Road. This photograph, taken in 1896, shows Fred B. Arnold and Joseph W. Arnold holding croquet mallets. Standing are Anne Arnold, F. M. Arnold, and Mrs. F. M. Arnold, nee Mary Ann Blood. In the background, Charles M. Arnold stands by the team of horses. Charles, Anne, Joseph, and Fred were children of Frederick and Mary Ann. (Stephen and Linda Arnold, 1995).

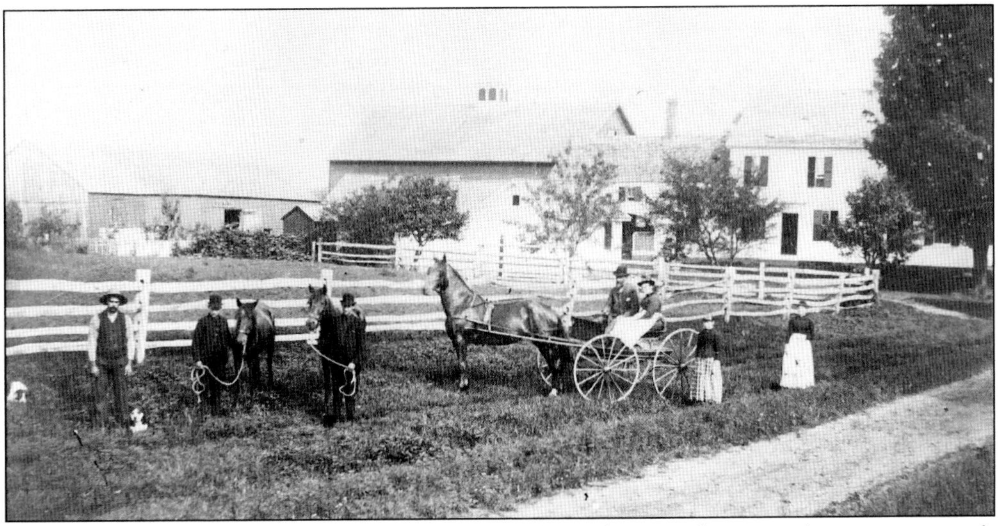

The Dibble House. Emerson C. Dibble and his wife Emeline are shown in their carriage, with their children: Albert, Arthur, Martha, and Flora. Daughter Dora is looking out the upstairs window. To the far left is John Kohlor, a hired man, listed on the 1900 U.S. Census as Yanos Kayla, who came to the United States in 1889 from Hungary. "Mattie" and Flora married William S. Barnes and George L. Warner respectively. Notice the beautifully groomed horses. The house is located at #59 North Longyard Road. (Stephen and Janice Tingley, 1995).

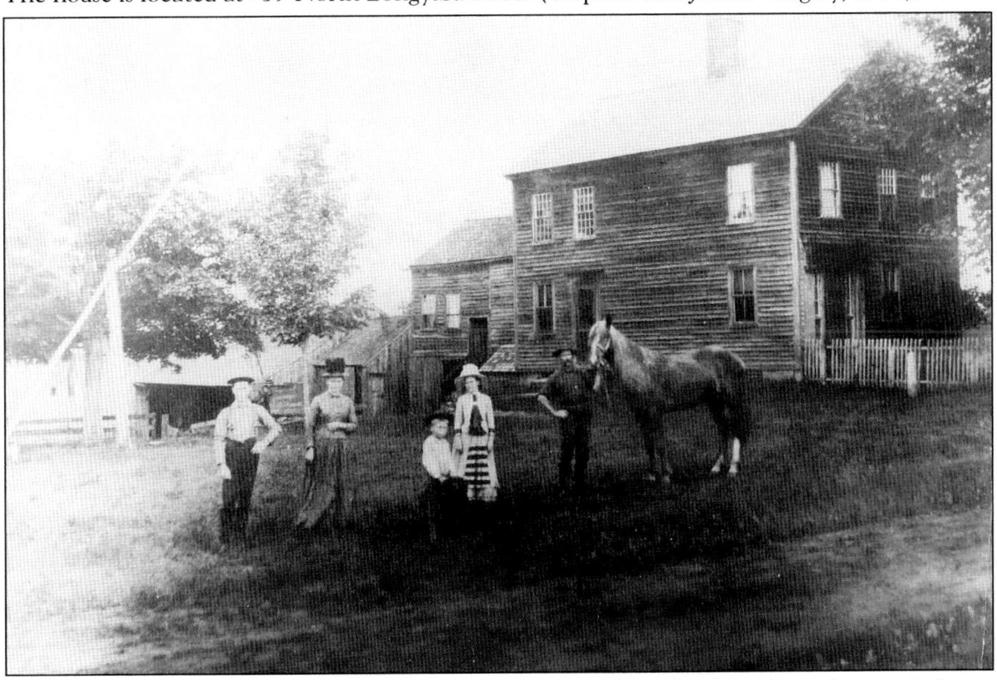

The Warner House. Solomon C. Warner served as a cook in the 8th Massachusetts Infantry during the American Civil War. He moved from the "X" in Springfield to the "country" on the advice of his doctor, and bought this farm from Charles Easton in March 1882. Lemuel Easton had owned the dwelling in 1854 and 1870. Shown are Herbert Warner, Mary Elizabeth (Kirtland) Warner (wife of Solomon), Franklin D. Warner, Alice Warner (later Mrs. Henry B. Hosmer), and Solomon C. Warner himself. (Stetson and Marjorie Arnold, 1995).

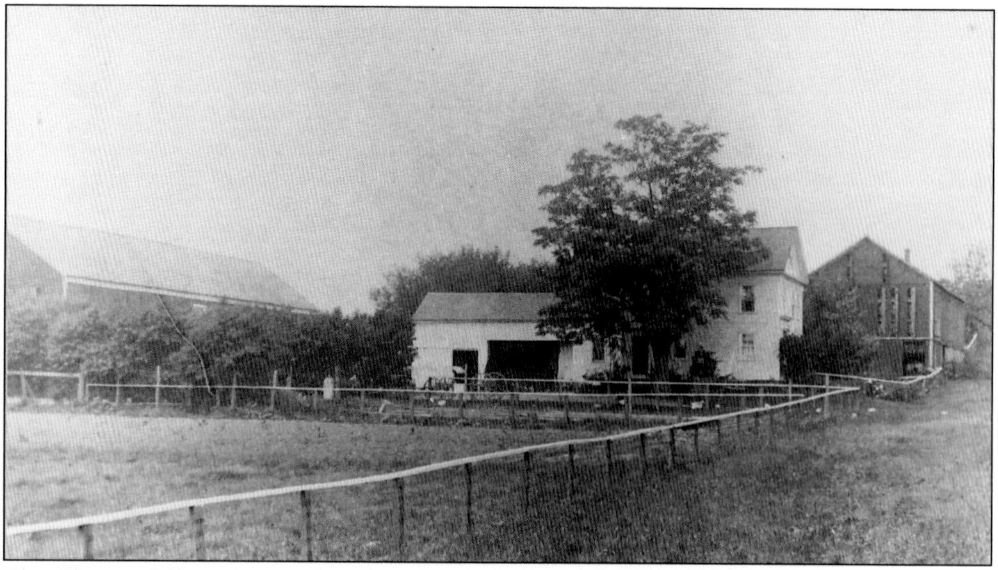

The Chester Gillett House. Chester Gillett and his wife Ida (nee Skelly) lived on this farm at 4 Rising Corner Road. One can see that tobacco is hanging in the woodshed and is undergoing the curing process in the barn at the right. This photograph, handed down in the family, was taken by the Howes brothers, whose collections are now held by the Ashfield (MA) Historical Society. (Don and Lydia Lepenas, 1995).

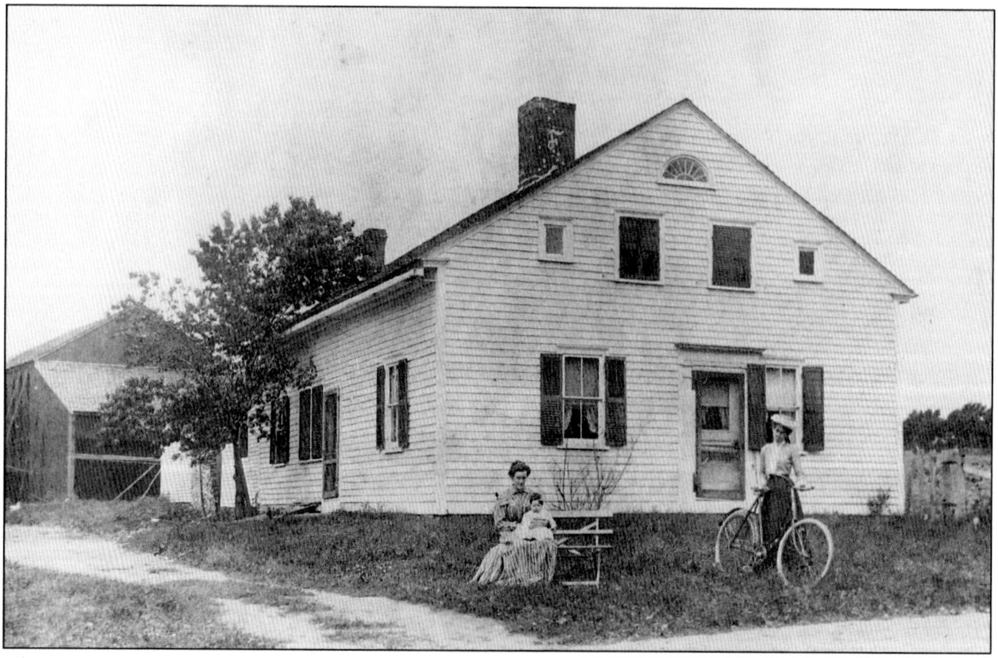

The James Skelly House, *c.* 1900. This home at 309 South Longyard Road was owned by the Barker family: Almond H. in 1854 and 1870, and A.R. Barker in 1894. Ida Skelly, daughter of James and Jane, displays her bicycle. James came to the United States from Ireland in 1864. The lady with the baby may be Ida's older sister, Elizabeth (Skelly) Austin. During Ida's married life with Chester Gillett, she lived very near here at 4 Rising Corner Road. (Francis and Bernadette Case, 1995).

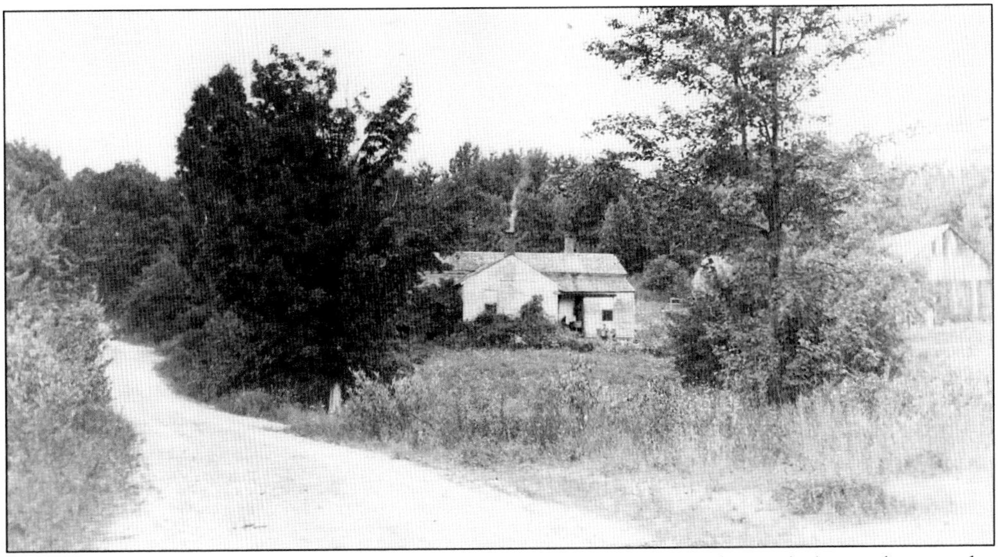

The A.J. Cushman House. This house, now #74-A Congamond Road, located near the junction of Sheep Pasture and Congamond Roads, is shown looking up the hill to the west. U. Camel (Campbell?) is listed as the 1854 owner. In 1870, George W. Hamilton, son of William and Caroline (Dewey) Hamilton, lived here with his wife Mary (nee Gillett) and their three children. By 1894, the owner was Arthur J. Cushman, a bachelor. (Lawrence and Lynn DeChesser, 1995).

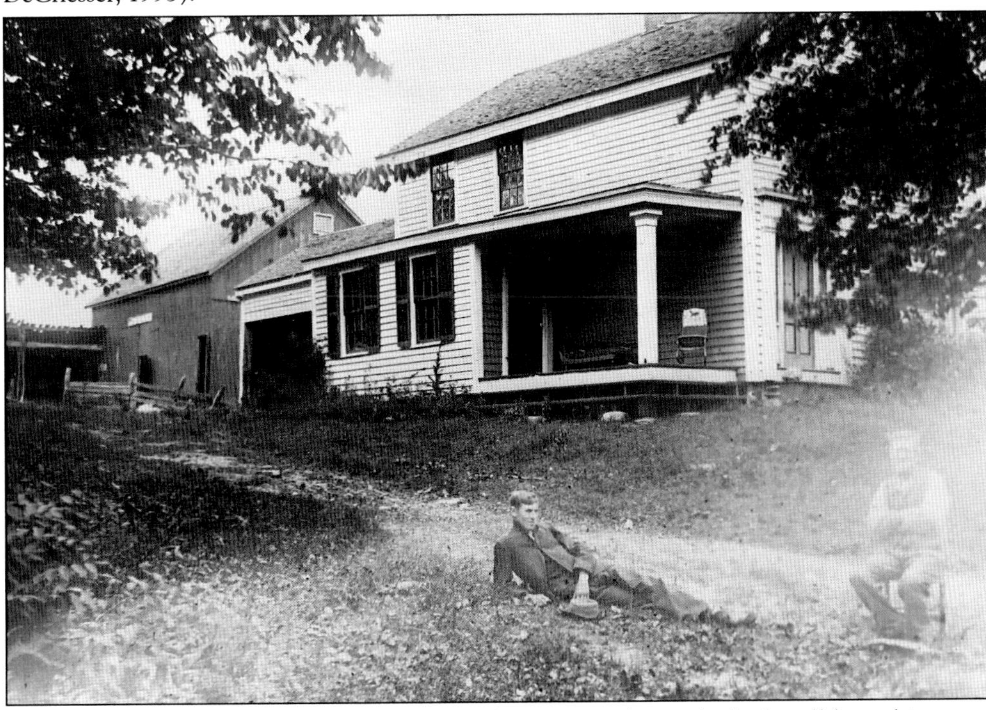

The Palmer House, c. 1890. Will Palmer lived at #43 on the road which still bears his name. The Palmer family had occupied this property off Hillside Road at least since 1854, when Mrs. C. Palmer was the owner. William G. Palmer, the owner in 1870, is shown here with his son Will. (Warren and Norma Baker, 1995).

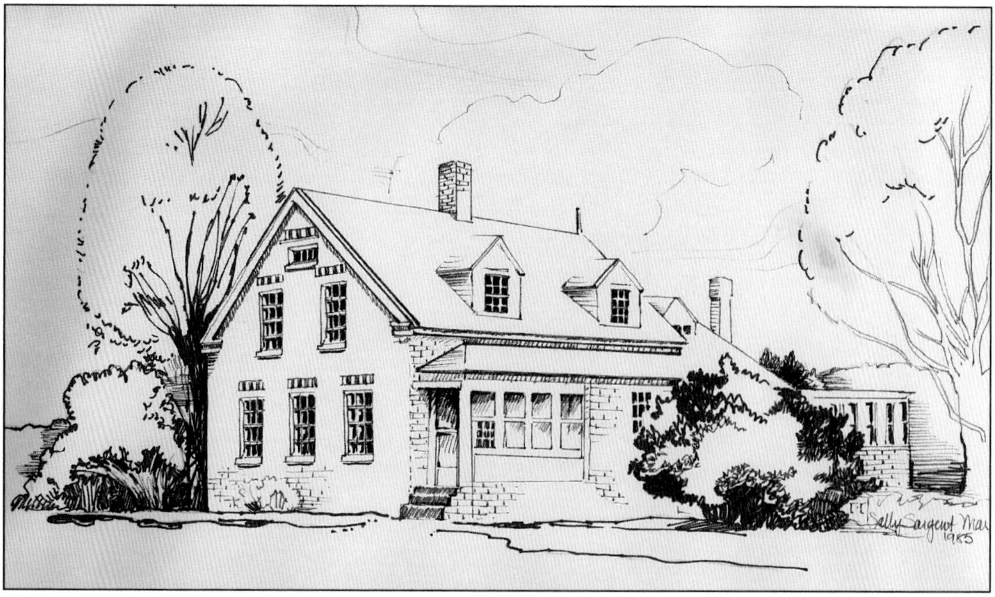

The Palmer Brothers Home. Located at 54 College Highway, this brick-faced residence was originally sided with clapboards. It appears on the 1854 map owned by S. Russell, and the Palmer brothers owned it in both 1870 and 1894. Herbert Webster has owned it since 1958.

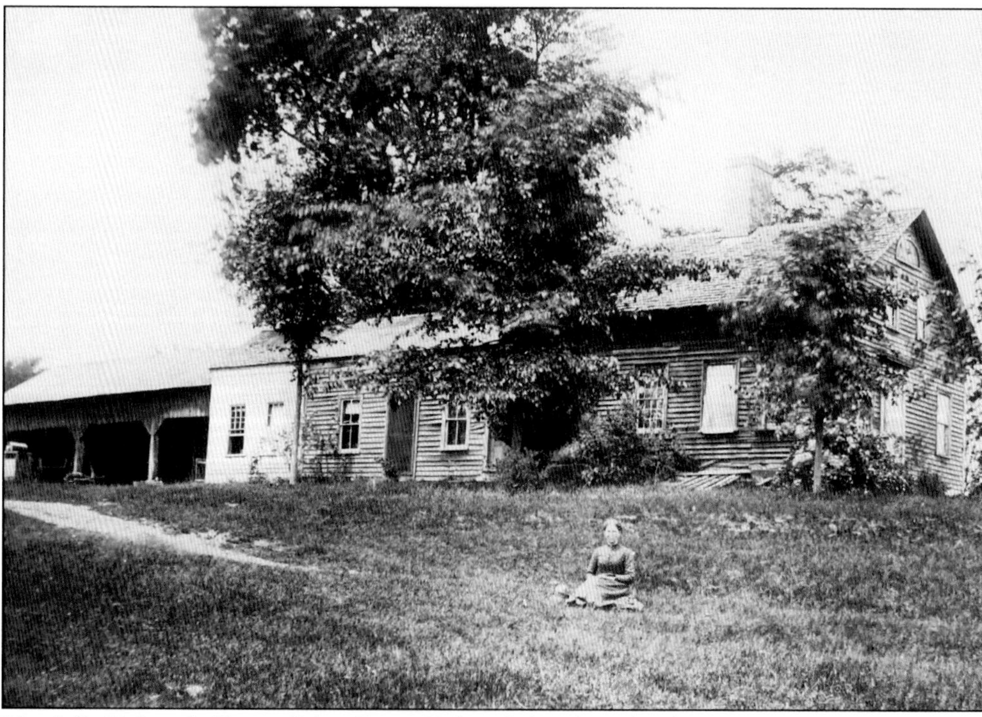

The J.O. Holcomb House. John Orrin Holcomb lived in this house at 253 South Longyard Road for at least twenty-four years; his name appears on both the 1870 and 1894 maps. The 1854 map shows H. Noble as the owner. Frank Orr Jr. lived here for a short time in more recent times. The half-moon window on the facade is an unusual feature. (Thomas and Diana Bazyk, 1995).

Chapter Five

People

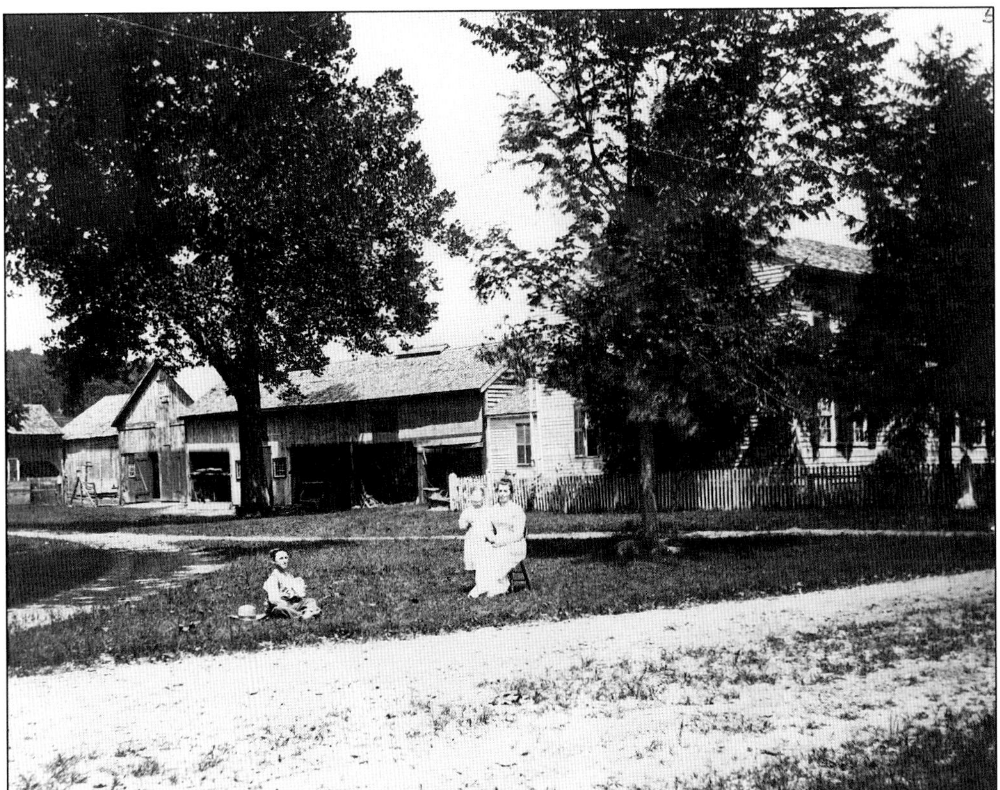

The Addison H. Coe House. On the site of the present Interstate Building Supply buildings, this dwelling appeared on the oldest map that the Southwick Historical Society, Inc. has available. On that map, which was made between 1808 and 1823, the owner was Richard Dickinson, after whom the Dickinson Grammar School was named. In 1854, H. Laflin was the owner; in 1870, the owner was B.B. Loomis. Addison C. Coe and Lillian Coe, children of Addison H. Coe, are pictured here with their mother.

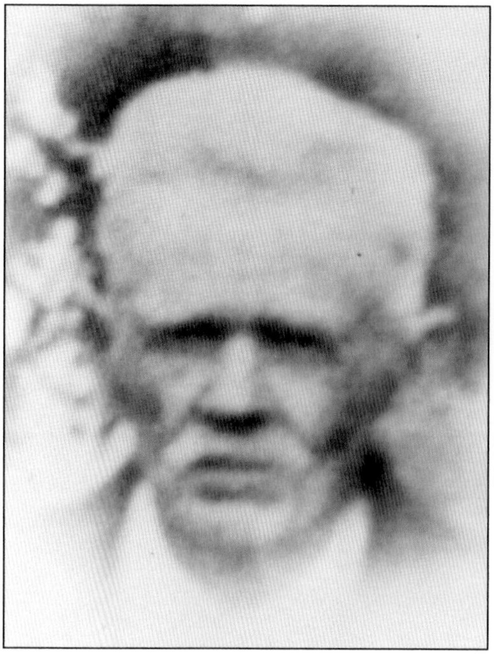 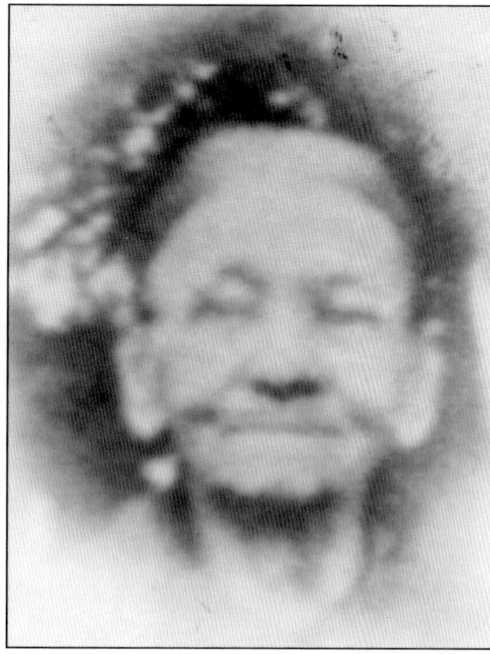

John and Hannah Peterson Anderson. John T. Anderson, born on November 26, 1859, in Ostergotland, Sweden, married Hannah Peterson at Ekehy, Sweden, on April 27, 1884. In 1888, they emigrated to the United States. Originally they settled in Perham, Maine, where several of their children were born, but at some time before 1910 they moved to Southwick. Their son Harold married Rose Sathory; their daughter Martha married Hjalmar Johnson.

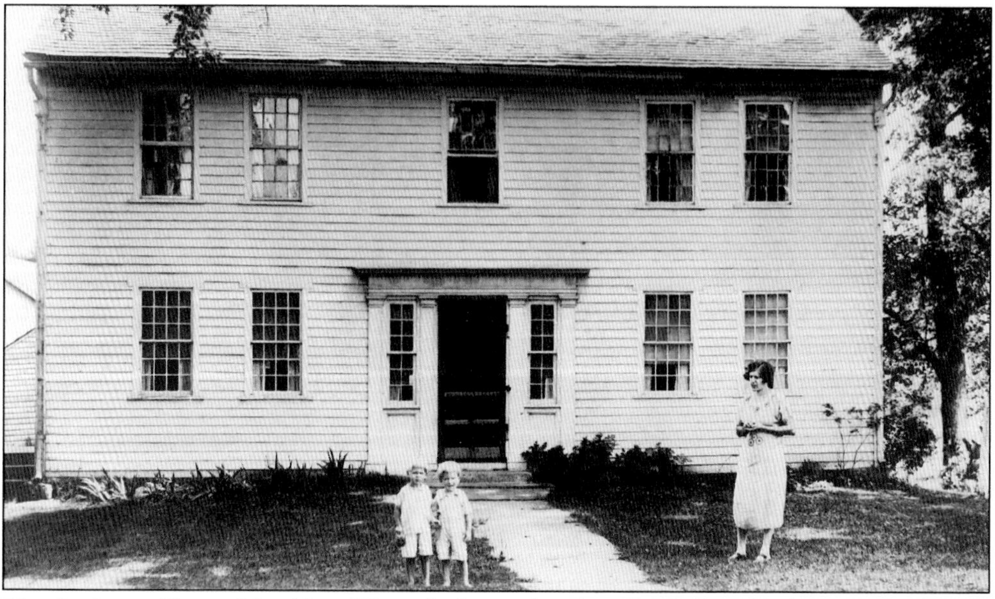

The Anderson House. Harold and Rose Anderson lived at 434 College Highway in this house, which was built for Dr. Levi W. Humphrey in the 1820s. Humphrey practiced *c.* 1820 to 1850. After Dr. Humphrey's death, his widow, Betsey (Stiles) Humphrey, lived here for many years. Rose (Sathory) Anderson is shown here with her nephew, Eldon Johnson (far left), and her son Elwood. (Benjamin Noga, 1995).

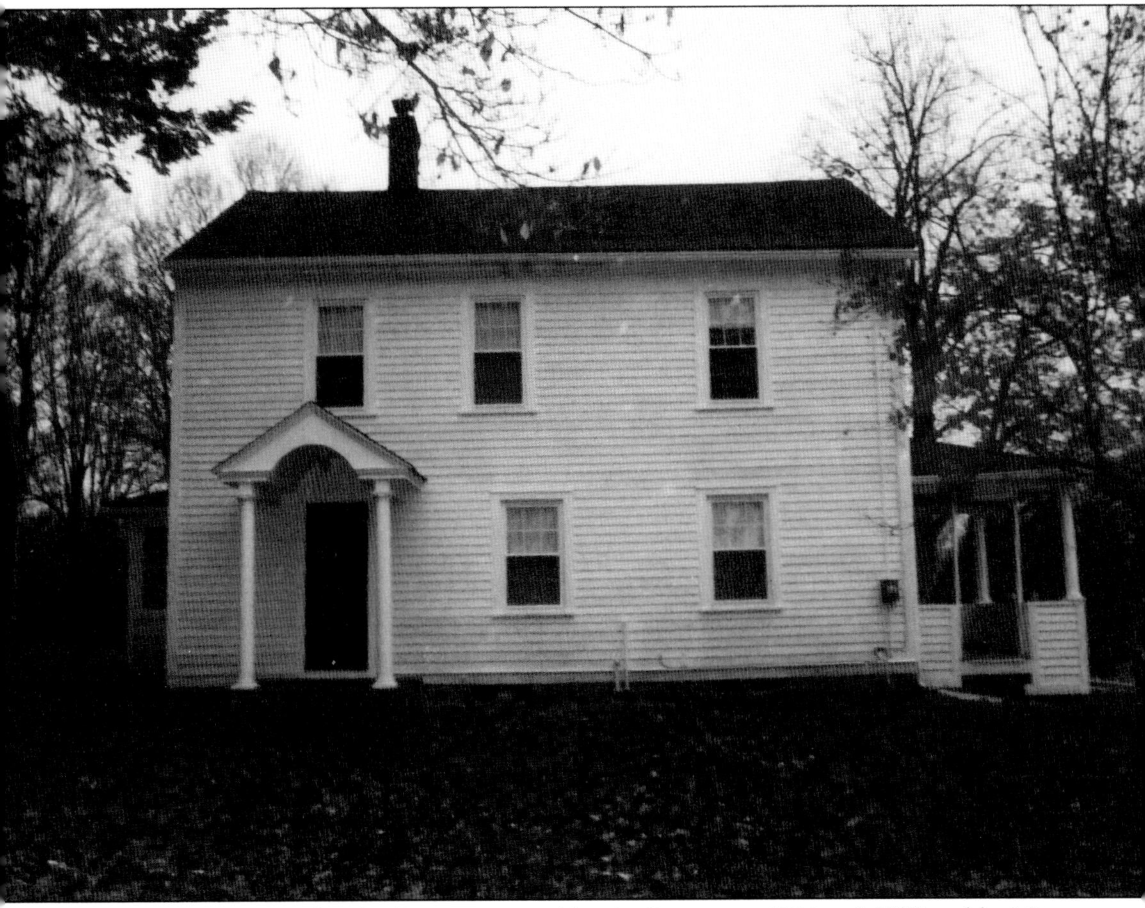

The Johnson House. This dwelling was owned by A. Granger in 1854 and 1870 and by Miss E. Granger in 1894. When a large group of people of Swedish descent settled in Southwick in the early 1900s, Hjalmar Johnson was among them. Hjalmar came to the United States in 1905 from his birthplace in Oland, Boda, Sweden, and bought this house at 441 College Highway. Hjalmar and his wife Martha (nee Anderson), who had been born in Perham, Aroostook County, Maine, raised their two sons, Elmer and Eldon, here. Eldon served as postmaster in the Town of Southwick for thirty years until his retirement. Eldon was deeply involved in attempts to preserve the town's unique history. A Life Member of the Southwick Historical Society, Inc., he was active in its work, and was also serving as chairman of the Southwick Historical Commission at the time of his death in 1994.

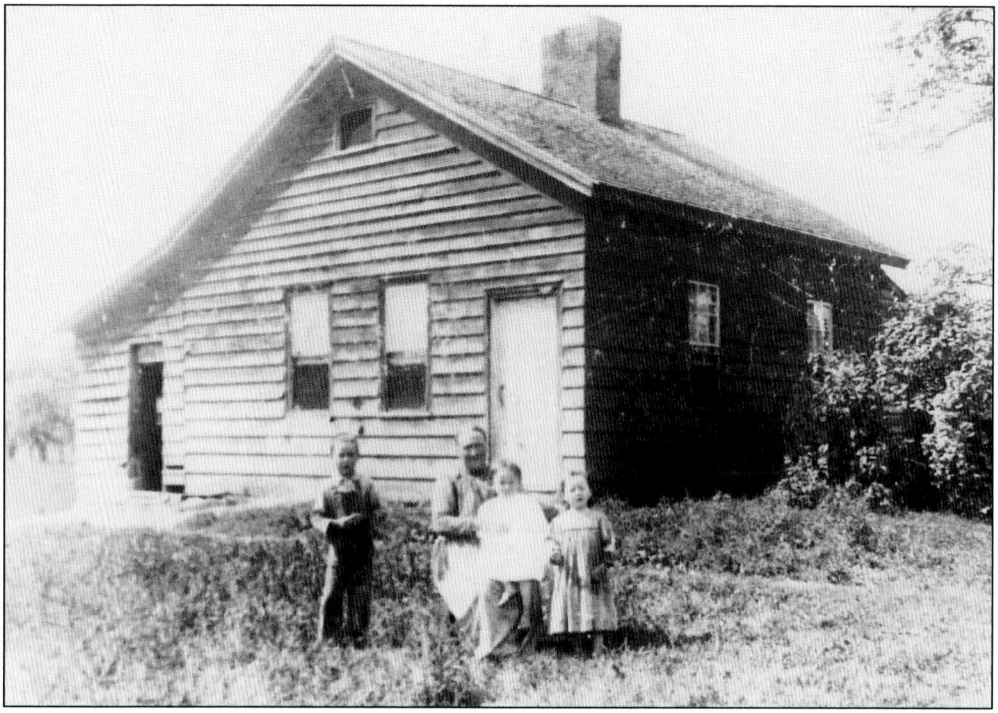

The Crowley House. Michael Crowley, who came to the United States from Ireland in 1881, lived in this house at 11 Feeding Hills Road. If the photograph was taken about 1900, then the people are John Crowley, Mrs. Michael Crowley, William D. Crowley, and Annie Crowley. (Richard and Lynn Power, 1995).

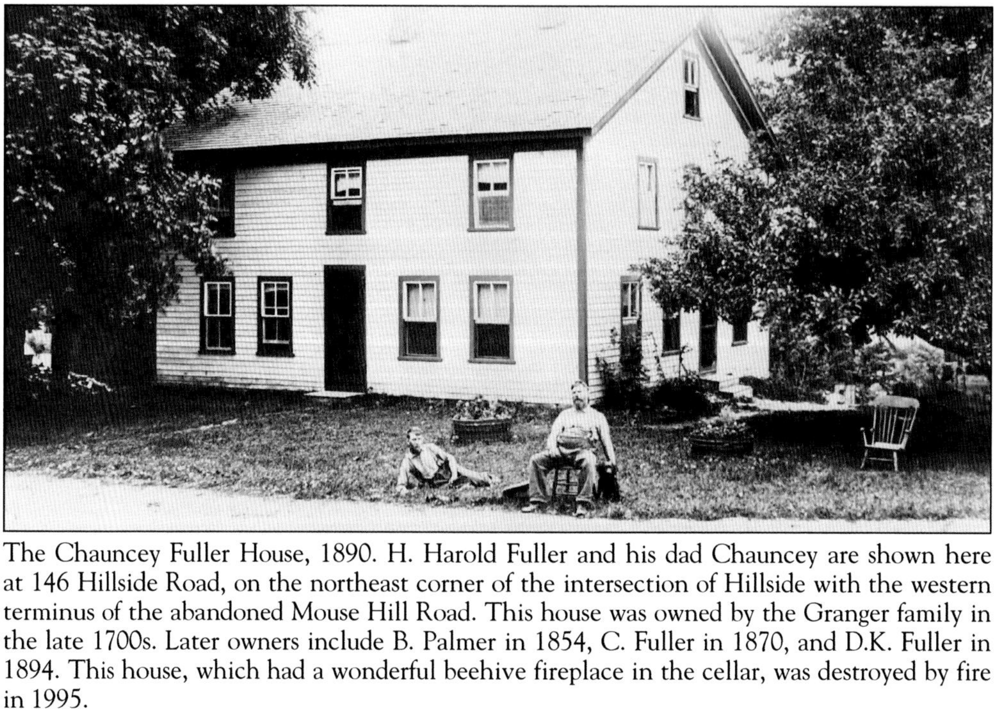

The Chauncey Fuller House, 1890. H. Harold Fuller and his dad Chauncey are shown here at 146 Hillside Road, on the northeast corner of the intersection of Hillside with the western terminus of the abandoned Mouse Hill Road. This house was owned by the Granger family in the late 1700s. Later owners include B. Palmer in 1854, C. Fuller in 1870, and D.K. Fuller in 1894. This house, which had a wonderful beehive fireplace in the cellar, was destroyed by fire in 1995.

Edith Chapman, 1889. The daughter of John and Eliza Chapman, Edith lived all her adult life in what was, in 1894, the only brick house in Southwick. She was an artist and naturalist, and preserved the area around her house as a sanctuary for the birds and animals she enjoyed watching.

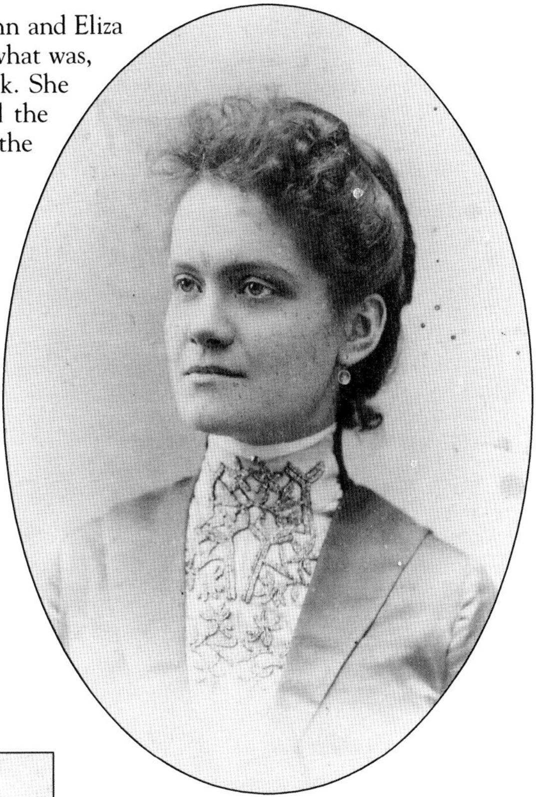

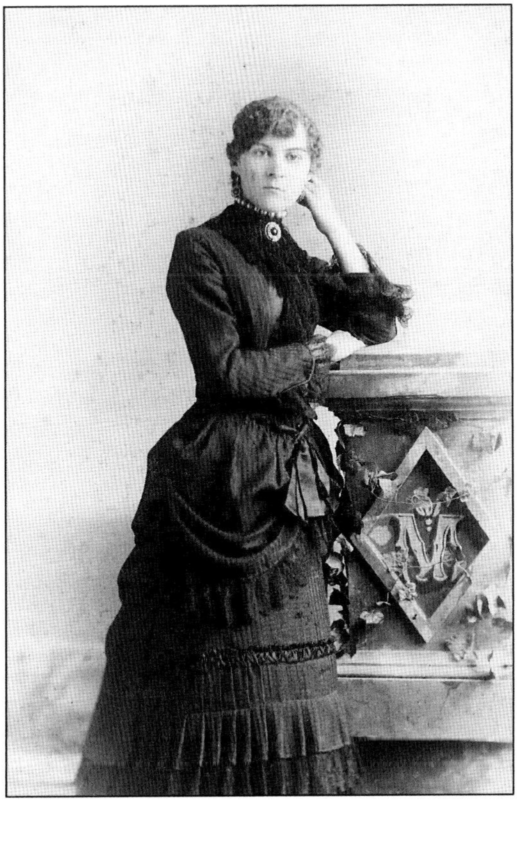

Frances Louise Malboeuf, *c.* 1900. The second wife of Canada native Napoleon Malboeuf, Frances raised at least five children, among whom was Gertrude, who became a teacher in the Southwick public schools for most of her adult life. The Malboeuf family lived on the east side of the intersection of Foster and South Longyard Roads, now the home of Martha Utzinger, who was also a Southwick teacher before her retirement.

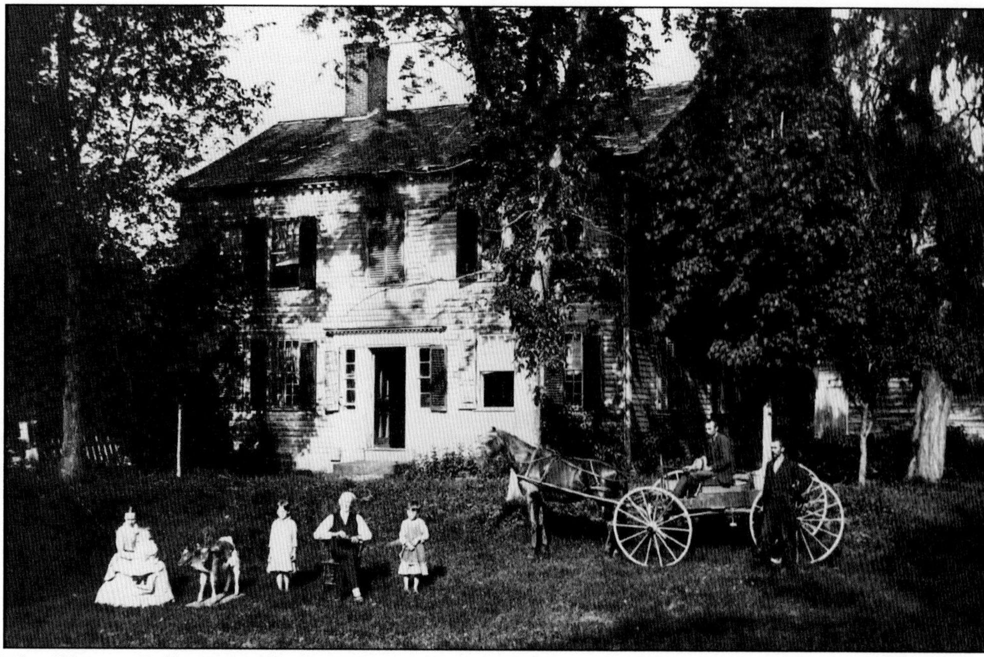

The Watson Fuller House before 1890. Almond Gillett built this house in the early 1800s for his wife Cynthia and their children: Isaac W., Chauncey S., Emeline, and Henry C. In 1870, Henry C. Gillett owned the house, which was located at the northeast corner of College Highway and Congamond Road. "Harry," who died on May 24, 1890, is the white-haired gentleman. His wife Adah, the daughter of Elam Goddard, had died three years earlier. The other people have not been identified. (Media City, 1995).

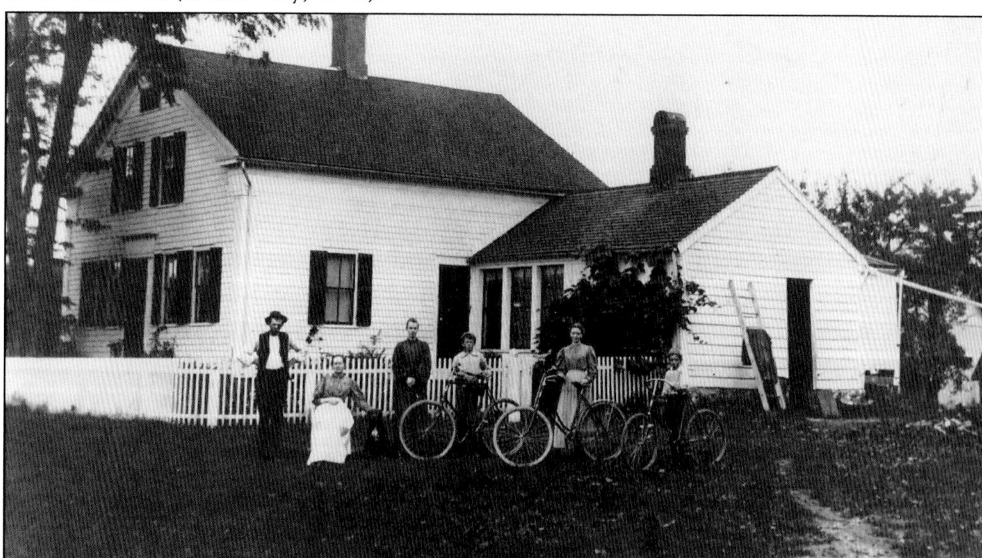

The Charles Gillett House. Socrates Gillett lived in this house, located at 8 Vining Hill Road, at least as early as 1854. Charles J. Gillett, the son of Socrates and Sophia (Holcomb), is shown in this photograph (taken after March 1897) with his wife Julia, daughter Hattie, son Chester, daughter Lucy, and son Arthur. C.J. was a cigar manufacturer and built a factory and warehouse (which still exists) near his home. (Roy and Marlene Benson, 1995).

Isabel Deming Root. Isabel Deming, the daughter of Ralph and Rose, was a 1926 graduate of Dickinson Grammar School. Here she wears fashions of the '30s and smiles at us as she stands near her favorite automobile. Isabel and her husband Richard lived on the north side of Feeding Hills Road.

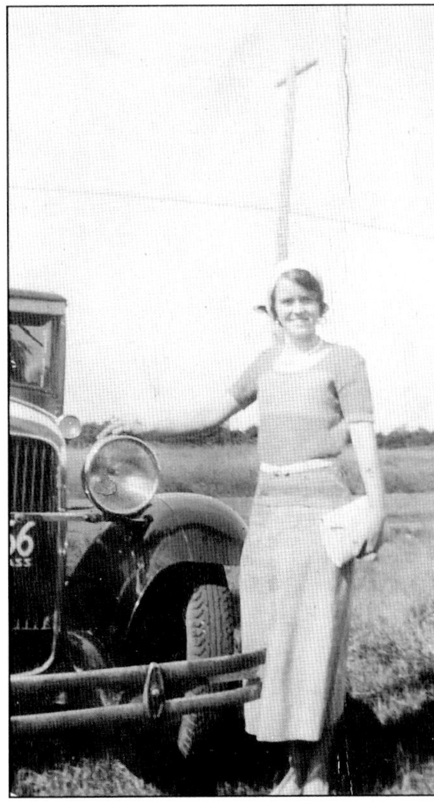

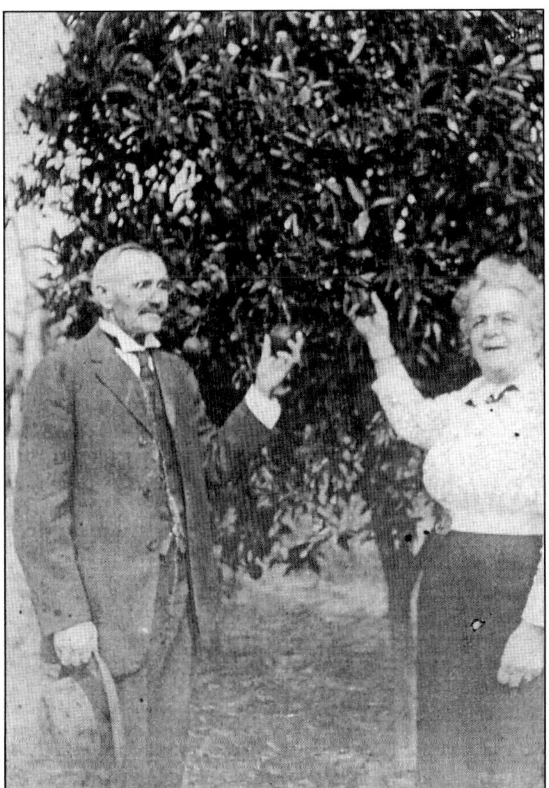

Luzerne and Jane (Simons) Fowler. Luzerne A. Fowler (1849–1932) and his wife Jane (1850–1941) were married in 1873. Luzerne grew up in Southwick, but in her youth Jane traveled with her family by covered wagon to homestead on the plains. When she returned east as an adult, she traveled in more comfort—by train.

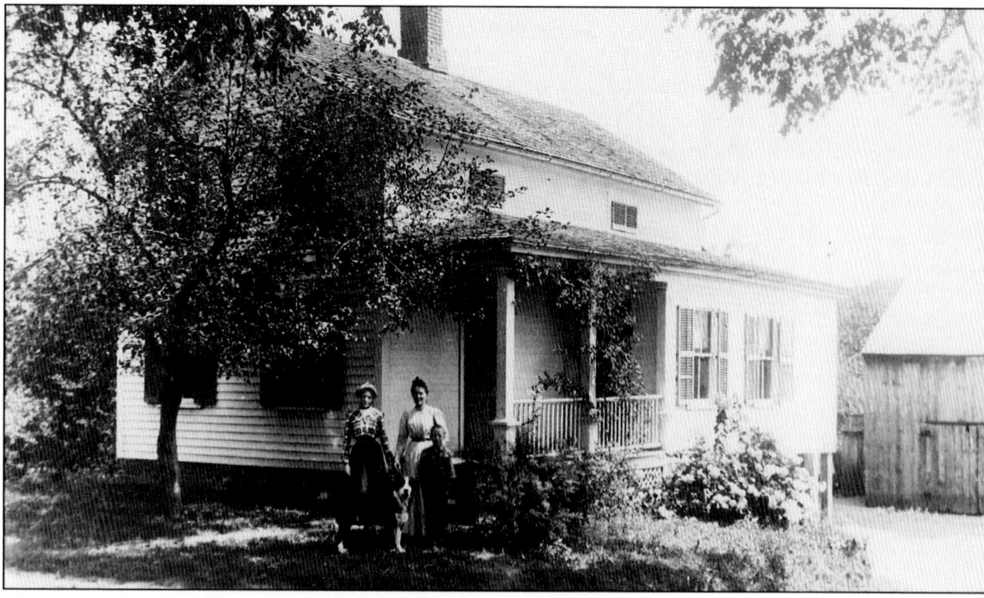

The Stone House. This dwelling, at 422 College Highway, was built in 1860; it was owned by Moses White in 1870, and by his son Andrew in 1894. When Andrew married Mary Black, daughter of Quartus, a prosperous local farmer, their pictures joined Black and White. The couple's youngest child Mary married Charles E. Stone in May 1893 and lived here when first married. Mary is shown with her son Cedric; the young lady has not been identified. (Elmer and Roxanne Cook, 1995).

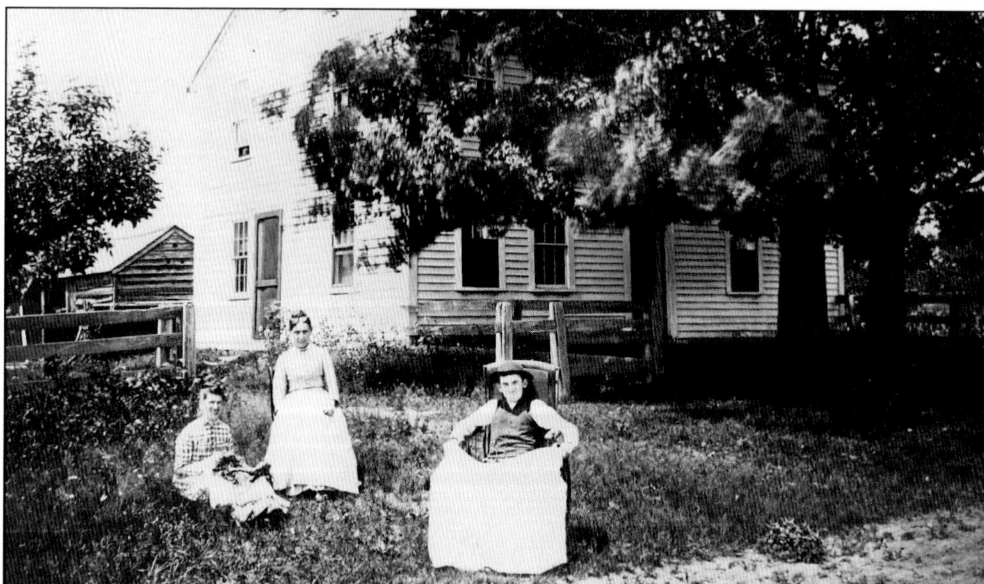

The Edwin Jackson House before 1893. Edwin L. Jackson, the son of Dewey and Adeline L. (Jones), owned this home in 1894; ownership eventually passed to Edwin's sister, Isabelle (Jackson) Deming, and subsequently to her son Ralph. The building, now part of the Captain Fowler Apartments, is located at 628 College Highway. Louis Jackson, in the wheel chair, was injured by a stone thrown by another boy while they were playing. Louis died in 1893. The women may be Louis' mother Adeline and his aunt Isabelle.

Chapter Six

School Days

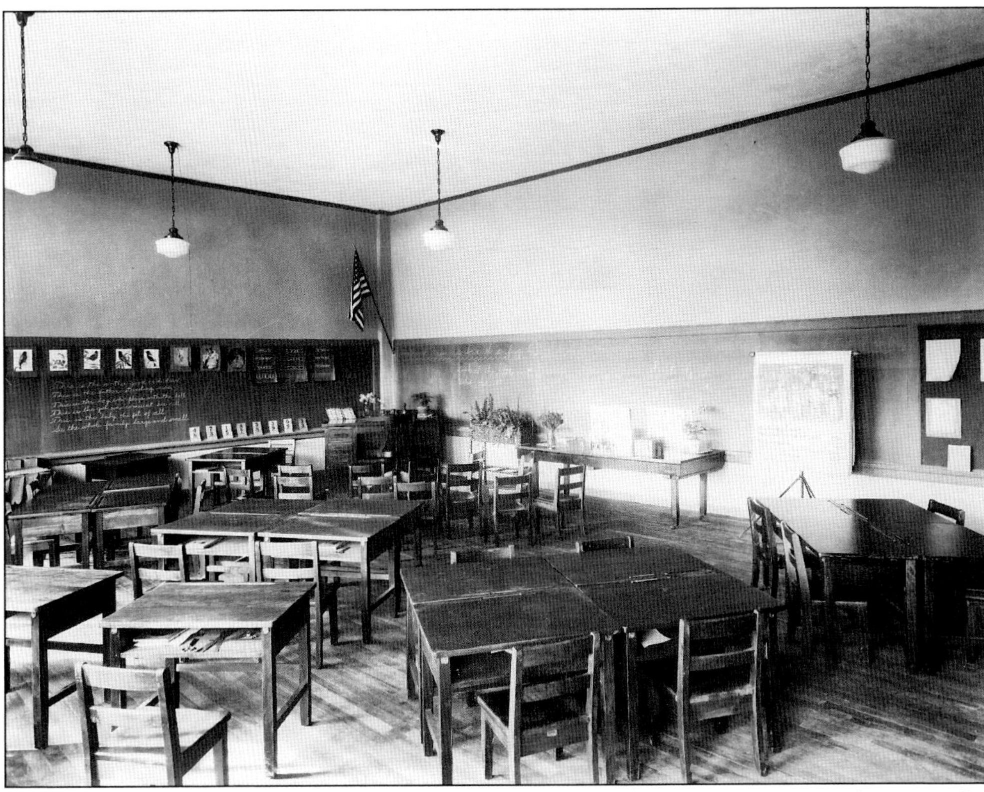

A First Grade Classroom after 1926. The Southwick Historical Society, Inc. has very few photographs of the interior of the Southwick Consolidated School. This image was donated by Helena Womboldt Duris, who taught in this classroom, and who later served for many years as the Granville historian.

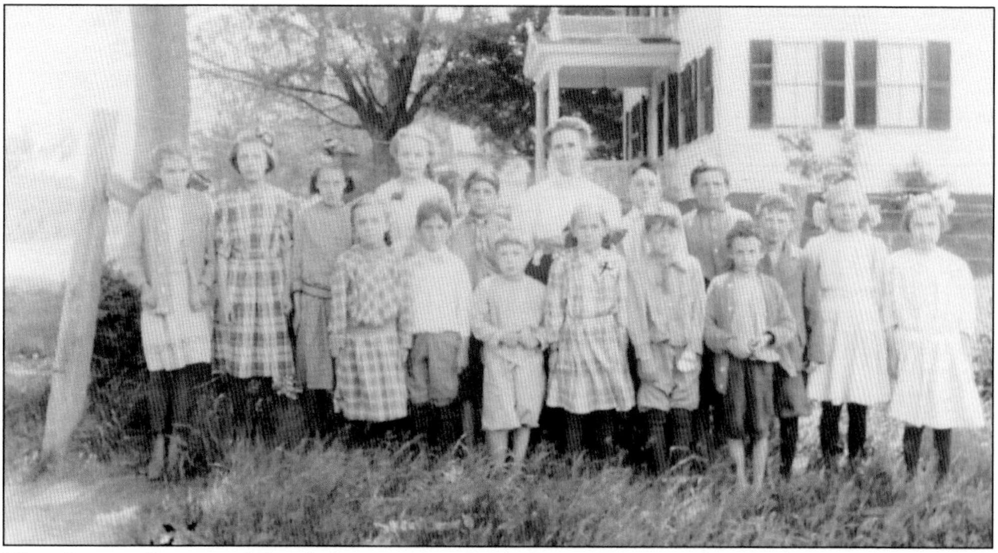

The Center Primary School, June 1911. Back Row: Bernice Weatherbee, Rose Sathory, Gertrude Jamellier, Mildred Phelps, John Sathory, Miss Cook (teacher), Donald Hollister, William Crowley, Albert Jones, Frances Lindquist, and Doris Griffin. Front Row: Rose Jarry, Coleman Moon, Neil Phelps, Edith Holcomb, Stanton Phelps, and George Jones. The school was located where the town hall parking lot is now. Notice the Fletcher residence and Adabelle (Langto) Crawford's home across the road from it.

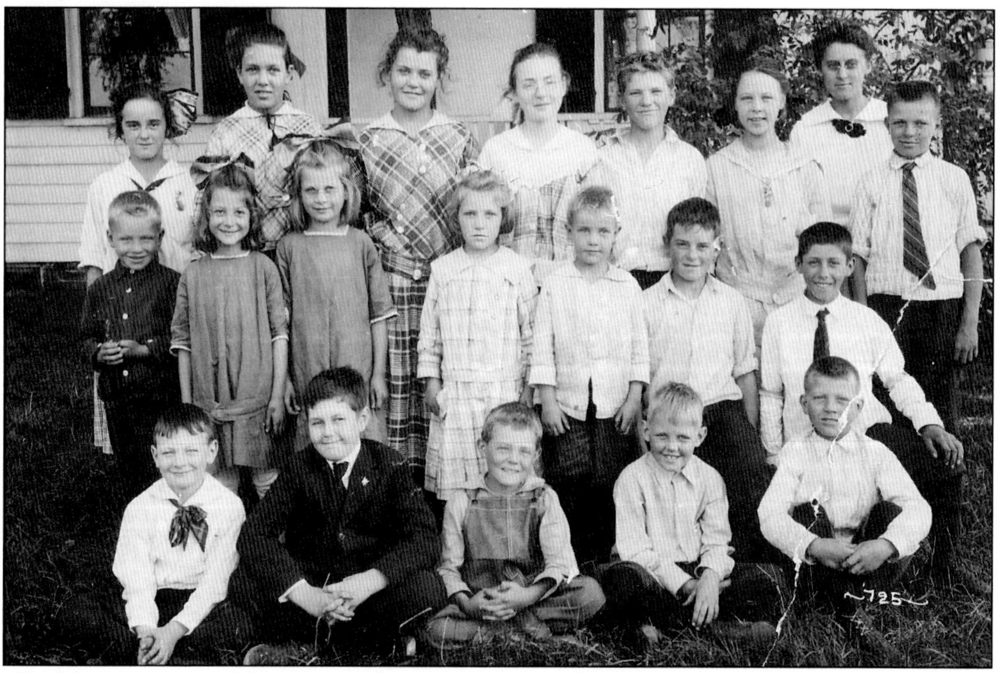

The South Longyard School, *c.* 1916. Back Row: Lucille Skelly, Beatrice Root, Elizabeth Lee, Grace Holcomb, Alvah Pearsall, Hazel Elder, Gertrude Malboeuf (teacher), and Herbert Root. Middle Row: Dorus Root, Marion Rising, Marjorie Rising, Myrtle Root, Leonard Rising, James Skelly, and Ernest Matthews. Front Row: Hobart Hosmer, Clifford Fowler, Roy Holcomb, Stanley Eskerka, and George Root.

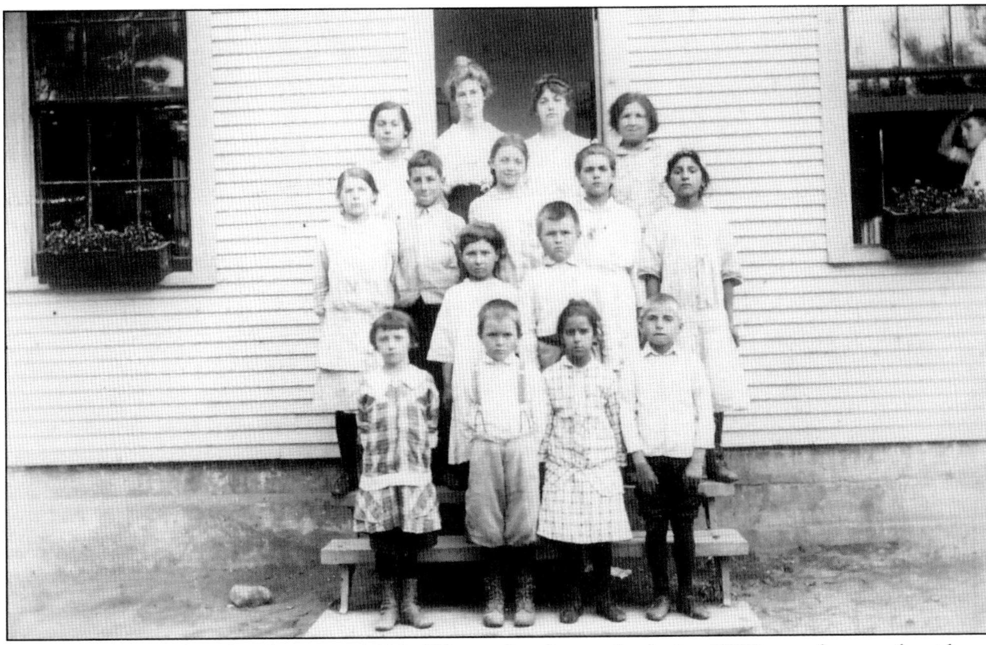

The Congamond School, 1914–1915. This school was built in 1912 on the south side of Congamond Road where Sheep Pasture Road intersects it. Back Row: Mildred Boero, Lucia F. Gleason (teacher), Josephine Mignotte, and Minnie White. Third Row: Lucy Mignotte, Oliver English, Doris Mills, Victoria Mignotte, and Lusina Pomina. Second Row: Valia Pomina and George Stalk. Front Row: Winona Desmond, Jack Stalk, Beatrice English, and Henry Mignotte. Iverson Warner is in the window.

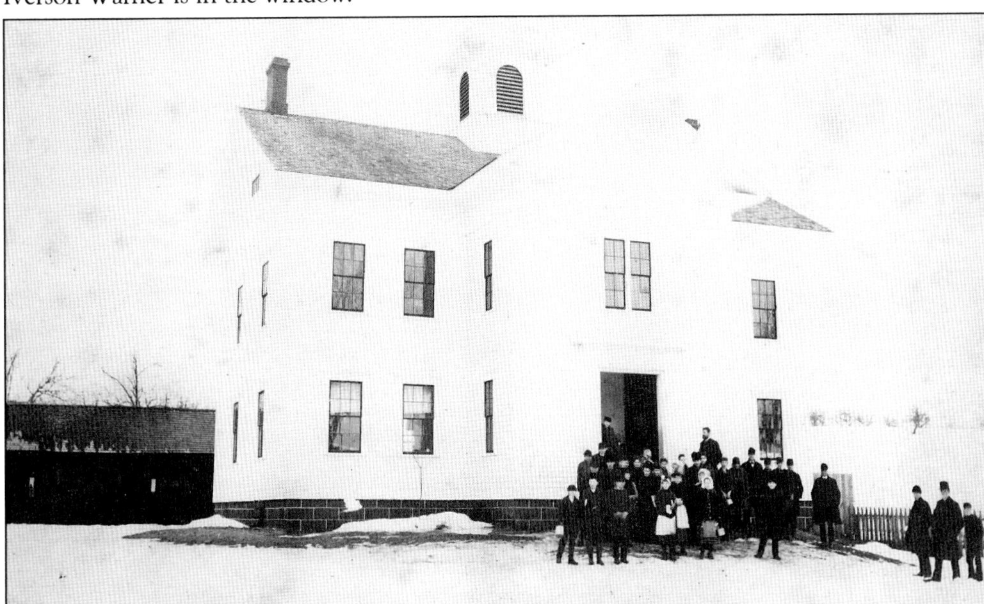

The Dickinson Grammar School, *c.* 1887. This is the earliest photograph we have of this building, which was rebuilt after the original structure burned in the 1860s. Leslie Luzerne Fowler and Lennie Hollister are among the students. Notice the sheds for the horses and carriages of parishioners of the Southwick Congregational Church.

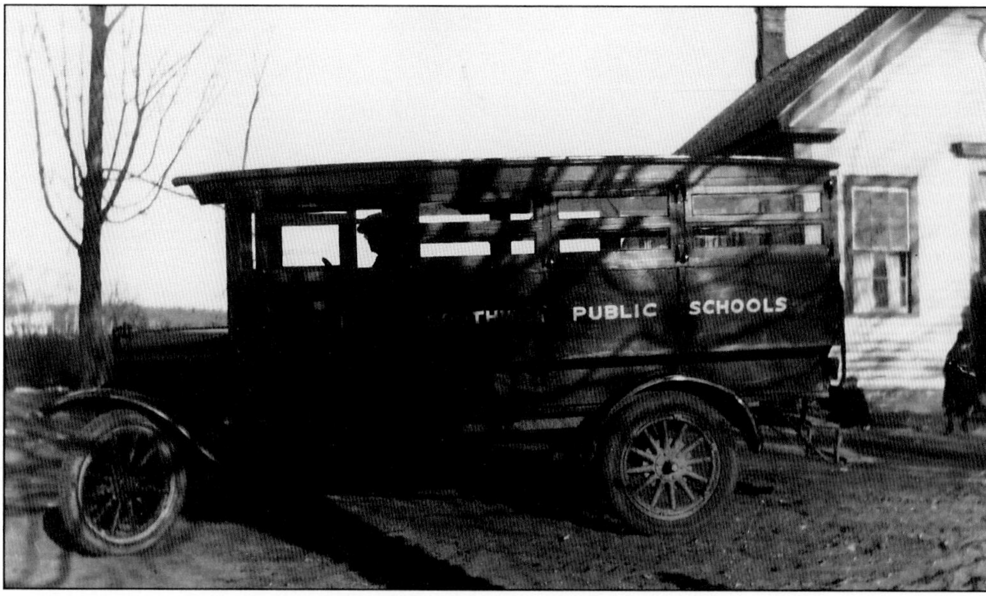

Southwick's First School Bus. When the Southwick Consolidated School opened on May 13, 1929, many children who had previously walked to the eleven neighborhood grammar schools boarded a school bus for the first time. Former Superintendent of Schools Roland Weeks donated this photograph.

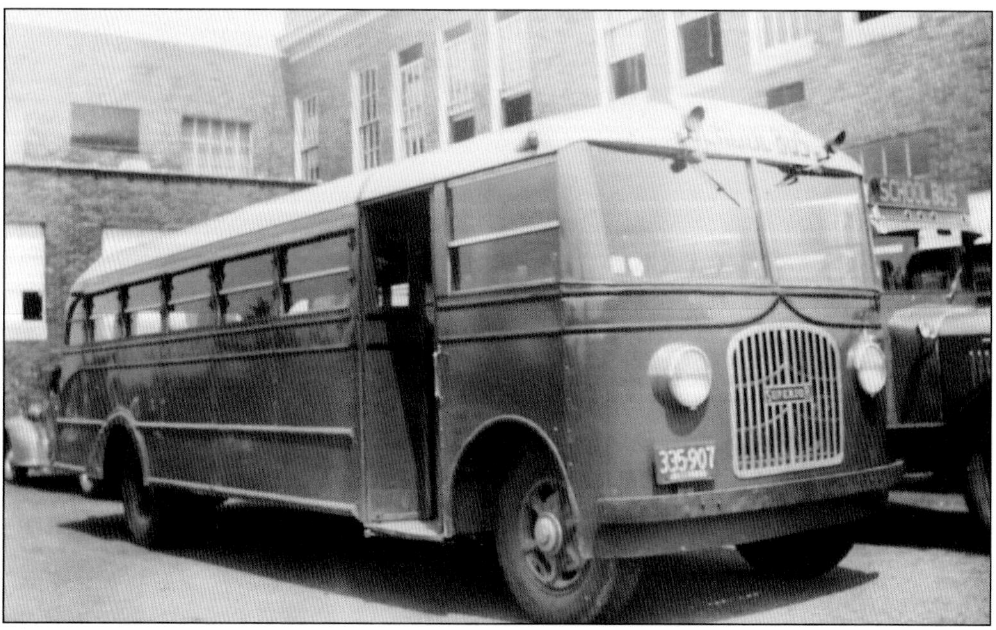

The "Queen Mary." The finest bus in the Southwick bus fleet was nicknamed the "Queen Mary" by drivers Laurence Johnson, Ralph Deming, Clarence Hudson, and William Arnold.

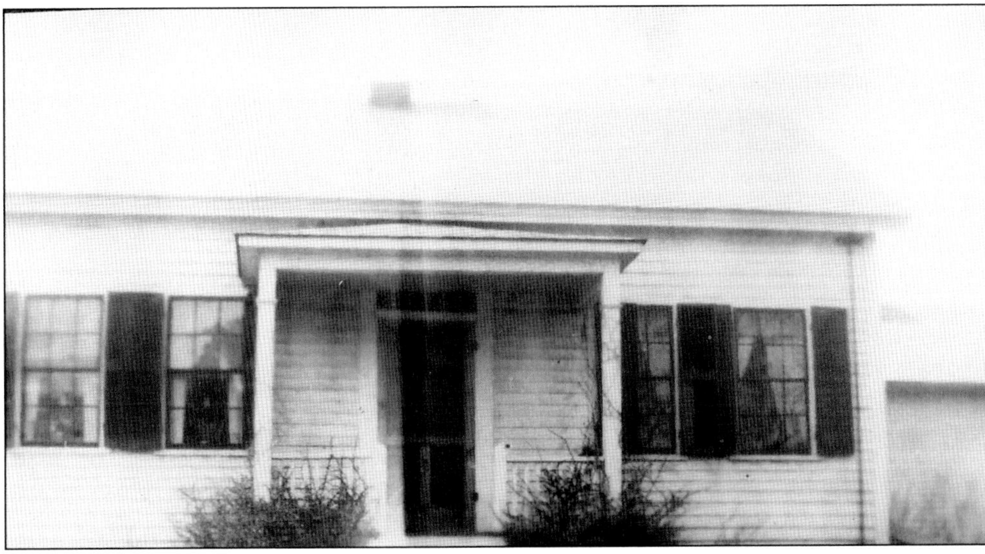

The John R. Boyle House. In the days when public school teachers were required to be unmarried, many boarded with local families. John R. and Fannie E. Boyle were one such family. Cora Moore, Ethel Wilcutt, and Dagma Fant were among their boarders.

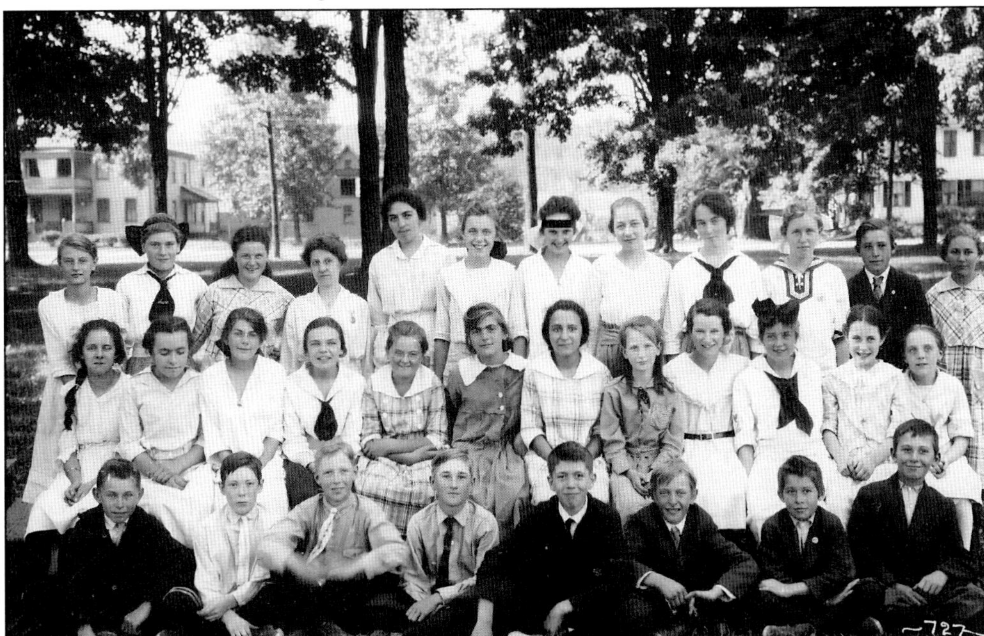

The Dickinson Grammar School and the Commercial School, 1917–1918. Back Row: Edna Elsey, Louise Maschin, Marjorie Storey, Mabel Wilson (teacher, Commercial School), Elizabeth Stetson (teacher, Dickinson Grammar School), Marion Hollister, Louise Yakes, Nellie Lambson, Winifred Palmer, Florence Anderson, Henry Wolfe, and Mabel Rising. Middle Row: Bessie Peebles, Rose Jarry, Lucy Mignotte, Ethel Curtis, Irene Storey, Victoria Mignotte, Lucina Pomina, Gladys Elsey, Helen Ferris, Doris Mills, Helen Phelps, and Dorothy Hollister. Front Row: John Sarat, Neil Phelps, Raymond Griffin, Iverson Warner, James Montovani, Thomas Klaus, Adolph Wolfe, and Herman Wolfe.

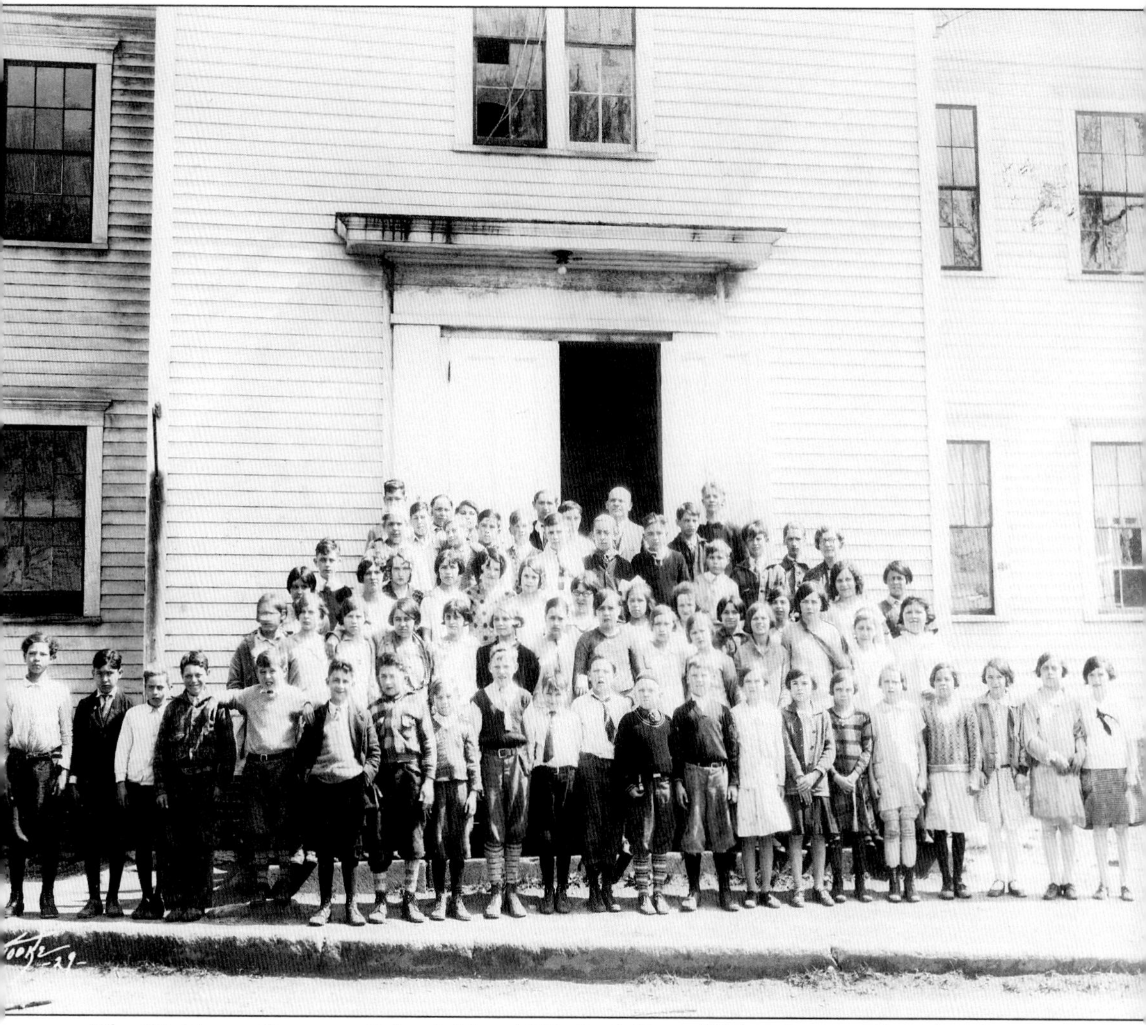

The Dickinson Grammar School, May 1929. Back Row: Walter Pierce, Edward Stiles, Frank Bernardara, Ernest Davis, Ernest Stone(?), Mr. Libby (principal), Peter Masiska, and Malcolm Wilcox. Fifth Row: Joseph Garcia, Sebastian Paroli, John Jackson, George Malone, Raymond Fletcher, Jr., Bruce Trench, Nuchi Prifti, John Brzoska, Walter Wolfe, Albert Ryll, Albert Davis, and Mildred Arnold (teacher). Fourth Row: Henry Tierney and Anna Dziengelewski. Third Row: Bertha Rogers, Madeline Maloney, Rose Madagusso, Frances Malone, Althea Saunders, Hazel Humphrey, Adeline Pierce, Angelina Ruffo, Olga Babeski, Ann Zanolli, Leila Bemis, and Angelina Tomassini. Second Row: Ida Semchruk, Josephine Backus, Margarite Gimchuk, Florence Dibble, Helen Battistoni, Clair Maraviglia, Lillian Henry, Ciela Sponberg (?), Martha Brown, Carolyn Arnold, Martha Babeski, Rita Malone, Marguerite Tierney, and Katherine Bernadara. Front Row: Earl Williams, Robert Ball, Elliott Phillips, Julios Consolini, Harry Libbey, unknown, Joseph Zanolli, Frank Jackson, Ralph Pihl, Ellis Hollister, Tige Arnold, Elmer Johnson, Carl Gough, Joshne Edwards, Catherine Sarat, Elizabeth Hollister, Ernestine Hardy, Mary Consolini, Mary Massoni, Adeline Babeski, and Shirley Malone.

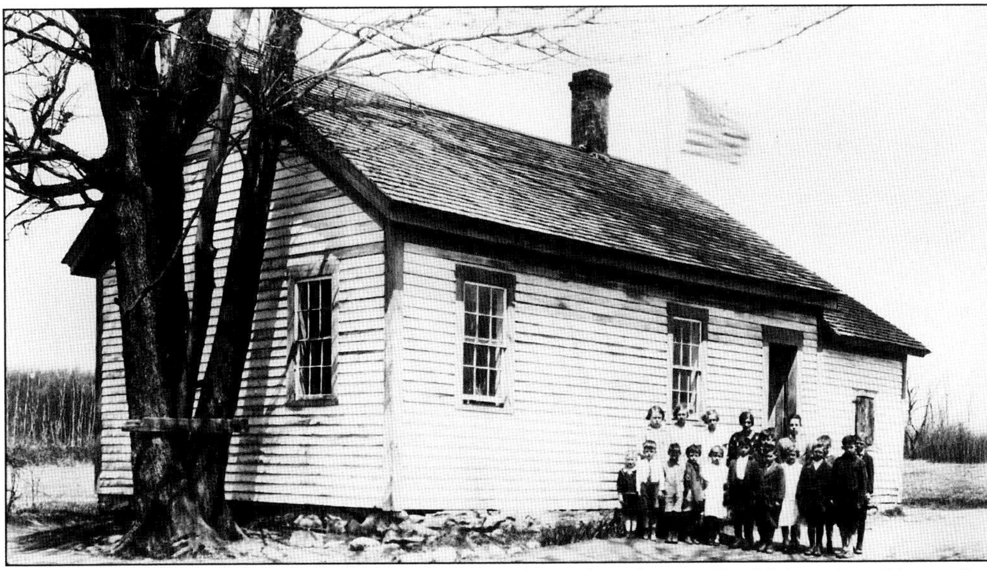

The Vining Hill School, 1925. Back Row: Wilda Holcomb, Winifred Monczka, Alexandria Monczka, Miss Hancock (teacher), Victor Monczka, Alvin Anderson, John Smith, and Ralph Holcomb. Front Row: Russell Smith, Richard Anderson, Joseph Monczka, Laura Holcomb, Sophie Monczka, Ludwig Monczka, Richard Smith, Florence Monczka, John Monczka, and Raymond Aldrich.

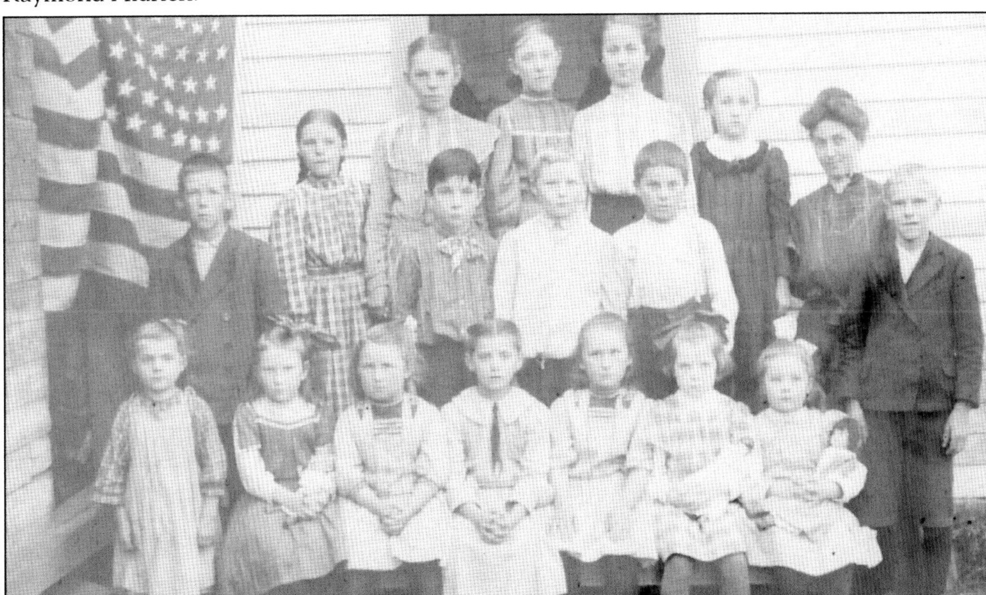

The Mooretown School, c. 1907. Back Row: George Steere (in front of the American flag), Myrtle Robinson, Helen Konopka, Hilda Larson, Lucy Nicholson, Marion Warner, Florence Marshall (later Vining, teacher), and Enfred Anderson. Middle Row: Miles Rogers, Amasa Steere, and Joseph Konopka. Front Row: Lucy Mignotte, Helen Larson, Minnie White, Josephine Mignotte, Margaret White, Elizabeth Rogers, and Alma Steere. Before the Congamond School was built in 1912, children from Sheep Pasture Road attended Mooretown School.

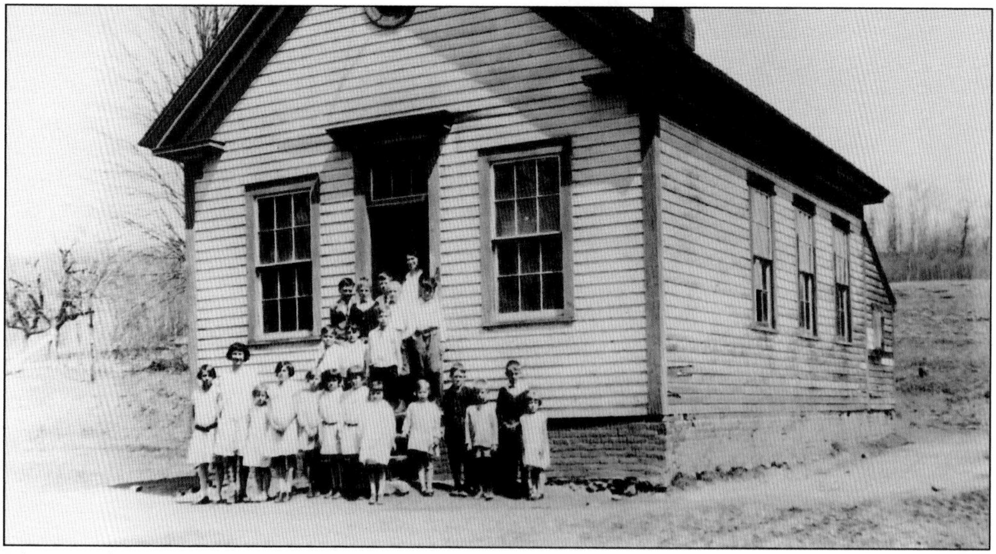

The North Longyard School, April 1929. Back Row: Wallace Tysz and Fannie Hosmer (teacher) Third Row: unknown, William Liese, Tony Godek, and Robert McMullin. Second Row: August Menard, George Scibelli, and Charles Chestnut. Front Row: Florence Buynicki, ? Buynicki, Stella Godek, Dorothy Foisey, ? Butler, Pansy Tysz, Fannie Tysz (twins), Mabel Bovat, Edna Butler, ? Rutherford, Bernard Liese, Henry Liese, and unknown.

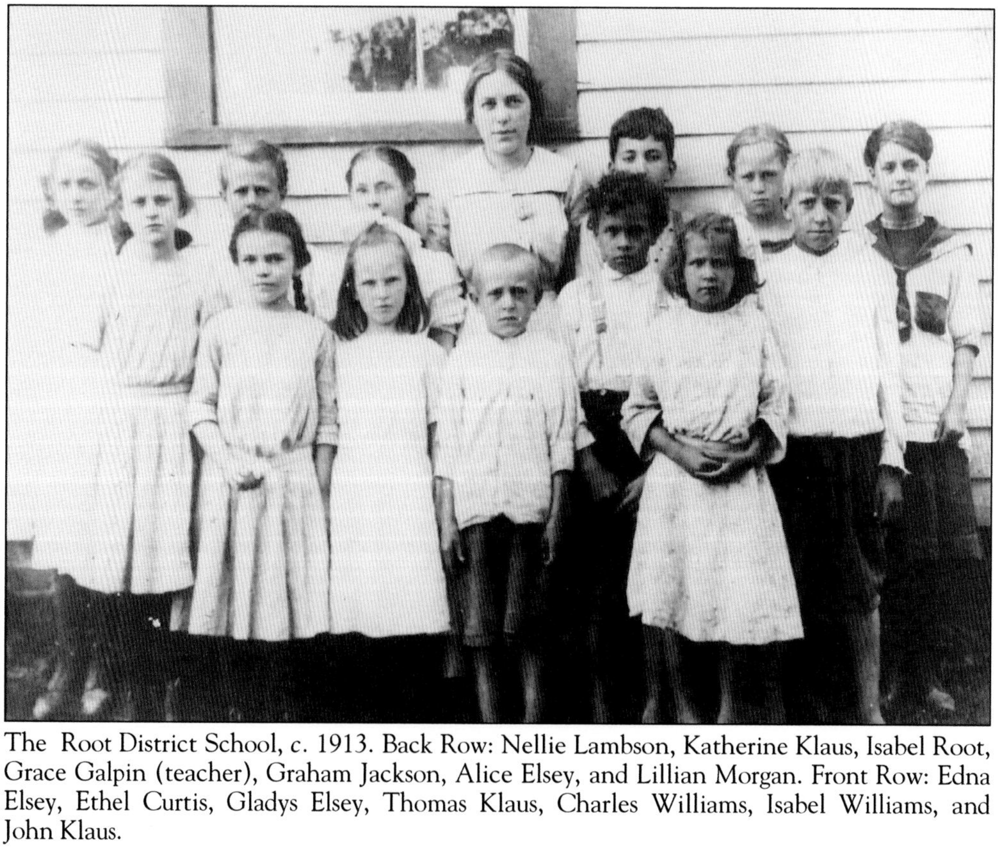

The Root District School, *c.* 1913. Back Row: Nellie Lambson, Katherine Klaus, Isabel Root, Grace Galpin (teacher), Graham Jackson, Alice Elsey, and Lillian Morgan. Front Row: Edna Elsey, Ethel Curtis, Gladys Elsey, Thomas Klaus, Charles Williams, Isabel Williams, and John Klaus.

Chapter Seven

Grammar School Graduates

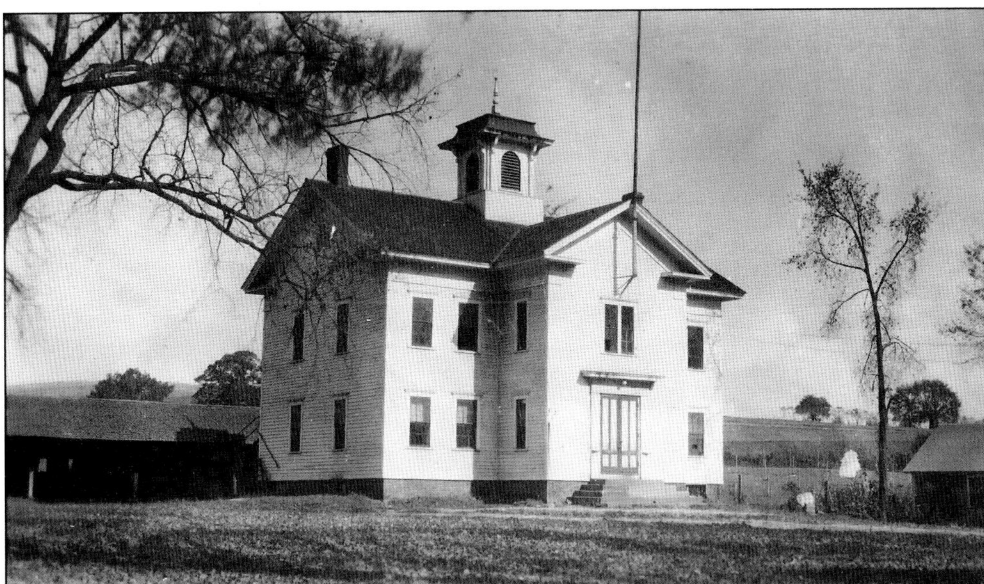

The Dickinson Grammar School. The Dickinson Fund for the Support of Schools in the Town of Southwick was established when the town meeting of May 1825 voted to accept the stipulations of the will of Richard Dickinson, who had died in May of 1824. At the same town meeting, the town voted to raise funds to build a "house for the purpose of keeping a Grammar School." That building, which also served as the town hall, burned in the 1860s, but an identical one, shown here, replaced it. Because Mr. Dickinson's document specified that only the interest generated was to be used for the support of the schools of Southwick, the Dickinson School Fund exists to this day.

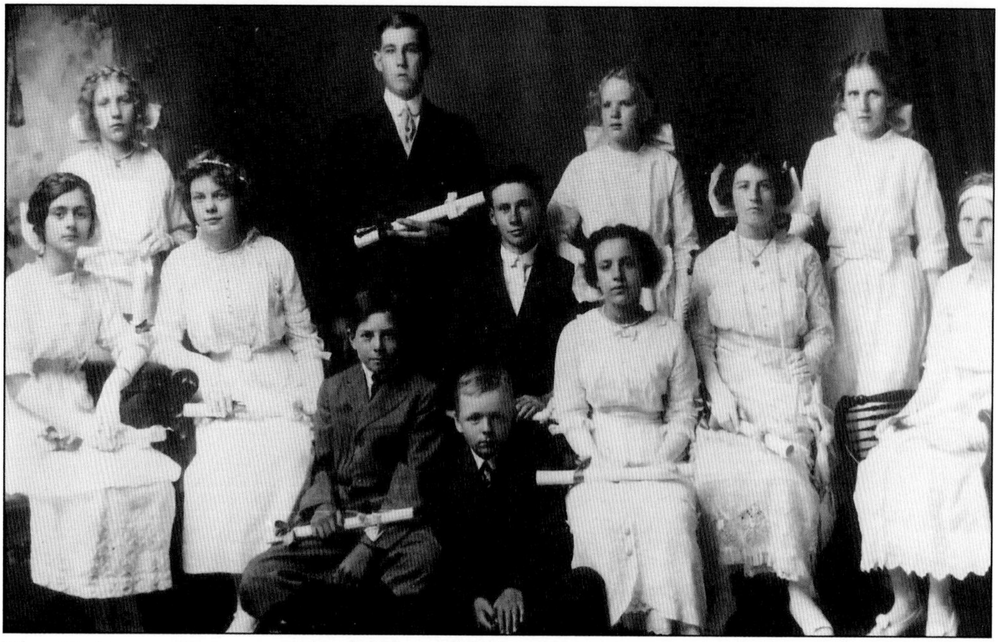

The Dickinson Grammar School Class of 1914. Graduations were held at the two center churches on alternating years. Back Row: Frances Lindquist, Leon Barnes, Ruth Foster, and Faith Foster. Middle Row: Maude Morgan, Gertrude Jamelier (Pratt), Austin Ferris, Marion Sharp, and Beatrice Hollister (Mellen). Front Row: Theodore Kellogg, Jessie Leonesio, and Charles Holcomb.

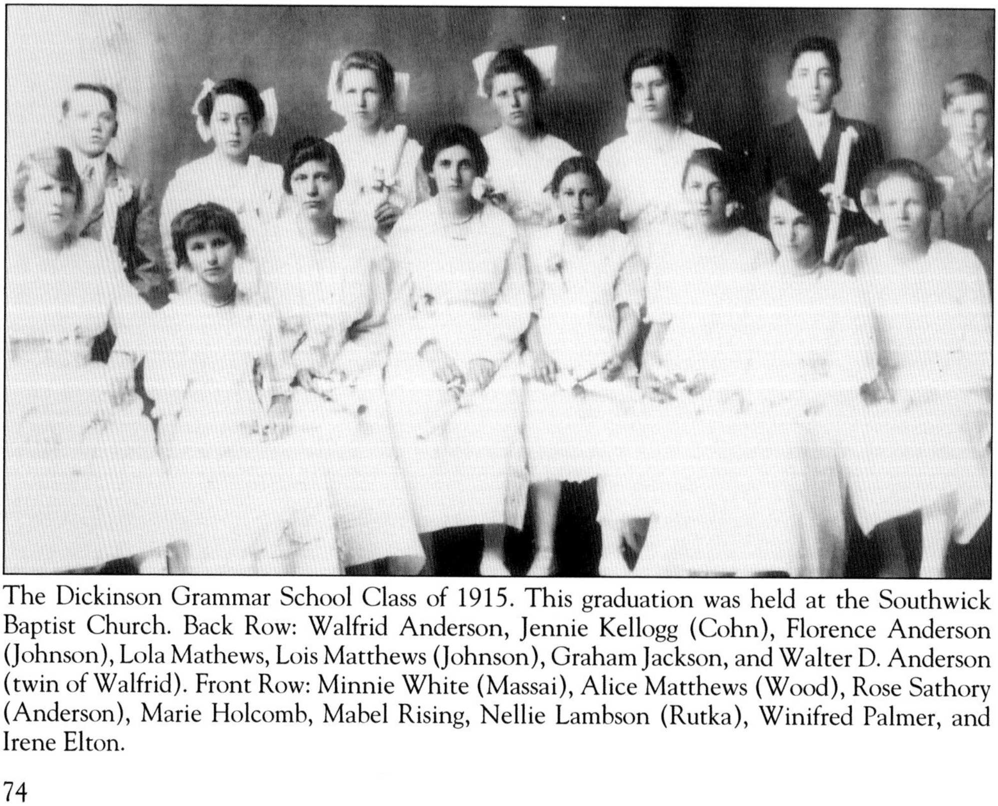

The Dickinson Grammar School Class of 1915. This graduation was held at the Southwick Baptist Church. Back Row: Walfrid Anderson, Jennie Kellogg (Cohn), Florence Anderson (Johnson), Lola Mathews, Lois Matthews (Johnson), Graham Jackson, and Walter D. Anderson (twin of Walfrid). Front Row: Minnie White (Massai), Alice Matthews (Wood), Rose Sathory (Anderson), Marie Holcomb, Mabel Rising, Nellie Lambson (Rutka), Winifred Palmer, and Irene Elton.

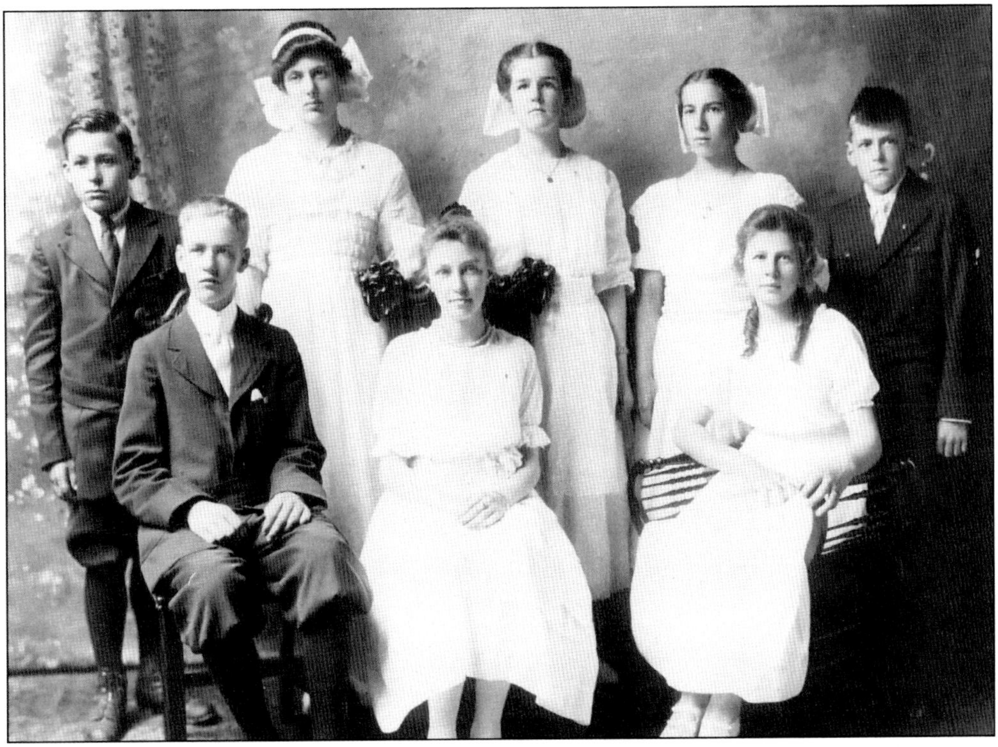

The DGS Class of 1916. Back Row: Henry Wolfe, Mildred Phelps, Marion Barnes, Edith Holcomb, and Stanton Phelps. Front Row: Walter S. Anderson, Doris Griffin (Valenti), and Alice Klous.

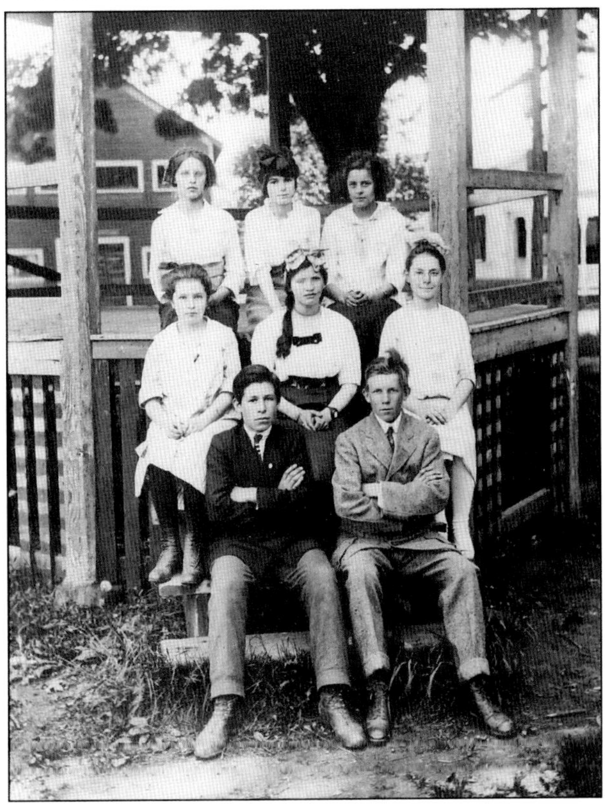

The DGS Class of 1917. Back Row: Esther Matthews, Bernice Weatherbee, and Irene Skelly. Middle Row: Alma Steere, Ruth Hosmer (Hastings), and Isabel Root (Carr). Front Row: Andrew Wolfe and Harold Hollister. Students were seated on the bandstand located near the school. Notice the buildings on the other side of Broad Street, now Depot Street.

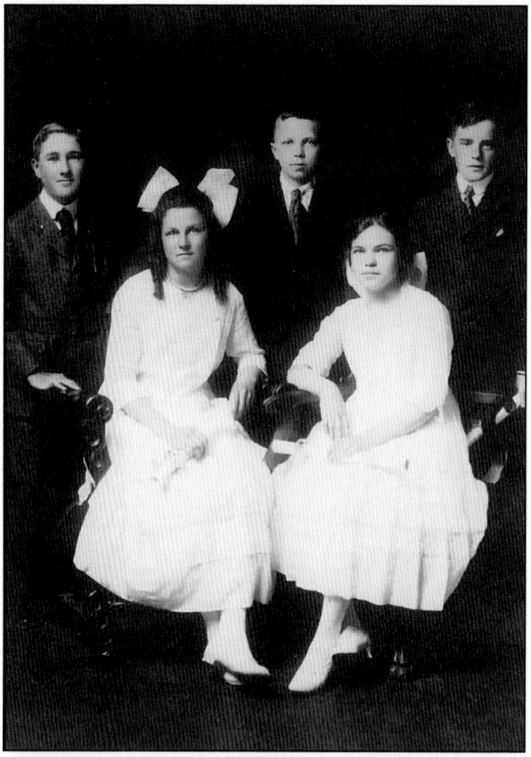

The DGS Class of 1918. Back Row: Iverson Warner, unknown, and ? Skelly. Front Row: Marjorie Storey and Ethel Curtis.

The DGS Class of 1919. Back Row: Rose Jarry, Samuel Bilsky, Edna Elsey, Seth Kellogg, Louise Mashin, and Cora Smith. Middle row: Dorothy Hollister, Raymond Griffin, Marion Hollister, Helen Ferris, Lucy Skelly, and Grace Holcomb. Front Row: Lucy Mignotte (Schmaling), Ernest Matthews, Neil Phelps, and Helen Phelps.

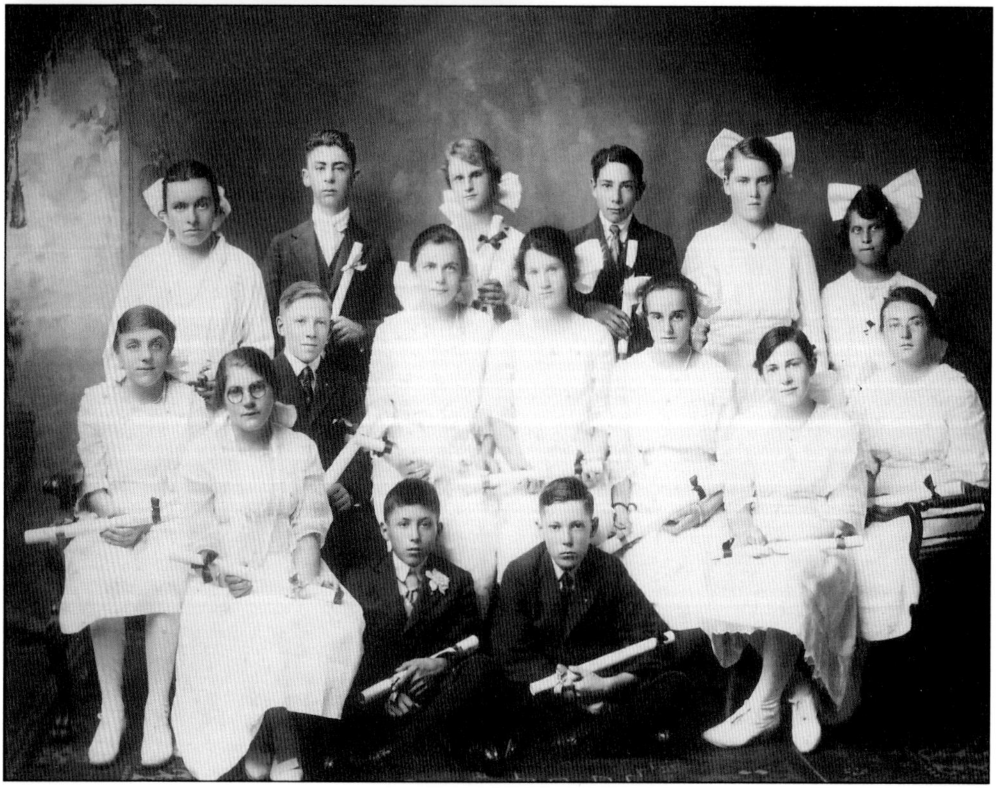

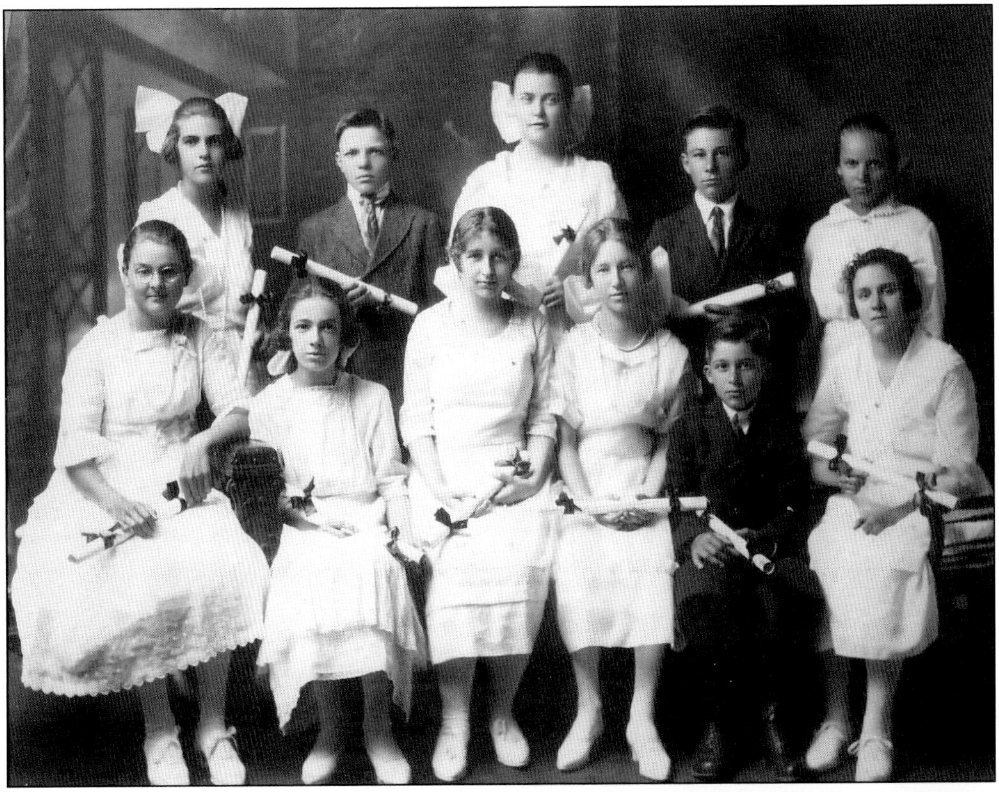

The DGS Class of 1920. Back Row: Victoria Mignotte (Mondelo), Herbert Root, Elizabeth Lee, Herman Wolfe, and unknown. Front Row: Irene Storey (Sponberg), Marion Brzoska (Cline), Doris Holcomb, Mary Lambson (Montovani), Adolph Wolfe, and Bessie Peebles.

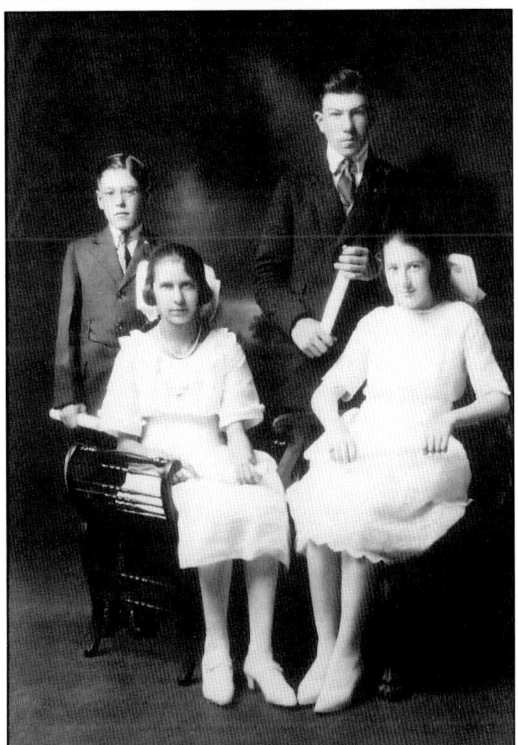

The DGS Class of 1921. Back Row: Reginald Phelps and John Hannon. Front Row: Elizabeth Silan and Katherine Hannon.

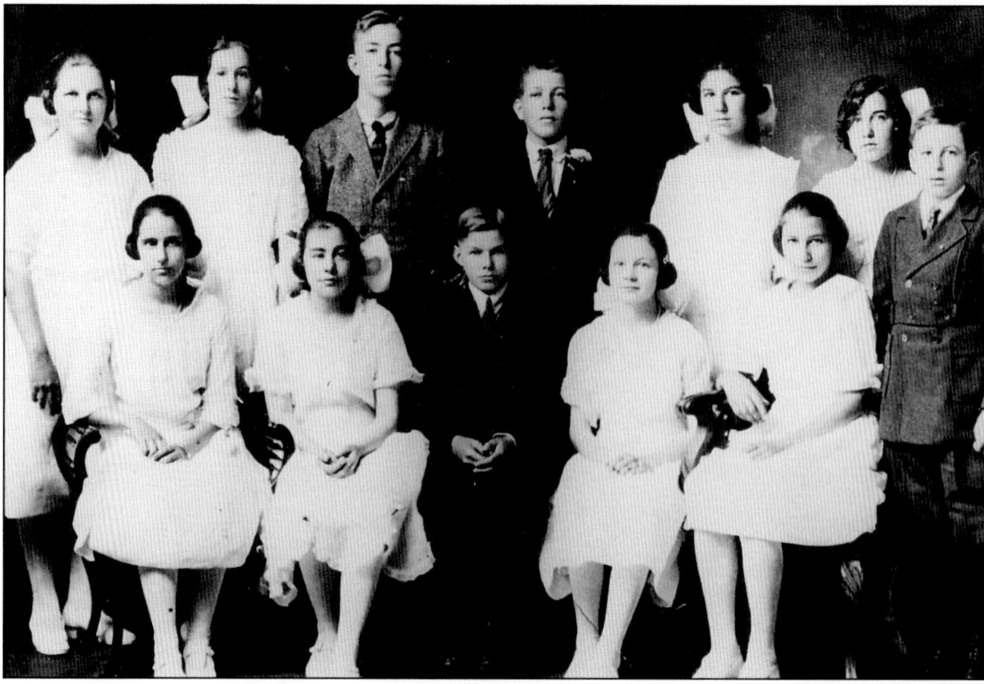

The DGS Class of 1922. Back Row: Myrtle Storey (Gravel), Caroline Shurtleff (Hughes), Lorenzo Lambson, George Root, Mary Swochak, unknown, and Merrill Mason. Front Row: Beatrice English (Root), Wealthy Sperry, Victor Sarat, Alva Peterson, and Anna Wolfe. Valia Pomina (Bonini) graduated with this class, but wasn't present when the photograph was taken.

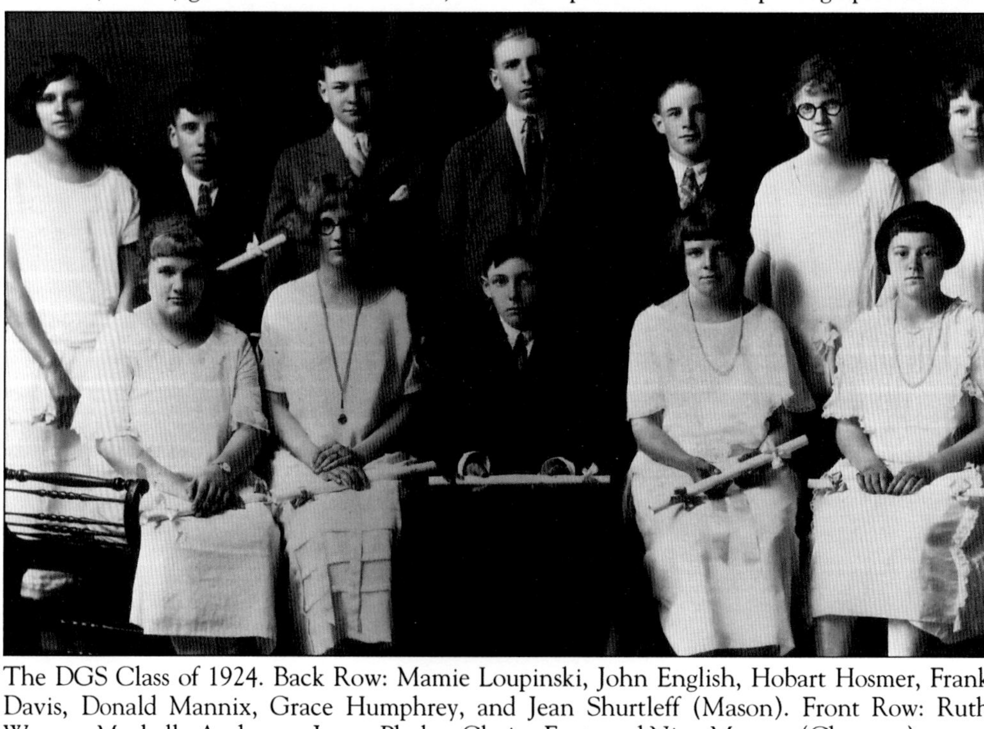

The DGS Class of 1924. Back Row: Mamie Loupinski, John English, Hobart Hosmer, Frank Davis, Donald Mannix, Grace Humphrey, and Jean Shurtleff (Mason). Front Row: Ruth Warner, Maybelle Anderson, James Phelps, Clarice Fant, and Nina Morgan (Chestnut).

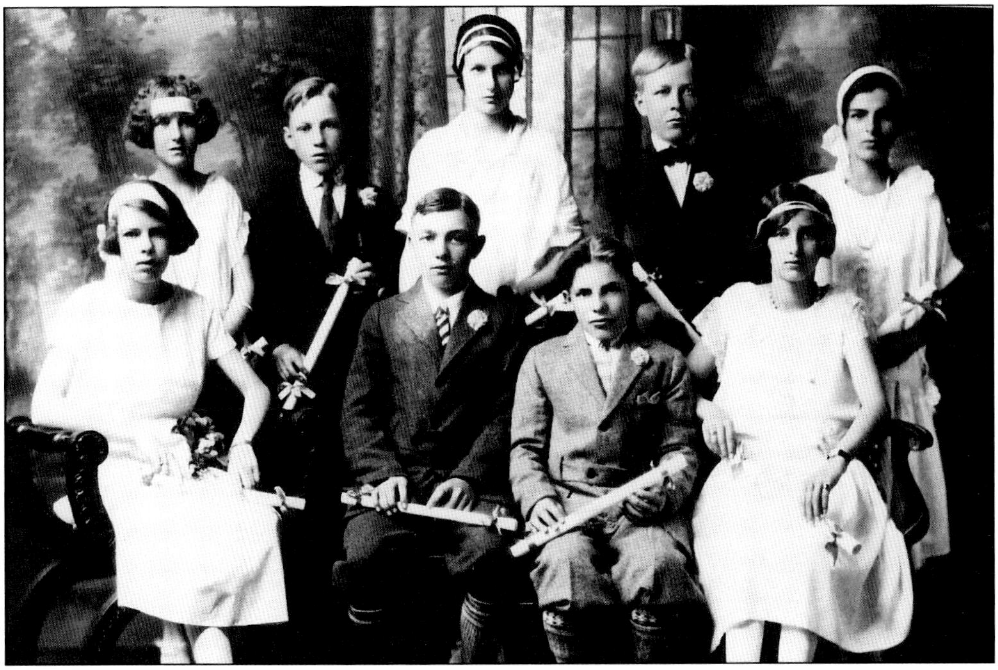

The DGS Class of 1925. Back Row: Muriel Root, Durus Root, Anne Battistoni, Waino Rantaman, and Bruna Gavioli. Front Row: Helen Eames, Richard Root, Anthony Gavioli, and Dorothy Wilcox (Little).

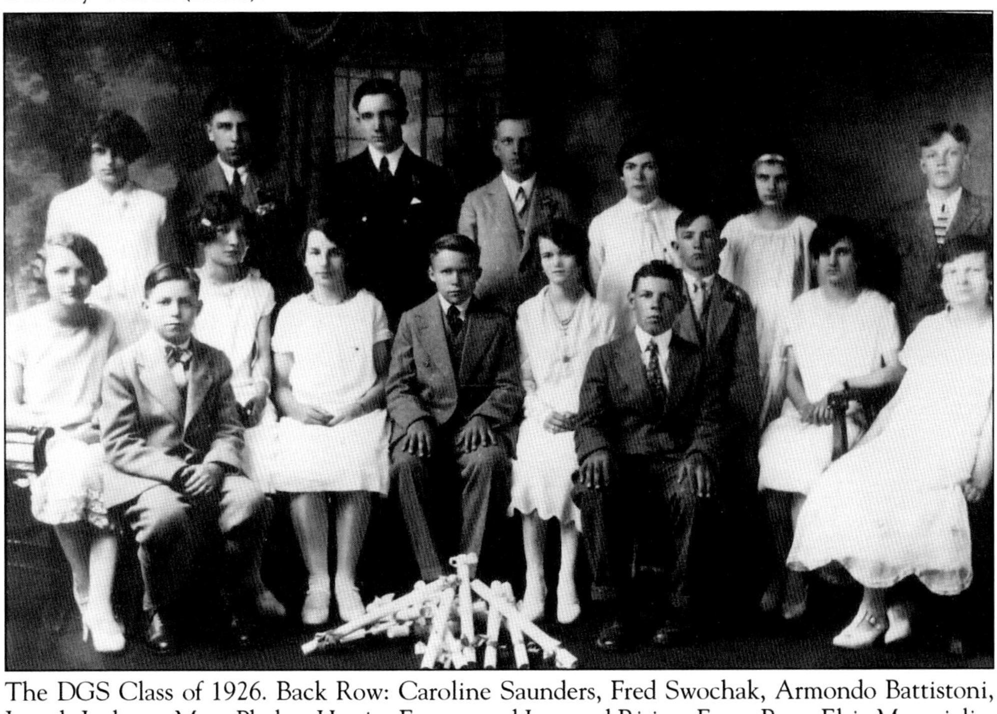

The DGS Class of 1926. Back Row: Caroline Saunders, Fred Swochak, Armondo Battistoni, Joseph Jackson, Mary Phelps, Harriet Eames, and Leonard Rising. Front Row: Elsie Meraviglia, George Newton Holcomb, Sophia Swochak, Helen Allen, Ernest Wolfe, Isabelle Deming, Osborne Gaugh, Chester Brzoska, Freida Dibble, and Netty Humphrey.

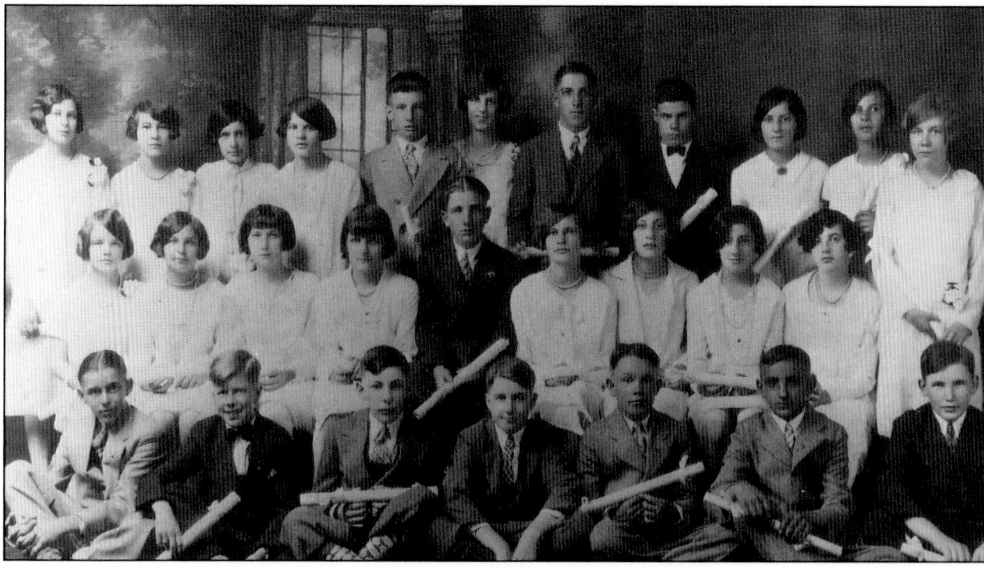

The DGS Class of 1928. Back Row: May Henry, Edna Wolfe, Vera Ball, Julie Mississco, Andrew Silan, Nona Abraham, James Humason, Fred Cigal, Agnes Brzoska, Christine Simchak, and Priscilla Arnold. Middle Row: Cederia Anderson, Lenore Anderson, Barbara Trench, Helen Owsianny, William Jackson, Ann Boswick, Dora Venotti, Mary Horkun, and Nora Battistoni. Front Row: Peter Sarat, Roderick Fletcher, George Phelps, James Lownds, Edward Ryll, Theodore Lecrenski, and Clifford Gibson. This was the last class to graduate from the Dickinson Grammar School.

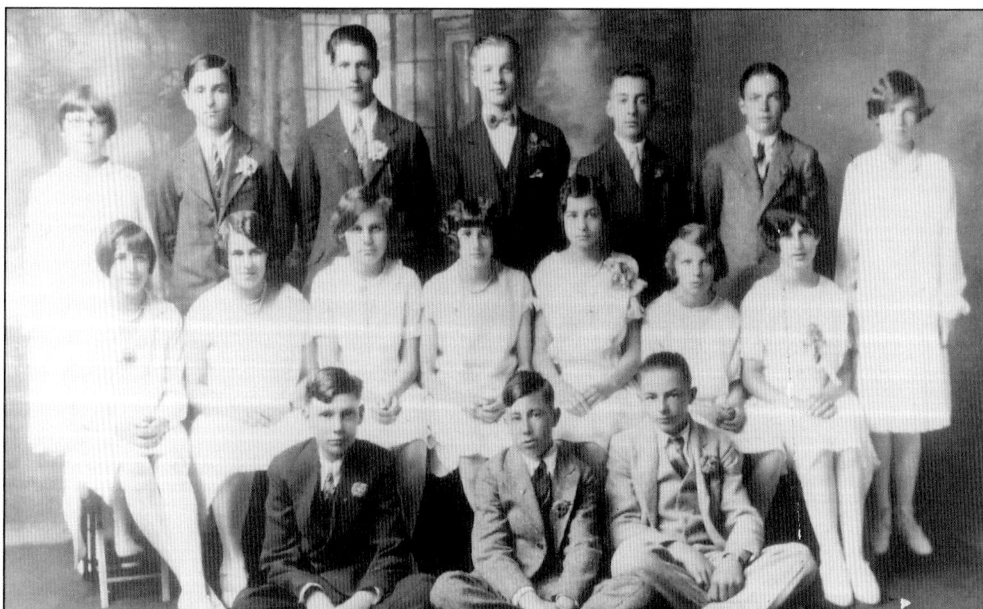

The Southwick Consolidated School Class of 1929. These students had attended their new school for only one month before they graduated from it. Back Row: Hazel Humphreys, Ernest Davis, Albert Davis, Malcolm Wilcox, Nuchi Prifti, Edward Stiles, and Margaret Swochak. Middle Row: unknown, Florence Dibble, Seila Sponberg, Helen Battistoni, Lillian Henry, Stacia Godek, and Bertha Rogers. Front Row: Bruce Trench, Sebastian Paroli, John Brzoska.

Chapter Eight

The Congamond Lakes

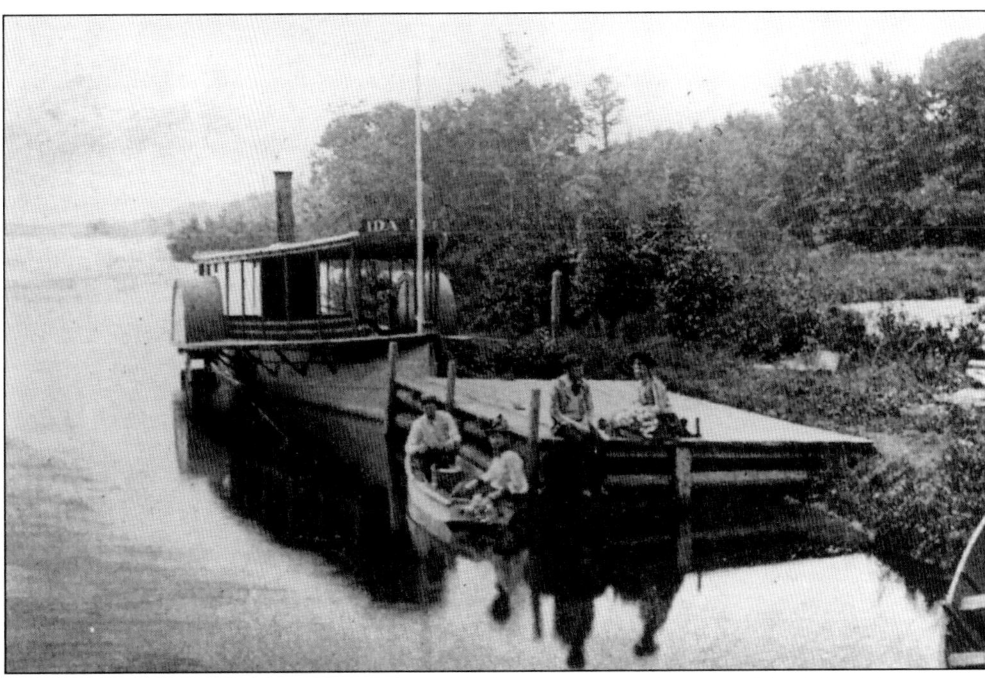

The *Ida Lee*. The side-wheeler steamboat *Ida Lee*, owned and operated by John Chapman, is anchored at her mooring at the north end of Middle Congamond Lake, as lake visitors enjoy fishing and the beautiful scenery.

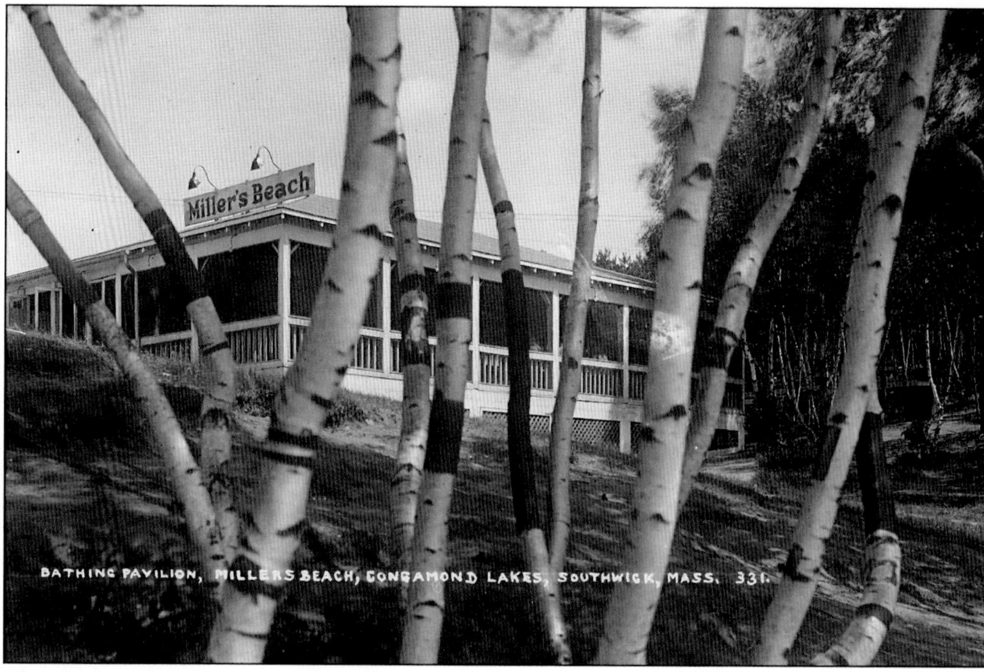

The Bathing Pavilion at Miller's Beach. Visitors to Miller's Beach had the opportunity to change into and out of swimming apparel at the bathing pavilion, set among the birches on South Pond.

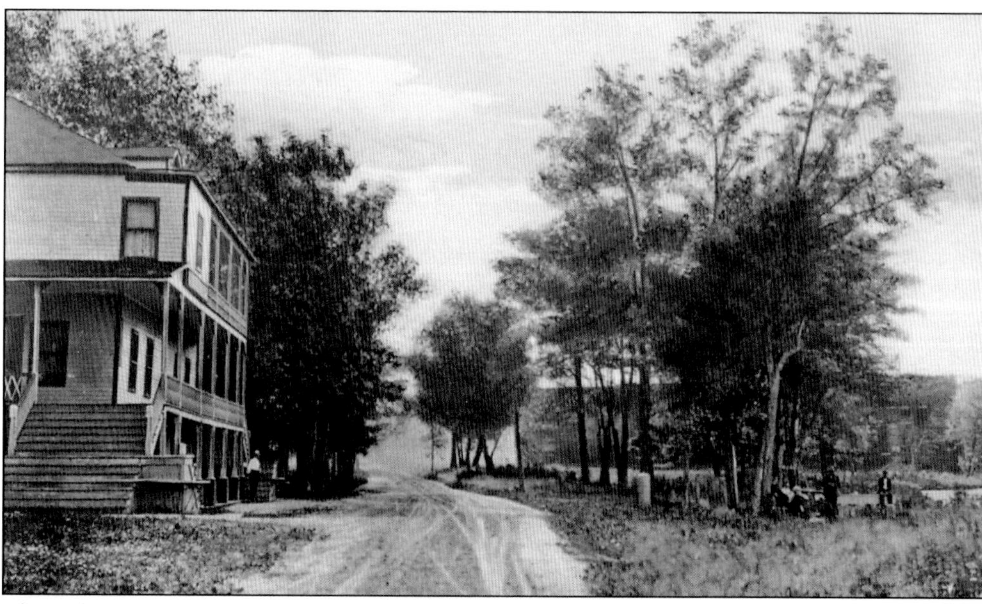
The Lake House. Located on the south side of what is now Congamond Road, across from Saunders Boat Livery, the Lake House began in the late 1800s as a small one-story hotel for summer visitors. It had easy access to the Congamond railway station. As the popularity of the lakes grew, the management of the Lake House added more floors. The building burned in 1925. Notice the Crystal Ice House in the right background.

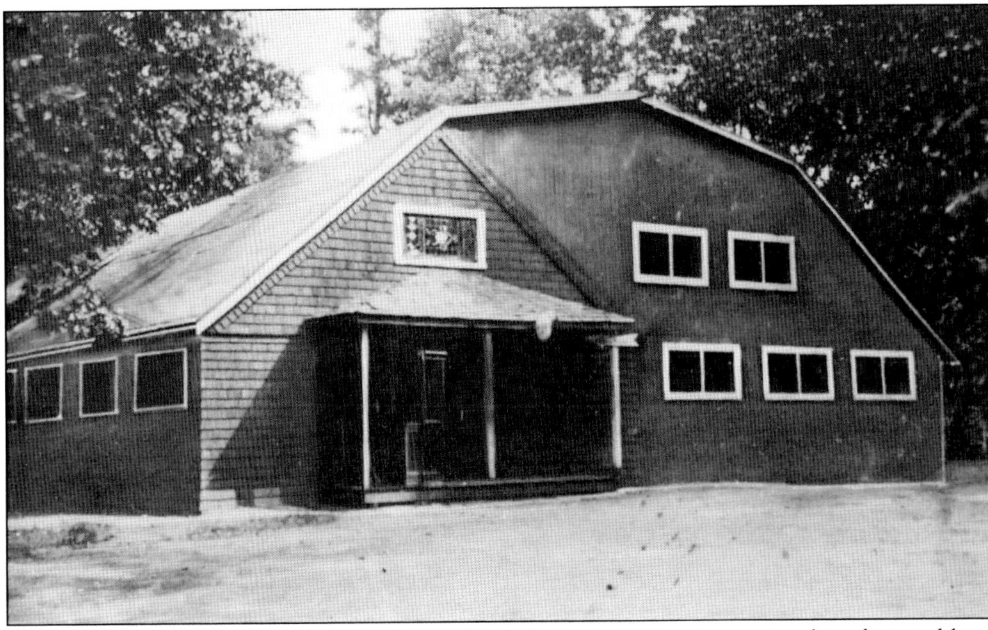

Babbs Dance Casino. The word "casino" did not in former days connote a place for gambling; this was a building in which people enjoyed an evening of dancing.

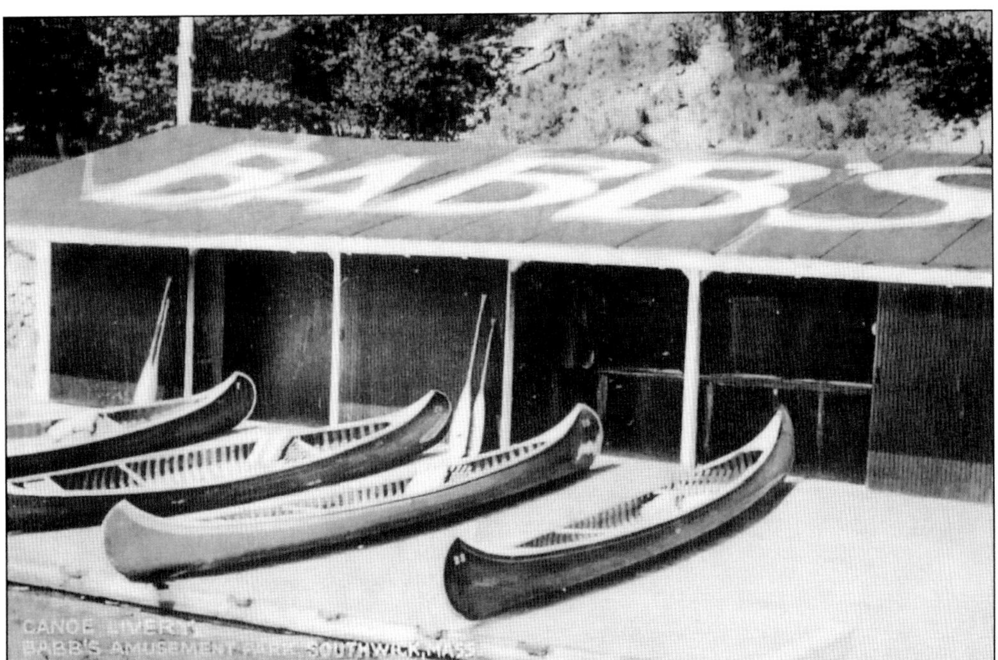

Canoes. Besides rowing, canoeing was another popular sport on the Congamond Lakes. Canoes could be rented at Babbs Beach for pleasant hours of recreation.

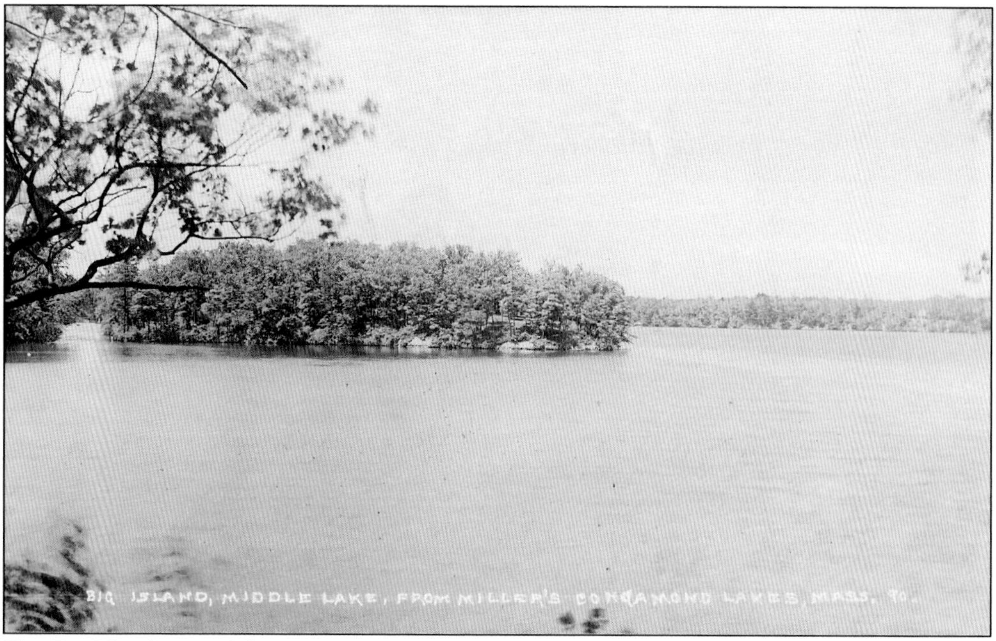

The Big Island on Middle Congamond Lake. The Big Island was created when the "Farmington Canal" was constructed linking New Haven with Northampton via Southwick. A pontoon bridge carried the towpath for the horses across the lake. The boats continued northward from the bridge traveling along the cut shown on the extreme left of the postcard.

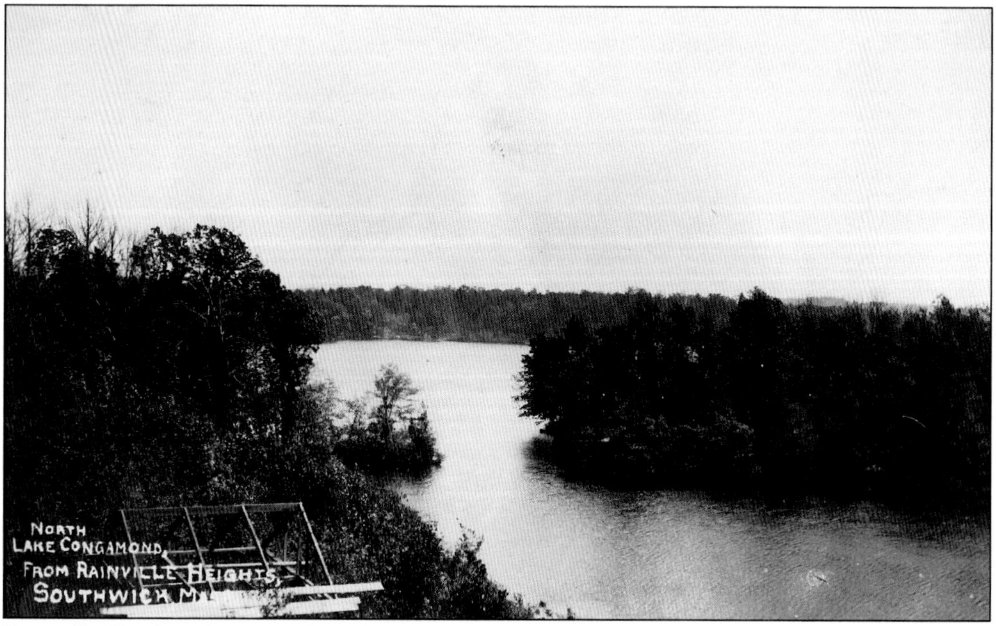

Rainville Heights. An area of North Pond where it greatly narrows is called "The Point." This view from Rainville Heights shows the locality.

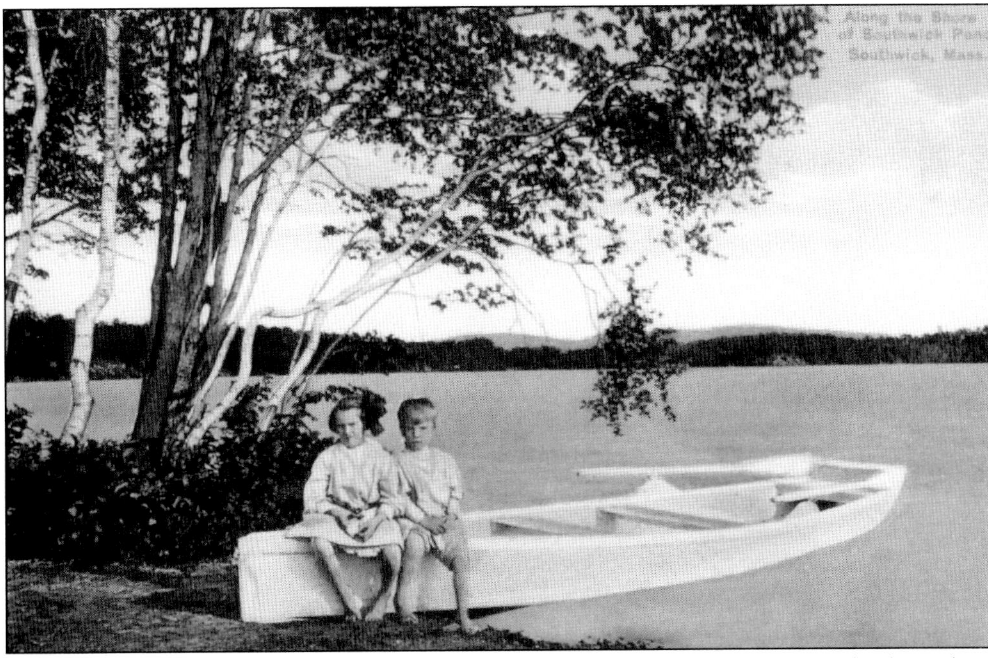

A Rowboat Beached. Even youngsters would propel a rowboat on the Congamond Lakes. These children's expressions suggest that it is the end of a long day of rowing.

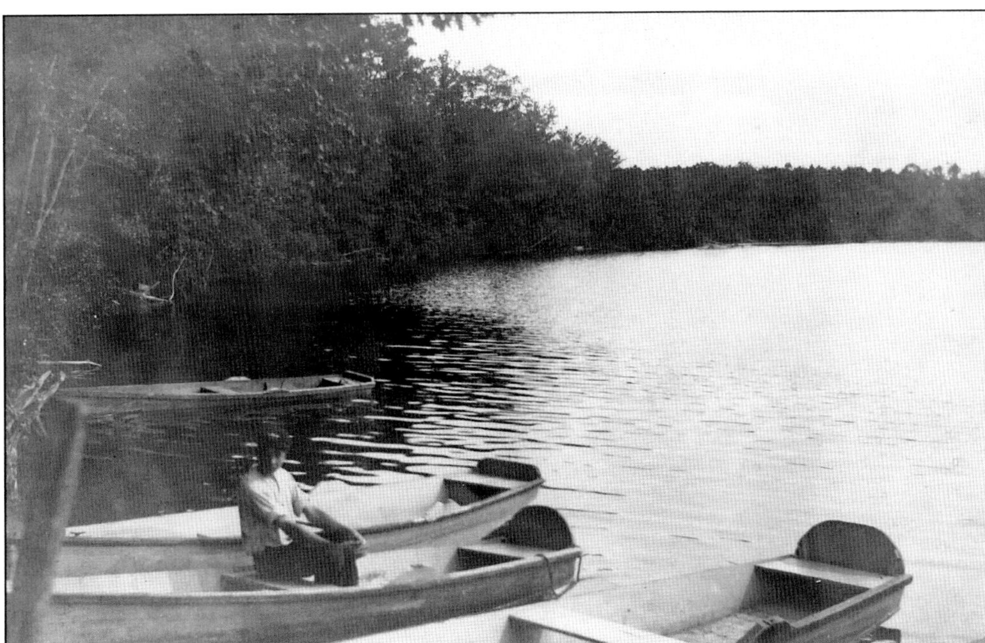

Rowboats at Cottage Grove. Cottage Grove, where the Babbs roller skating rink was located until its closing in 1996, was a site where rowboats could be rented.

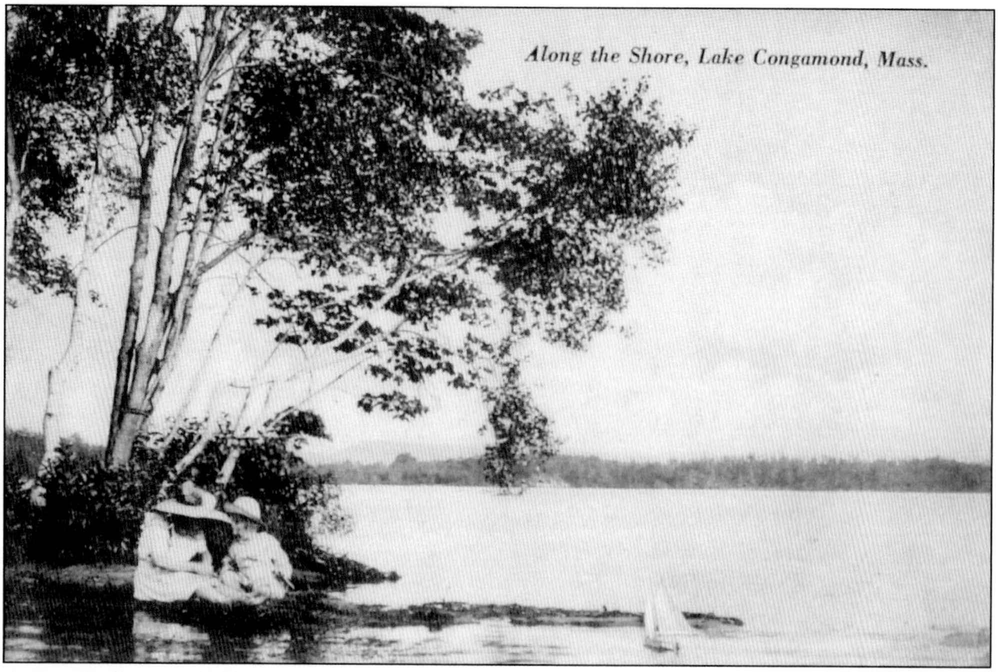

A Toy Sailboat. Children liked to sit near the water and cuddle a dog or watch a toy sailboat glide along on the waters of any of the three Congamond Lakes.

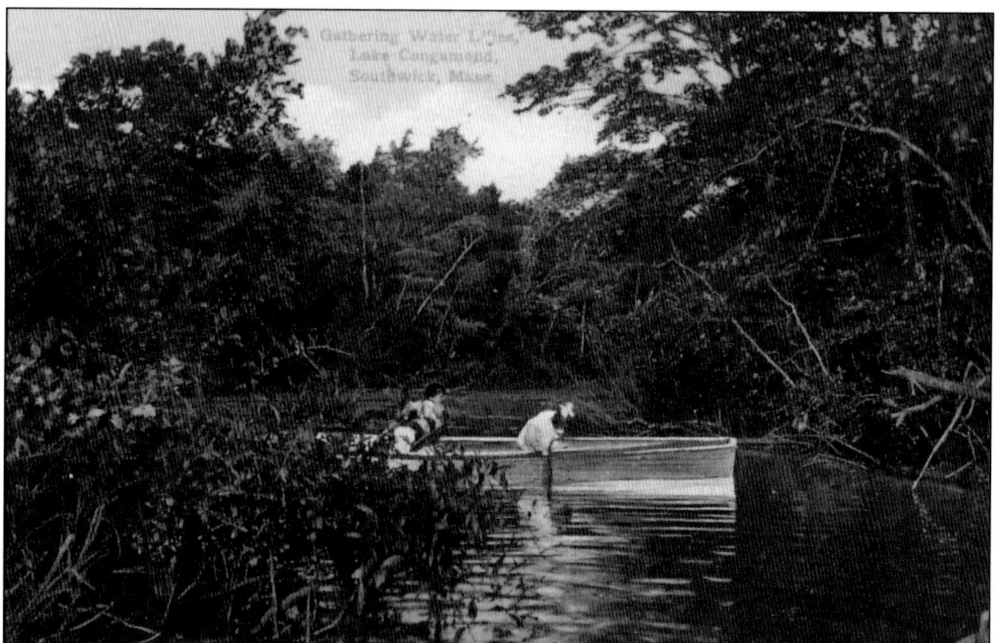

Another activity on the Congamond Lakes. Gathering water lilies after rowing a boat to the special spot was a pleasant occupation of the old days. It is still possible to rent a rowboat from Saunders Boat Livery, and find a few water lilies that have escaped the weed-eater.

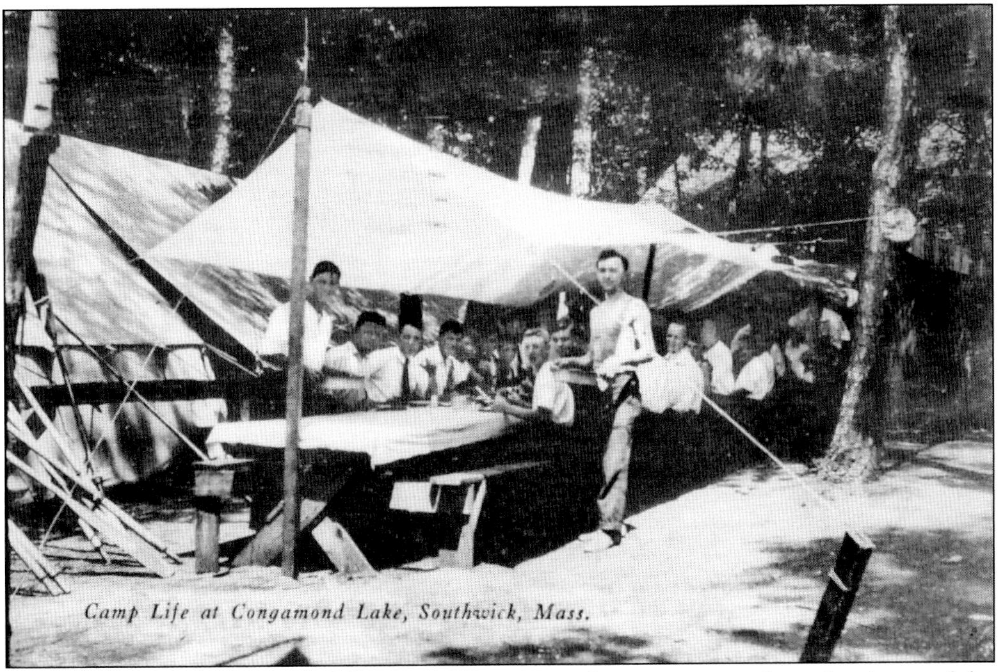

Camp Life. In the early part of this century, some people set up camp along the shores of the Congamond Lakes. It was common to have community meals.

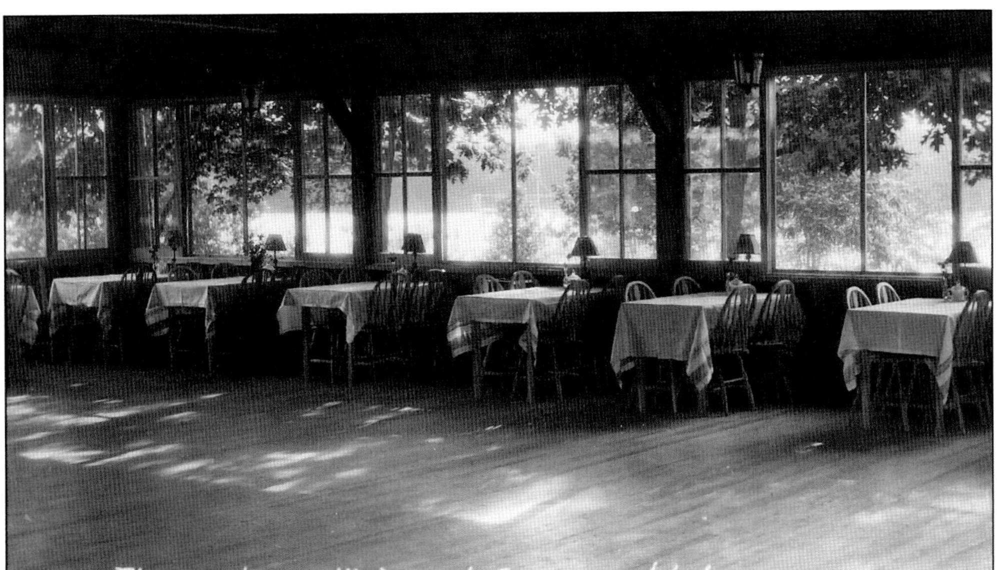

The Interior of the Manitou Restaurant. The Manitou Restaurant at Miller's Beach where South and Middle Congamond Lakes come together was the scene of many a pleasant social gathering Businesses in this building have included Ovid's, Gepetto's, and now the Round Up.

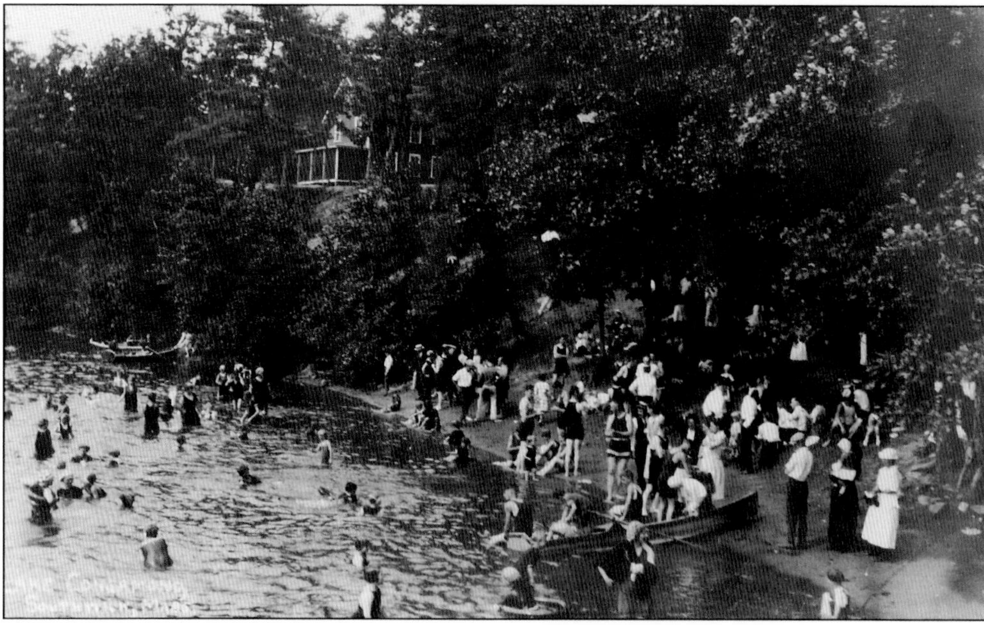

Babb's Swimming. Babb's Beach on the northeast side of Middle Congamond Lake offered a variety of activities, including rowboats and swimming. Notice the male swimmers dressed in bathing apparel which covered their chests as well as torsos.

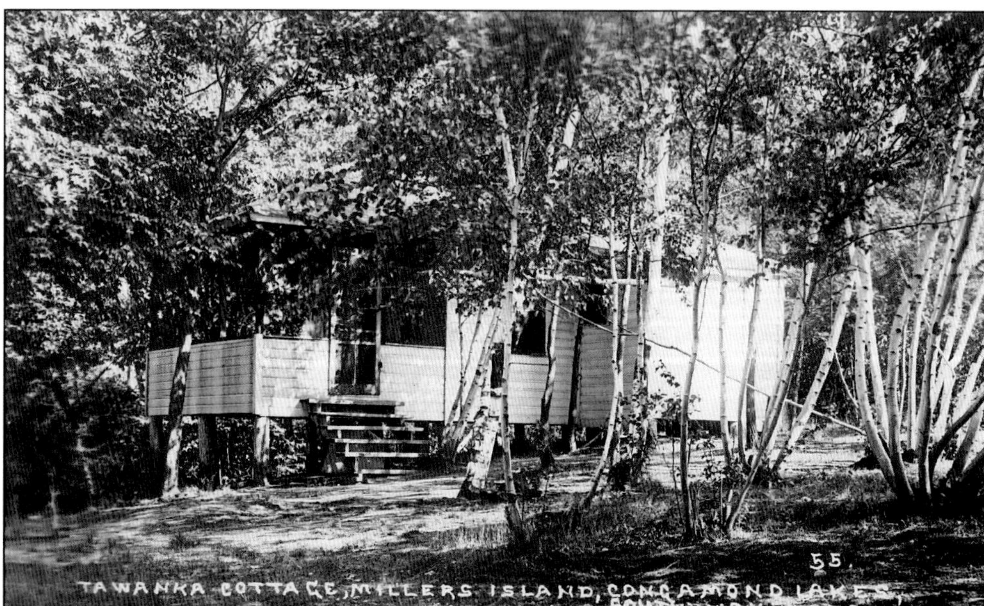

A Summer Cottage. Then, as now, many families rented a cottage by the week or month for their summer vacation. Most former summer cottages on the lakes have been winterized and made into year-round houses.

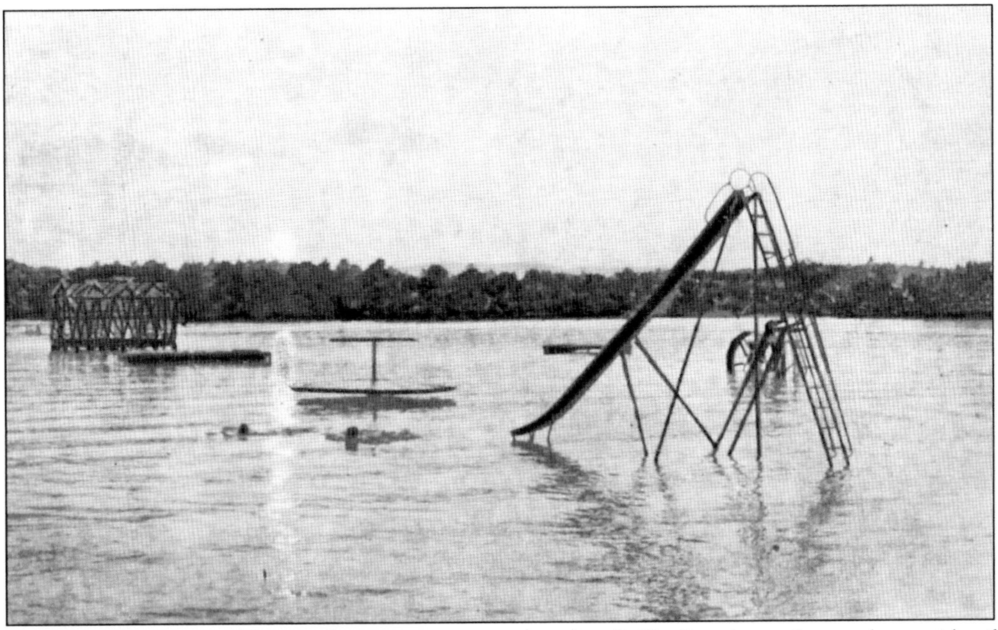

The Water Slide at Babbs Beach. Swimmers were lured to Babbs Beach on the northeast side of Middle Congamond Lake by the presence of a water slide near the diving platforms.

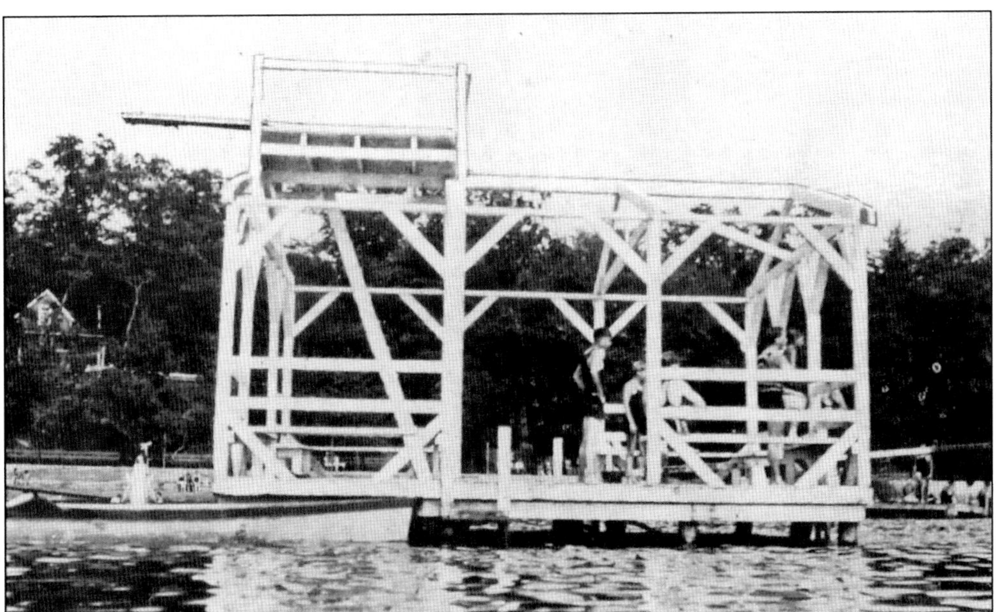

The Diving Platform at Babbs. Swimming and diving were part of a day's outing at the Congamond Lakes. These elaborate platforms were once a familiar sight from the beach at Babbs.

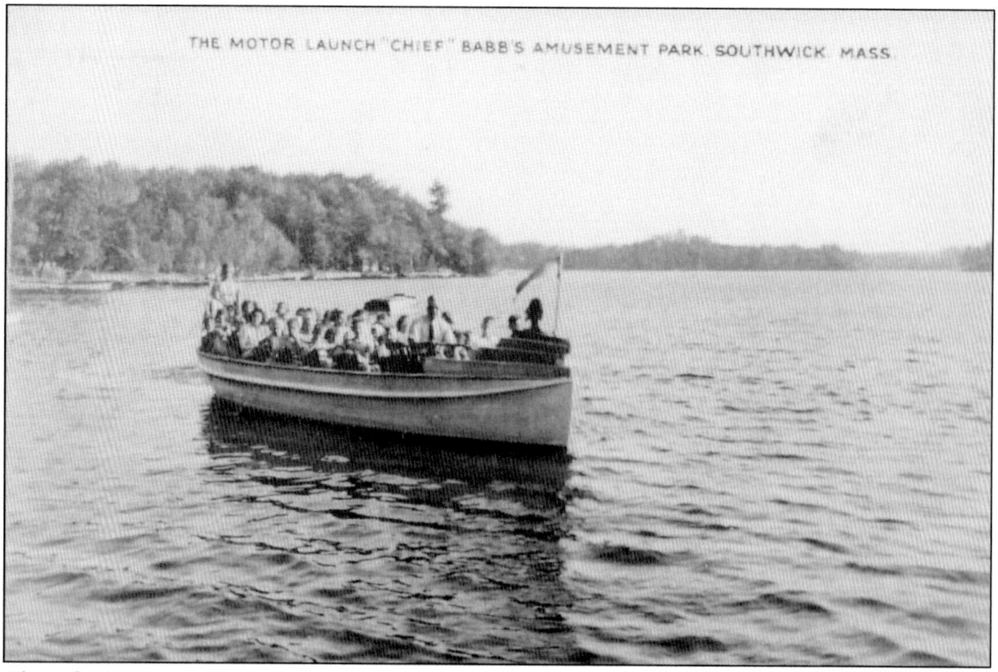

The *Chief*. When the larger steamboats were no longer running, the smaller motorboat *Chief* carried passengers to see the sights on Middle Congamond Lake.

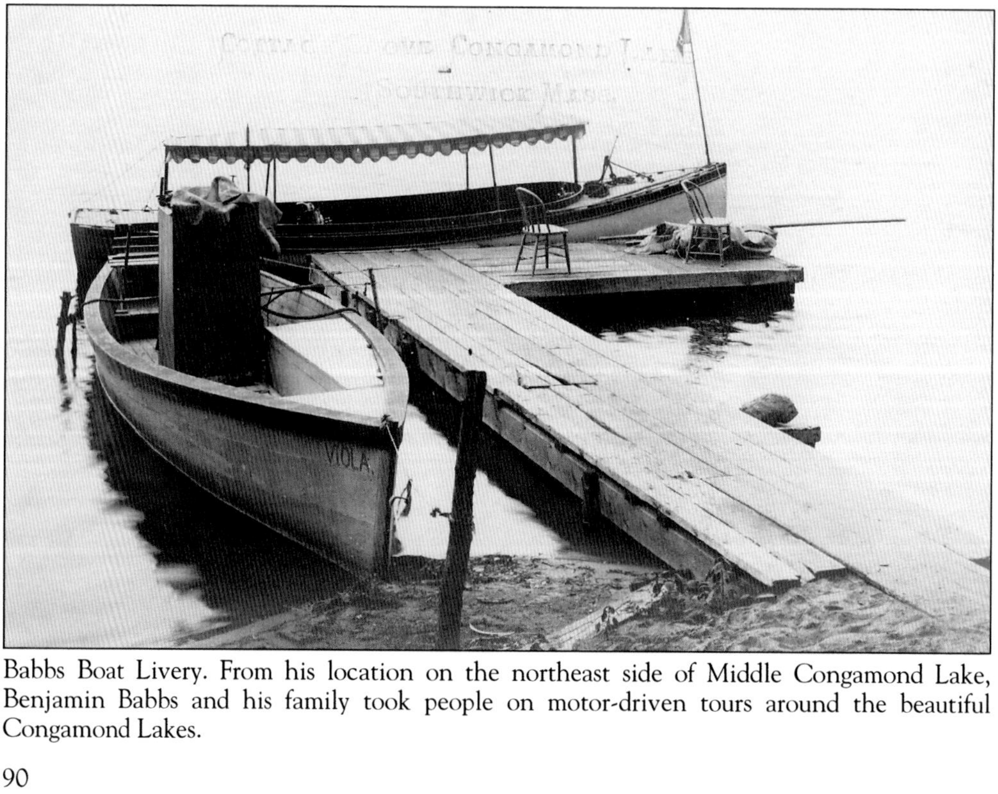

Babbs Boat Livery. From his location on the northeast side of Middle Congamond Lake, Benjamin Babbs and his family took people on motor-driven tours around the beautiful Congamond Lakes.

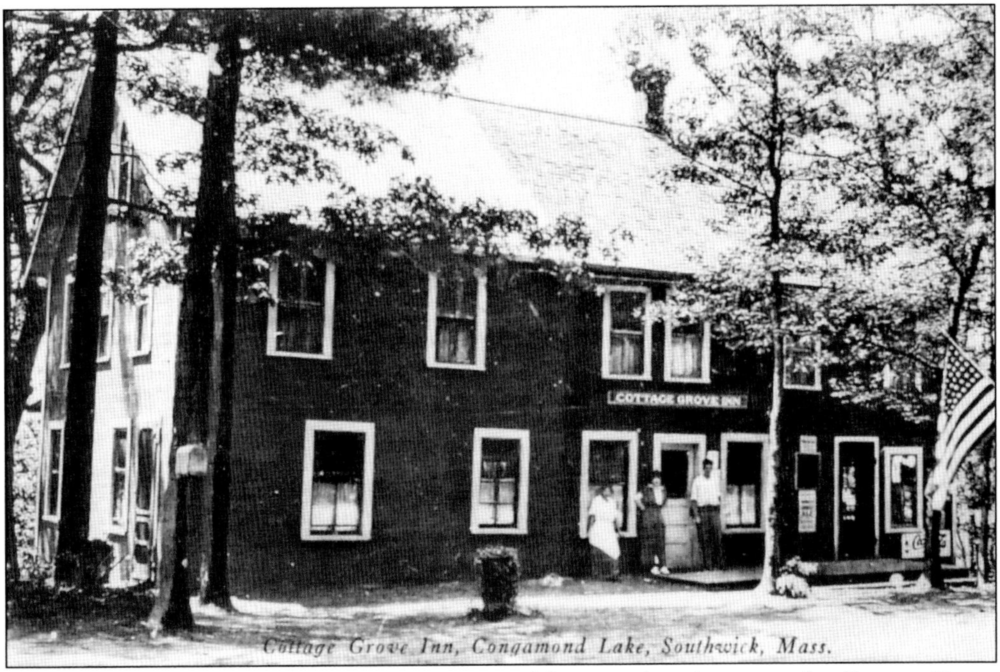

The Cottage Grove Inn. Many vacationers stayed for a week or longer at the Cottage Grove Inn on the northeast side of Middle Congamond Lake.

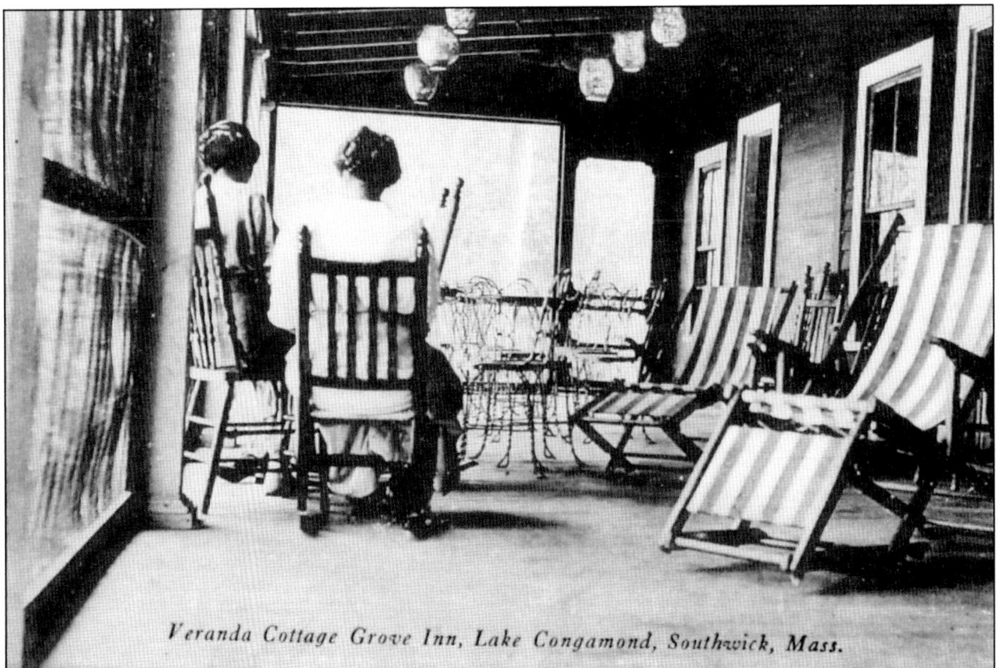

The Veranda of the Cottage Grove Inn. Enjoying the pleasant surroundings and fresh air of the "country" was one of the delights of sitting on the veranda of the hotel.

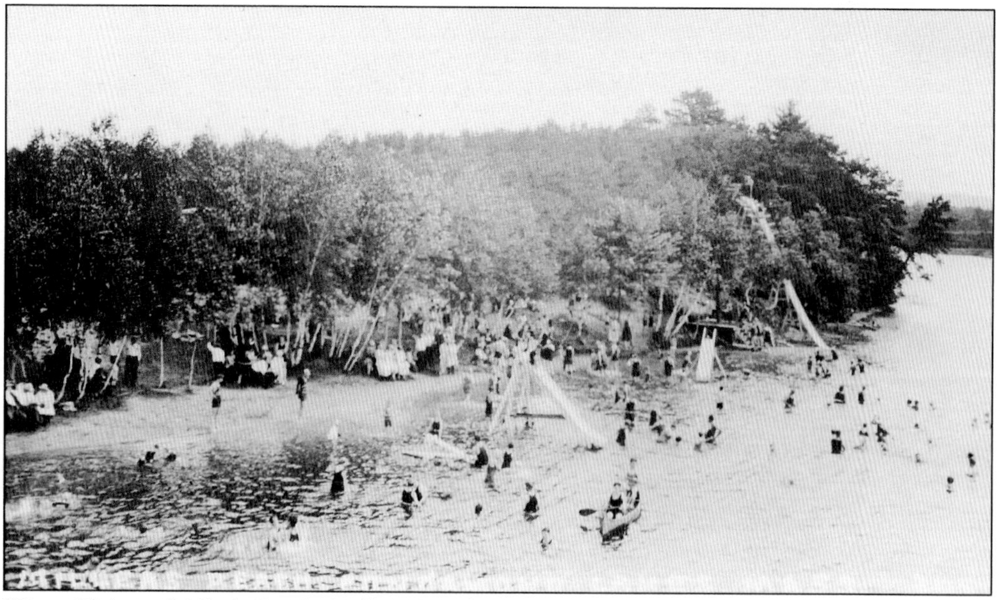

Water Slides at Miller's Beach. Miller's Beach offered swimmers a choice of several water slides in the stiff competition for the tourist dollar.

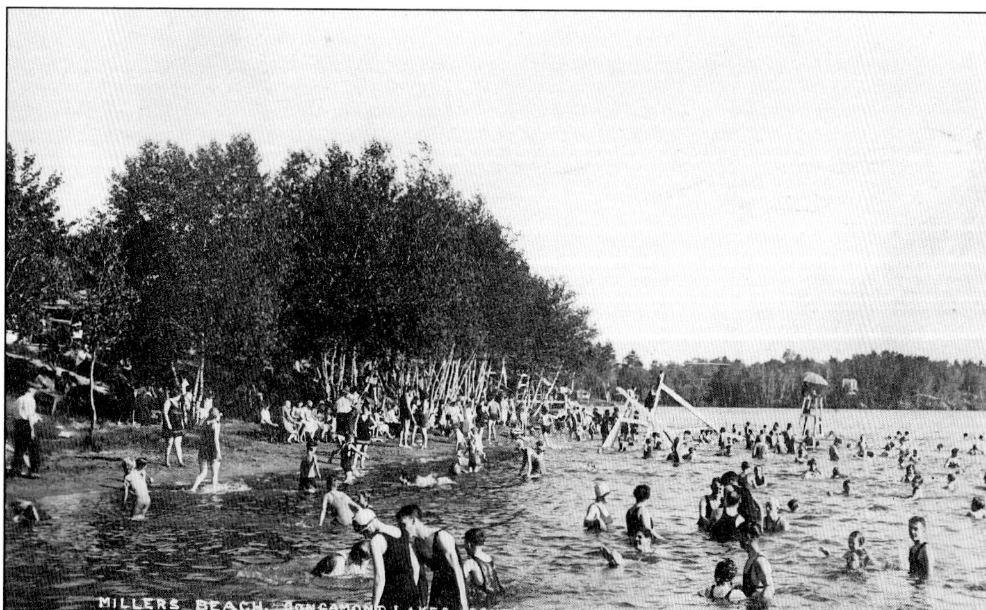

Swimming at Miller's Beach. Swimming was a popular summer pastime. Many residents recall frequent weekend visits to Miller's Beach before their families settled in Southwick.

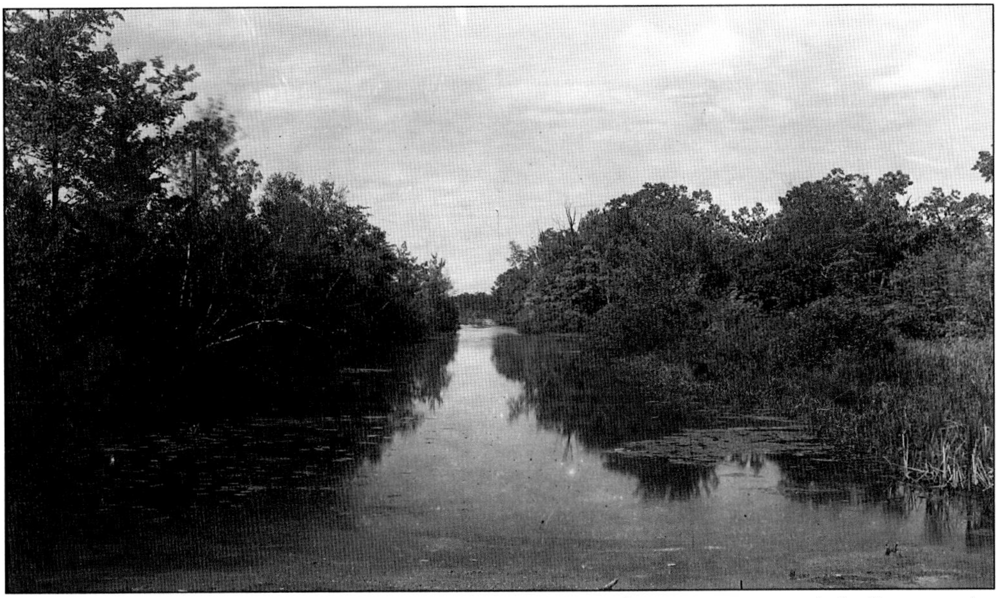

The Old Canal at Miller's. That the "Farmington Canal" was narrow and shallow can be surmised from this postcard taken at Miller's Beach. When the members of the Southwick Historical Society Inc. traveled to the Town of Plainville, Connecticut, to visit the Canal Museum there and view the 700-foot portion of the Connecticut section of the canal which has been restored, members discovered for themselves that the surmise was correct.

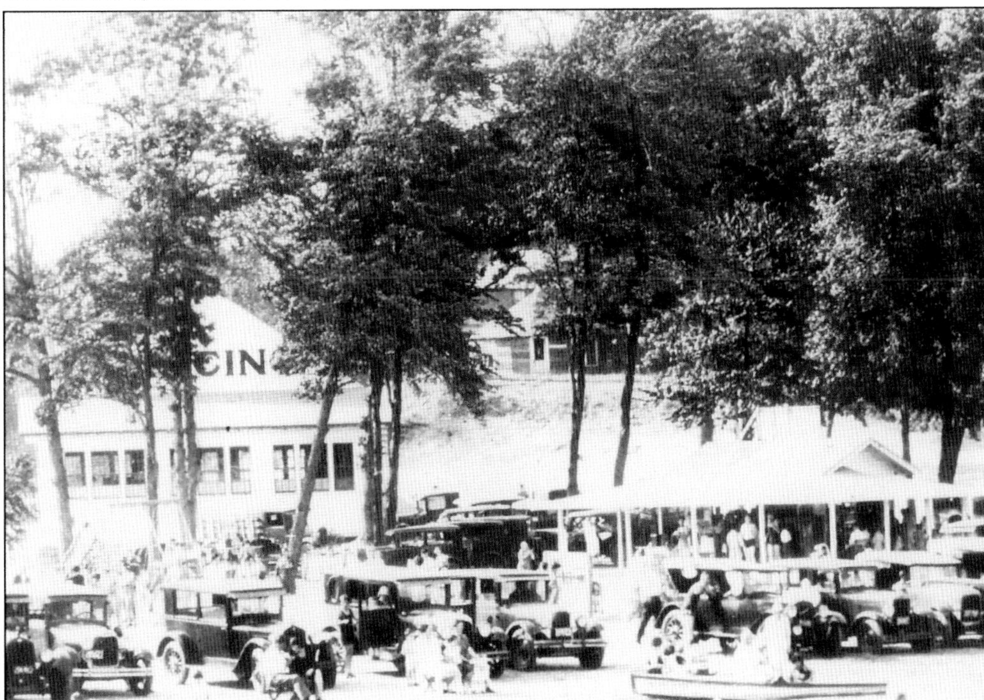

Balch's Beach. Because it was at the north end of Middle Pond, quite a distance from the Congamond railroad depot, Balch's Beach was popular at a later date, when automobiles could be used to get there. Notice the Merry-Go-Round in the background.

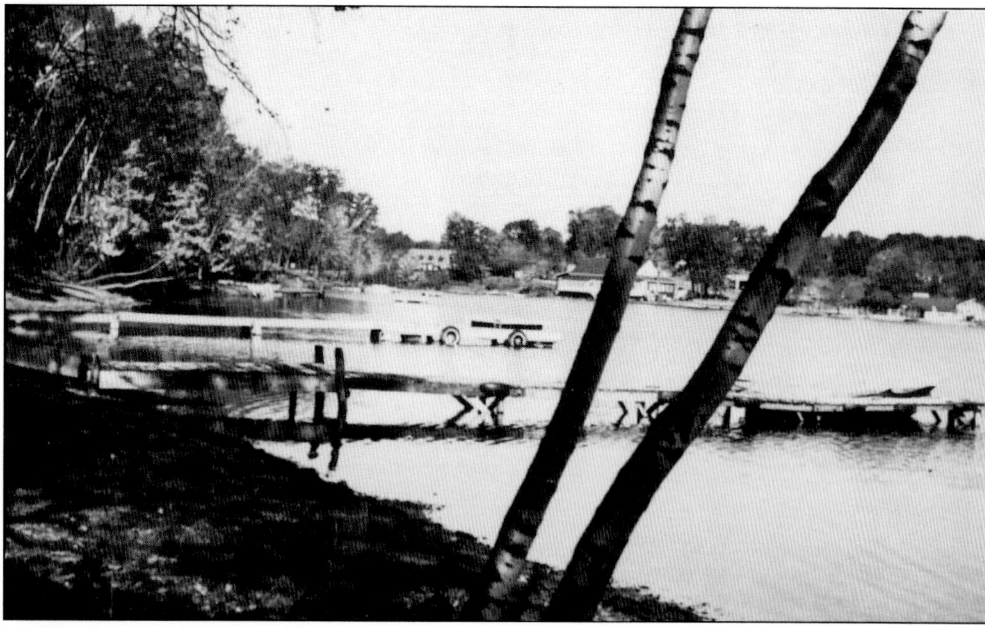

Middle Lake with Docks. In this more recent postcard, looking north from the west side of Middle Congamond Lake, one can see long docks to moor motor boats. The Brass Rail and several other lake-side businesses are visible in the background. The sites of the former Babb's Anchor and Merry-Go-Round are on the farther shore in the "V" formed by the birches.

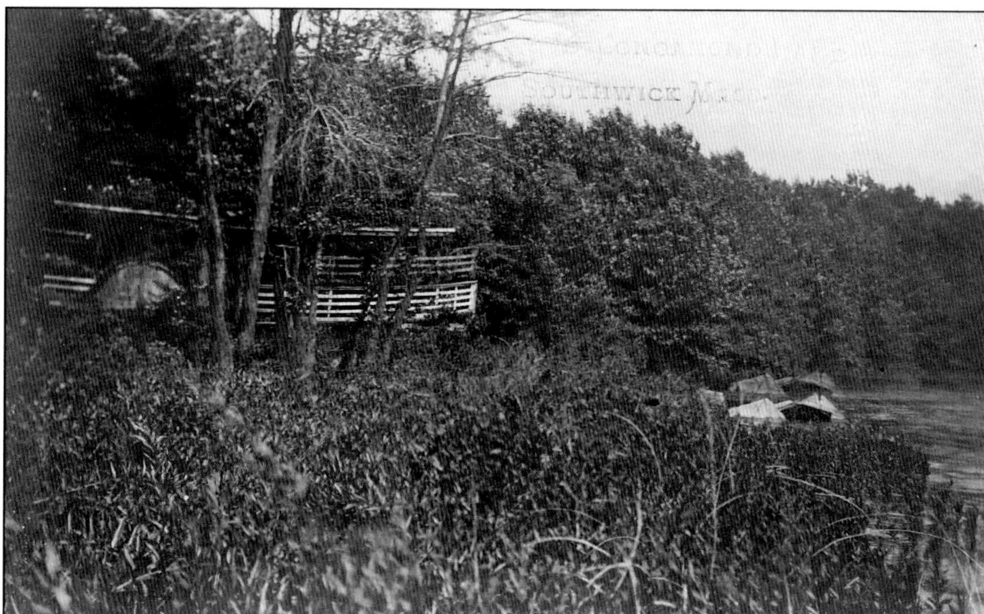

The Steamboat *Josephine*. John Chapman had at least two steamboats, the *Ida Lee* and the *Josephine*, which carried passengers to see the sights on Middle Congamond Lake from about 1890 to the 1920s.

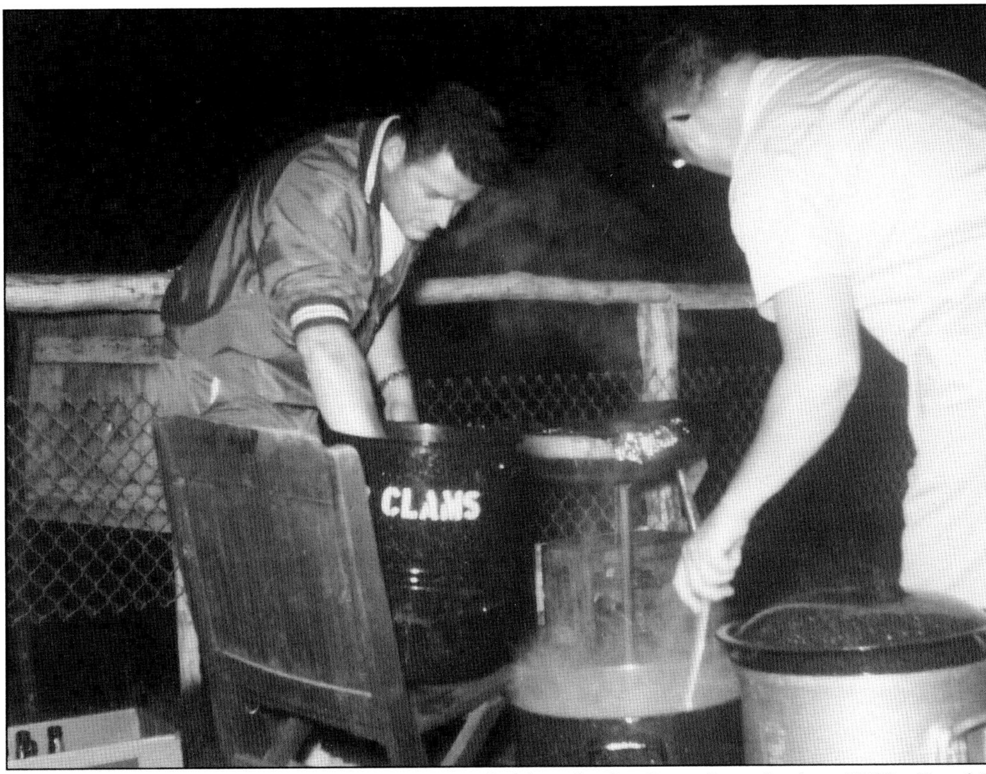

A Clambake at Smith's Beach, *c.* 1940. Founded by Charles Baiardi in the late 1930s, Smith's Beach offered clambakes to its beach patrons and the general public. While Charles served in World War II, his wife Alice continued the business, located at what is now the Town Beach on South Pond. The Baiardis offered "bathing, boating, fishing, dancing, picnicking, food and beverages, cabins, cottages, and motel" during many years of business at Smith's Beach.

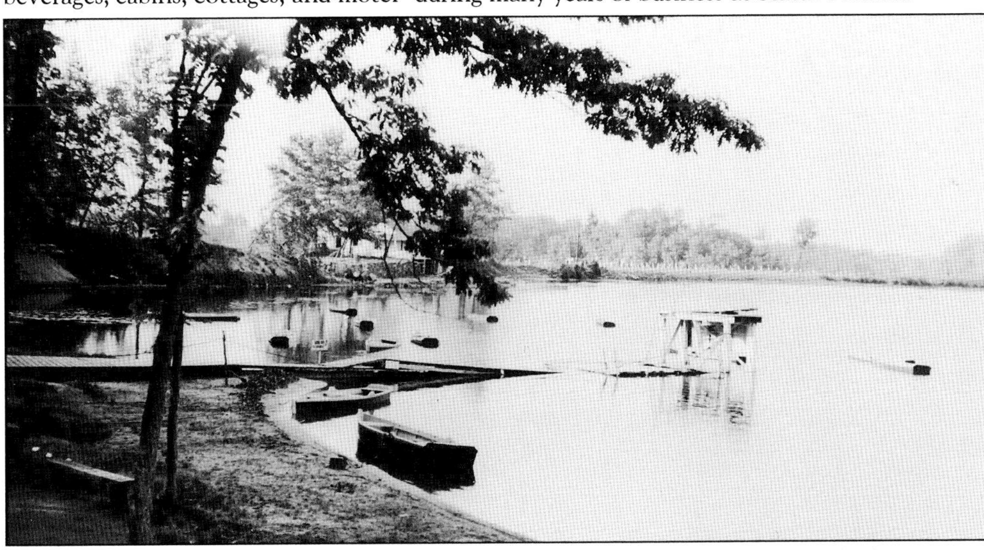

Smith's Beach, *c.* 1940. Smith's Beach, on South Pond, is shown here in a view looking toward the Connecticut side of the Congamond Lakes. The waters of Middle and South Ponds connect under a small bridge in view in the middle background. Ovid's Restaurant can also be seen.

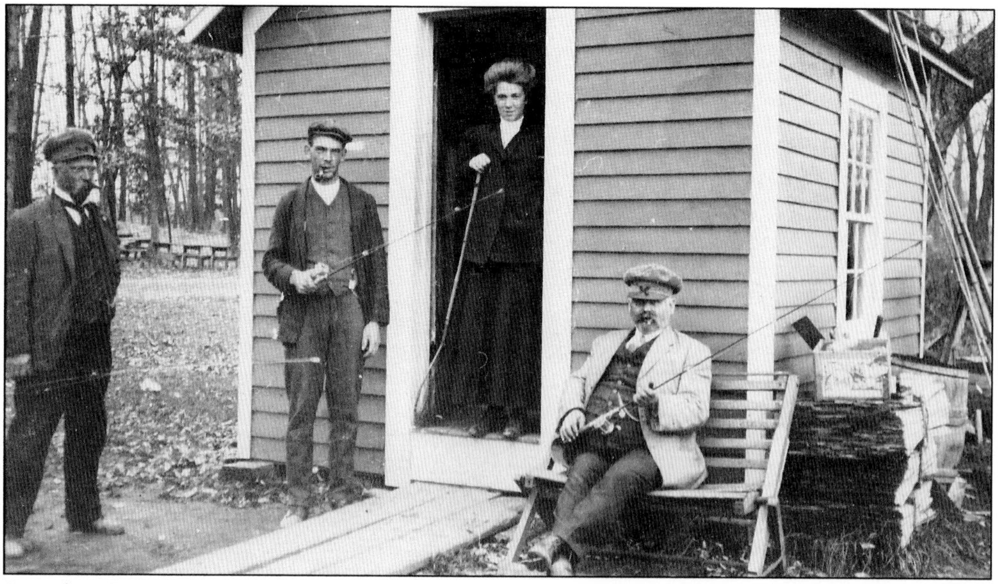

Saunders' Boat Livery. Owner William Saunders, his son John and his daughter Cornelia, along with John Borthwick (proprietor of the Lake House, shown here displaying his fishing pole), pose in front of the small building where the business began. Notice the poles stacked on the side of the building.

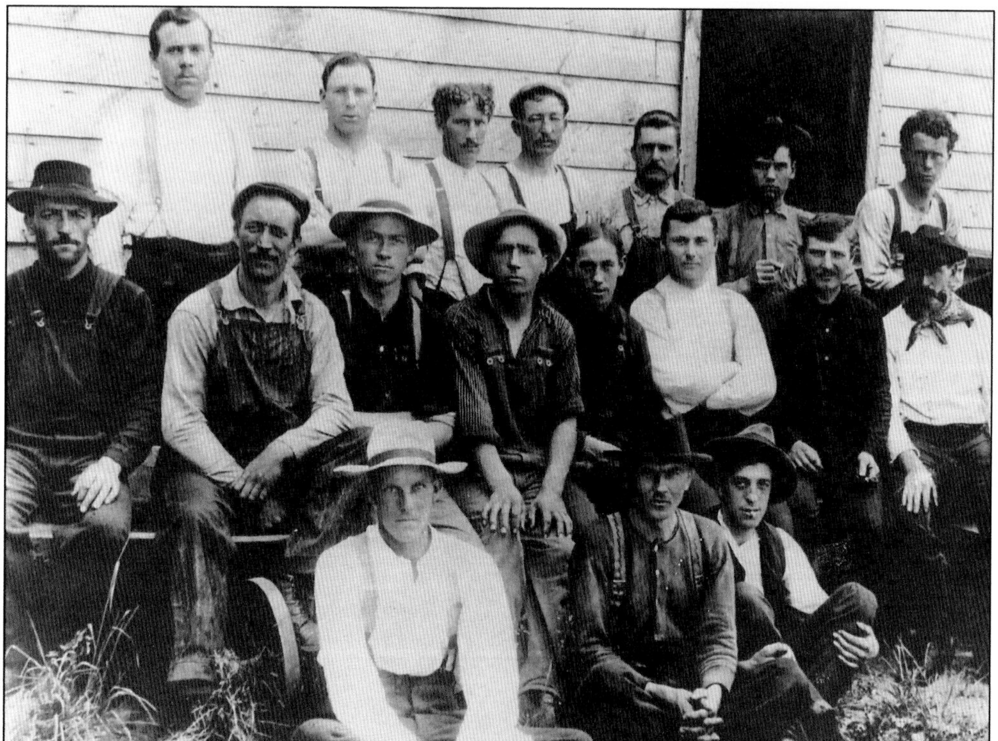

Ice House Workers in the Summer, *c.* 1910. Many workers were required in summer to transfer the cakes of ice from the ice houses to the waiting railroad cars for transport to cities such as Hartford, New Haven, and Bridgeport.

Chapter Nine

Winter

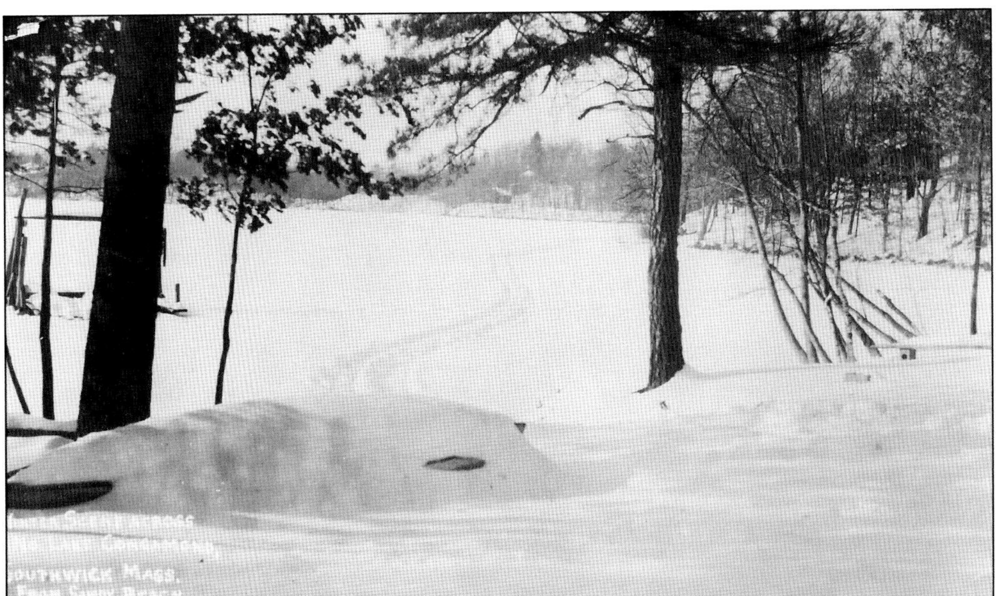

North Lake in Winter, c. 1920. The Sandy Beach of the North Congamond Lake provides a vantage for this snowy scene. Many people still enjoy hiking over the snow-clad lakes.

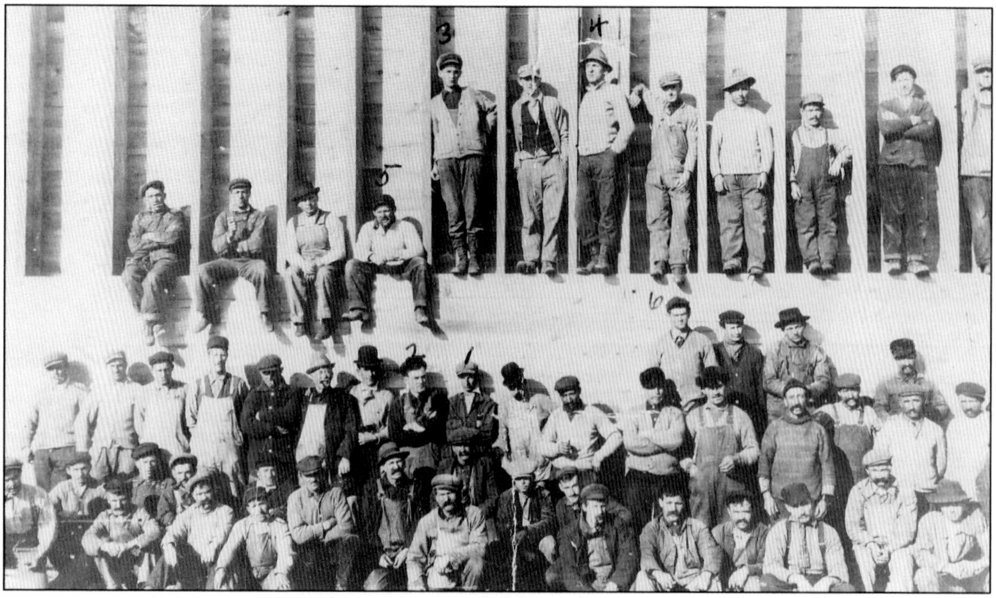

Ice House Workers, *c.* 1908. Between four hundred and seven hundred men worked at the five ice houses located at the Congamond Lakes (four on Middle Pond and one on South Pond). A few of the men are pictured here, during construction of the Walker Ice House.

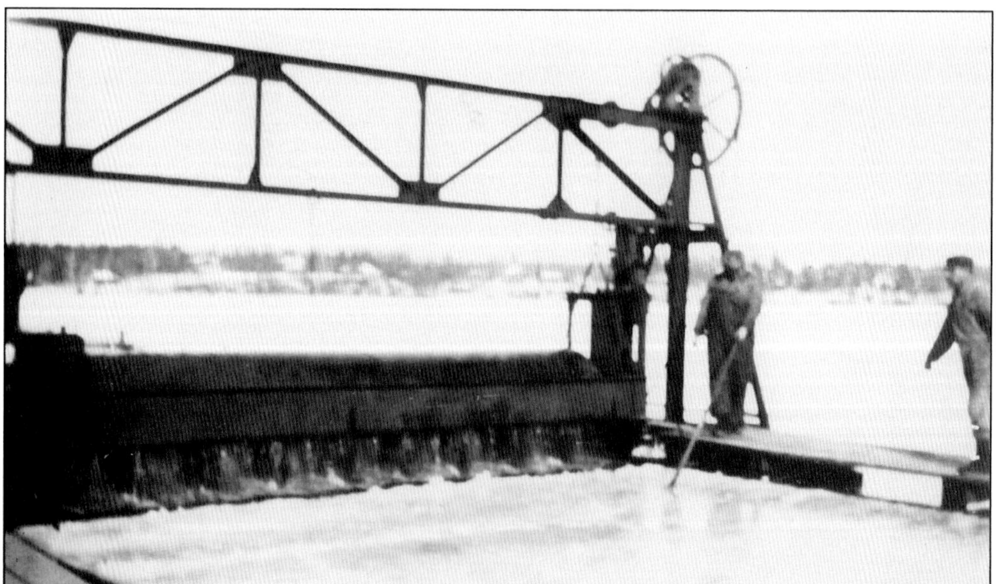

An Ice Planer and Saw, 1913. The machine shown is an ice planer, which was used to level the blocks so that they were all the same height, before it cut the pre-grooved blocks into cakes measuring 22 inches wide, 32 inches long, and 12 inches high.

Preparing Ice for Sawing, 1913. Enoch Mollander, Enfred Anderson, Hjalmar Johnson, and August Wolfe are marking off the ice for sawing. Before the advent of machinery, a hand cross-cut saw was used to cut the ice blocks into cakes.

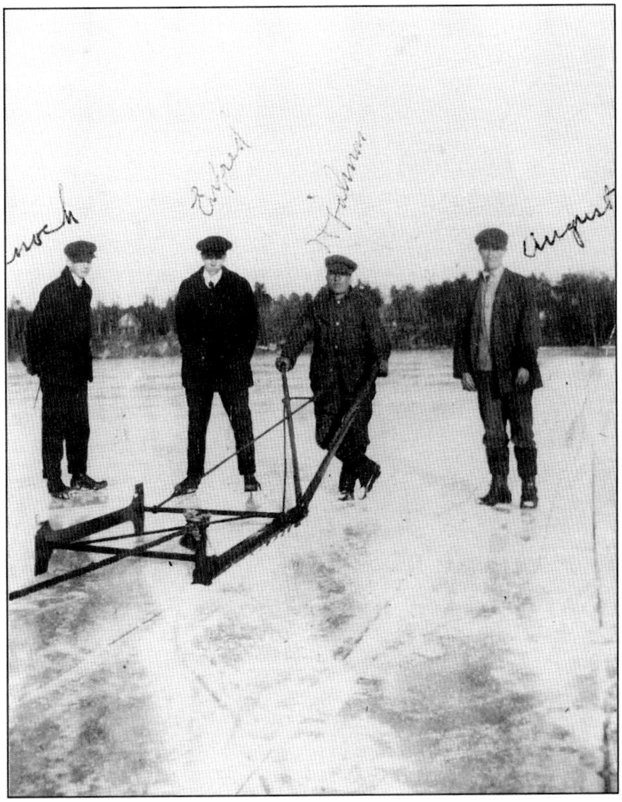

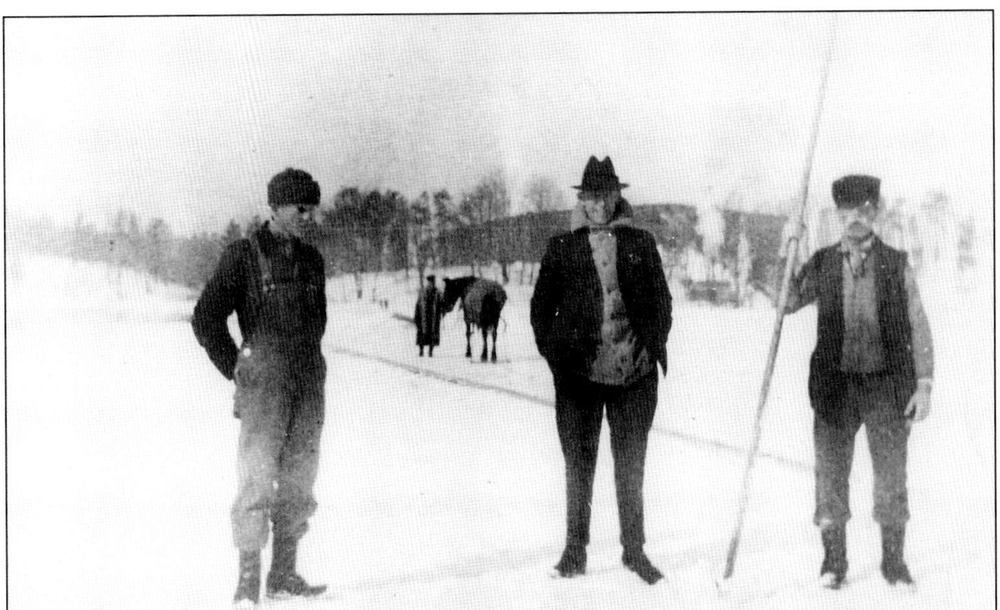

Guiding the Ice Blocks, 1913. Ice pikes were used to guide the blocks along the canal toward an ice house. Fred B. Arnold, Clarence Brooks, and Xavier Mignotte pose for Mrs. Brooks' camera. Mr. and Mrs. Brooks, who came east from Fresno, California, for President Wilson's inauguration, were fascinated by the ice harvesting operation.

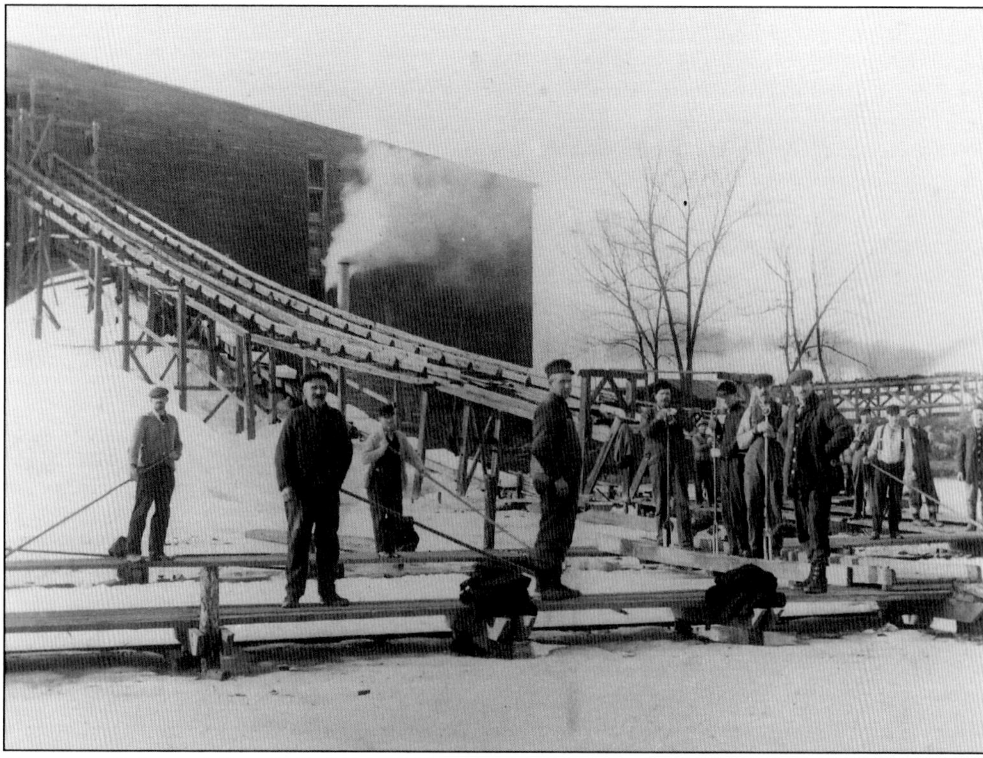

Conveyor Belts and Canal Workers, 1913. Conveyor belts carried the ice blocks from the level of the lake up into the ice house. Many workers were needed to guide the blocks down the canal and onto the conveyors. The men stood on wooden staging above the open water.

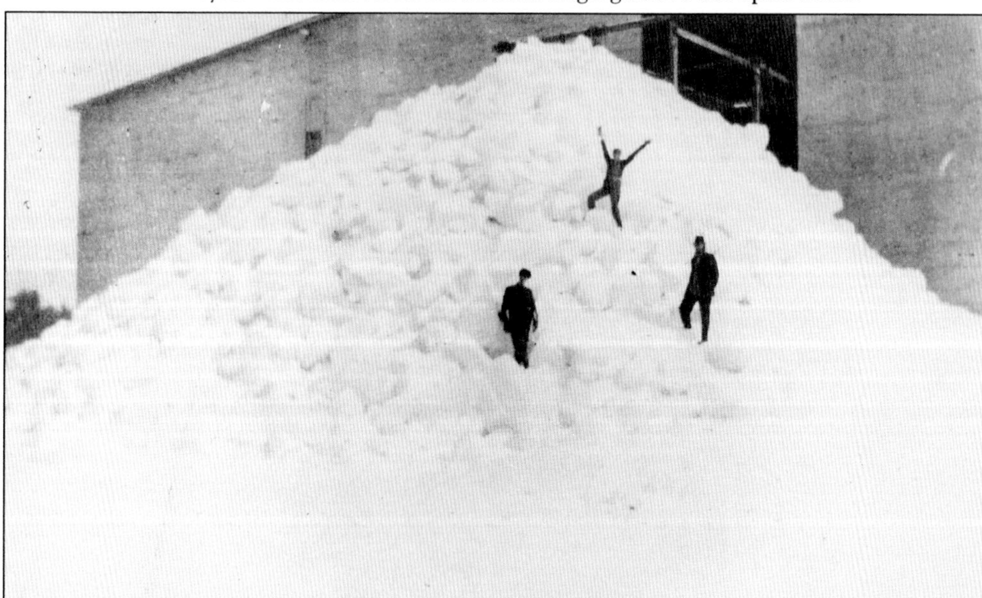

A Pile of Waste Ice, 1913. When the ice blocks were cut to size for shipment, the waste ice was pushed out of the ice house, making a huge mound which took many warm months to melt. Joseph Arnold, Fred B. Arnold, and Clarence Brooks pose here for the camera of Mrs. Brooks.

A Conveyor Belt Inside the Ice House. Conveyor belts carried the ice blocks down to the bottom level of the ice house first, filling each room at that level. Then the conveyor was raised to fill the second floor and succeeding floors until the ice house was full.

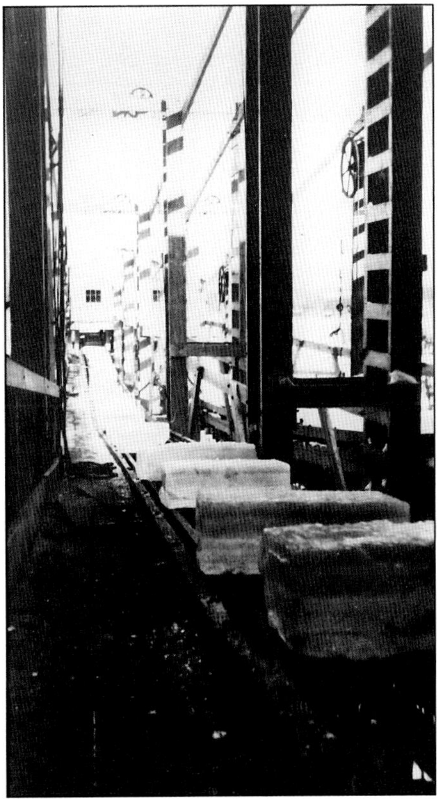

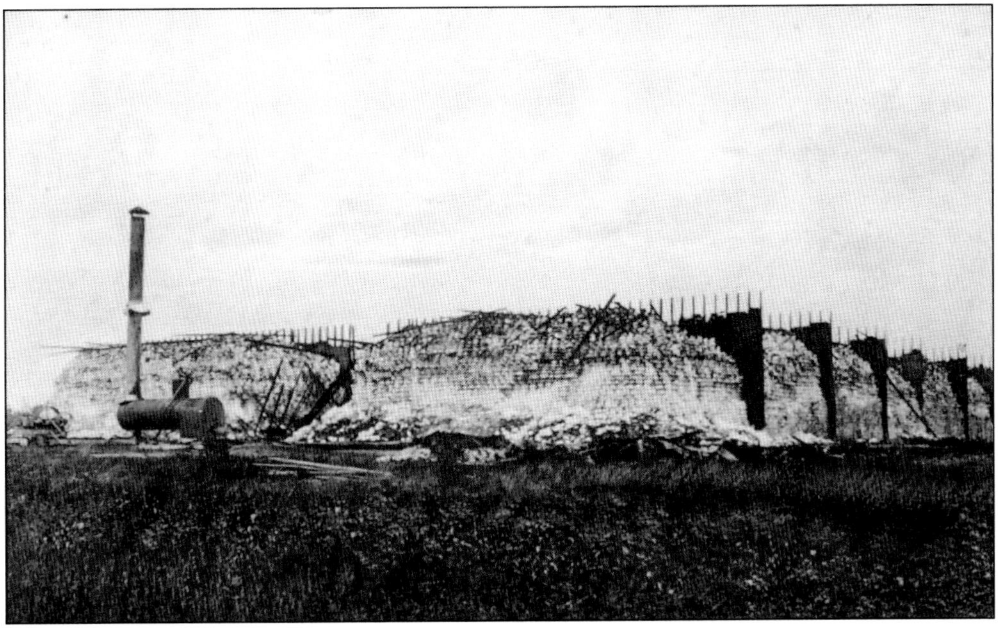

The Smoking Ruins of the Congamond Ice House. When the Congamond, or North, Ice House burned, the Carnazolla home nearby was also engulfed and destroyed. Notice the partitions between the various rooms and how much ice remained despite the tremendous heat of the fire.

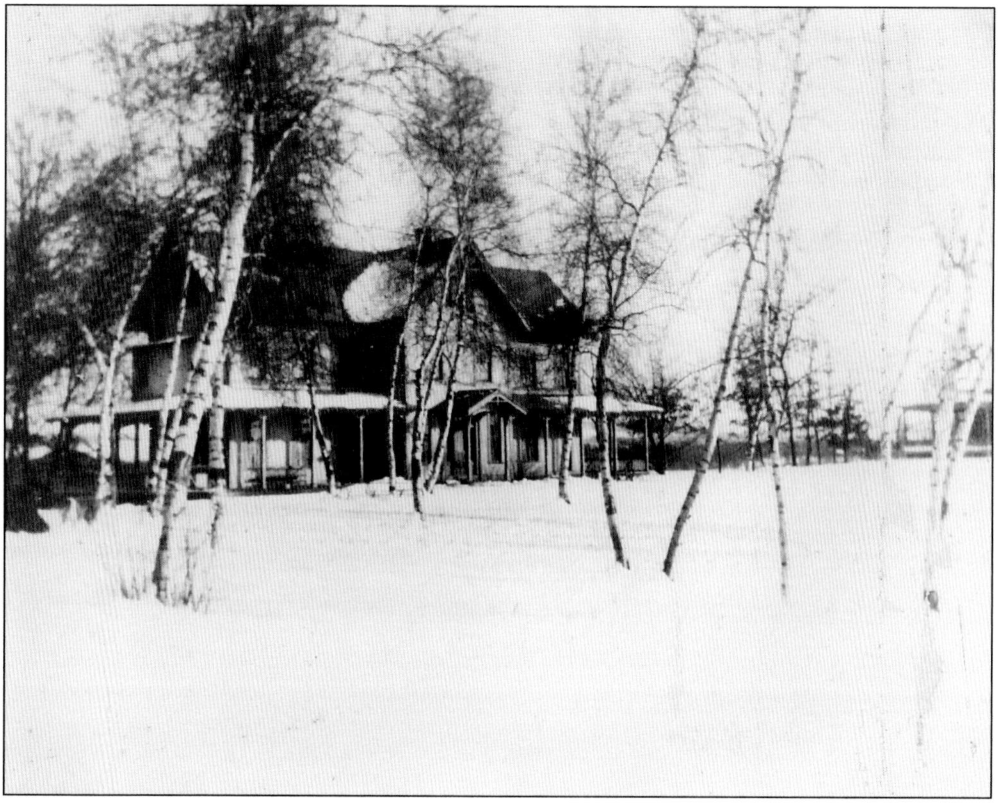

The Railroad Hotel. The Railroad Hotel in winter, without the summer crowds of people, presents a rather forlorn appearance.

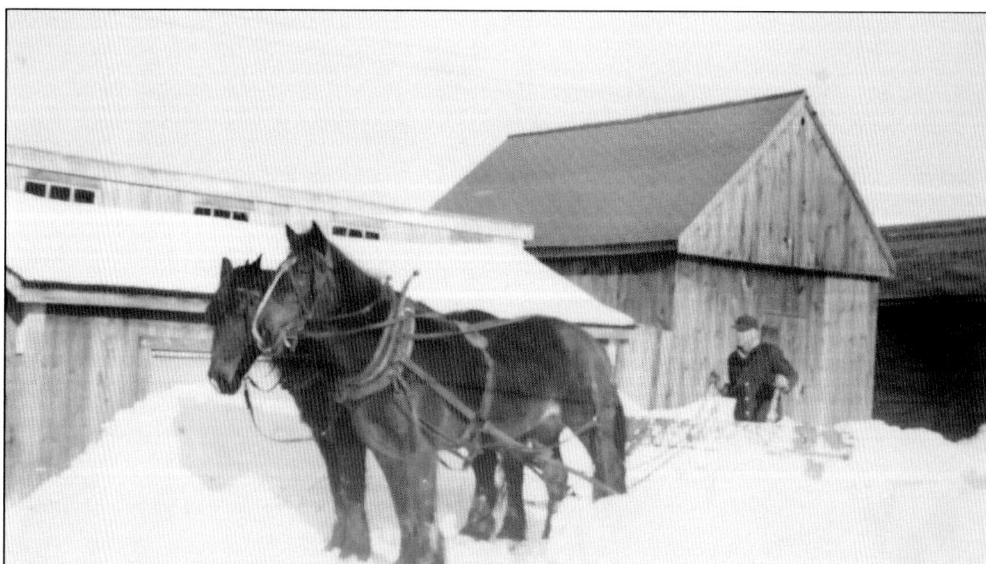

Plowing the Pathways. A two-horse team pulled the plow to clear the roadways on the Steere farm at 18 Vining Hill Road.

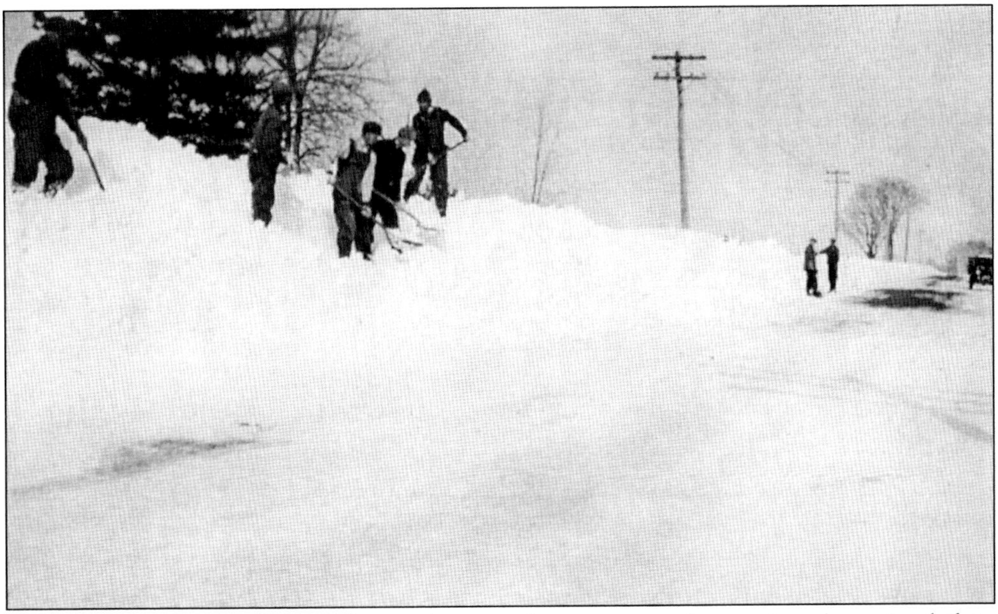

Clearing Snow from College Highway. A group of men got together to clear the major drift in the dip in the road to Westfield, just north of what is now the Southwick Country Club. The primitive plows of that era could not handle high mounds of snow.

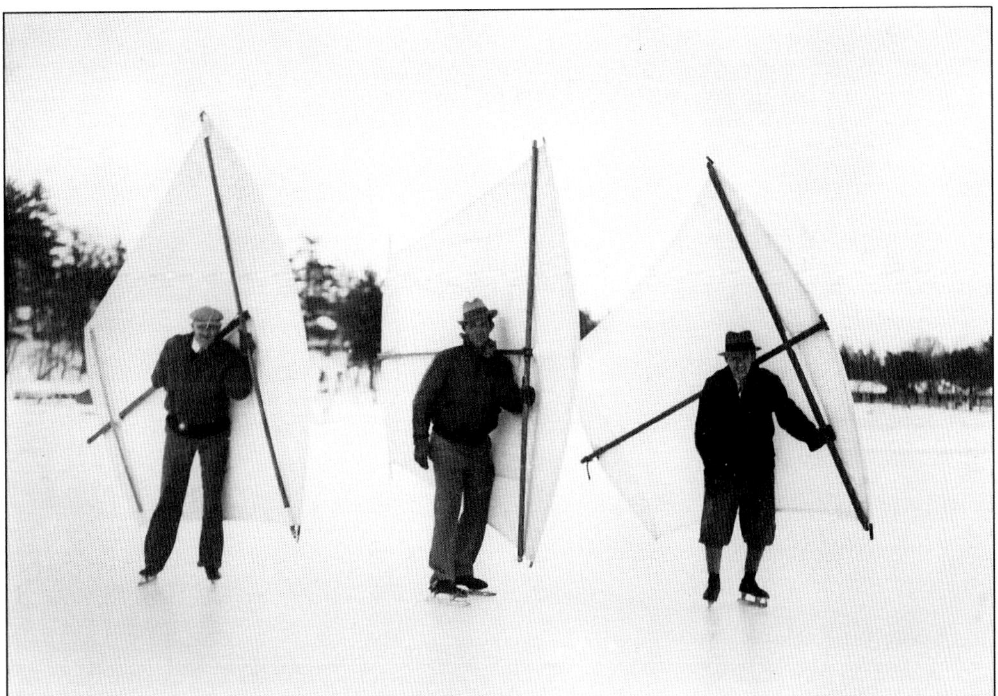

Sail-skating on Middle Congamond Lake, 1935. These young men, Arthur Roberts, Bradford Stannard, and Merrill Mason, made large kites to catch the wind and propel themselves swiftly over the ice-covered lake.

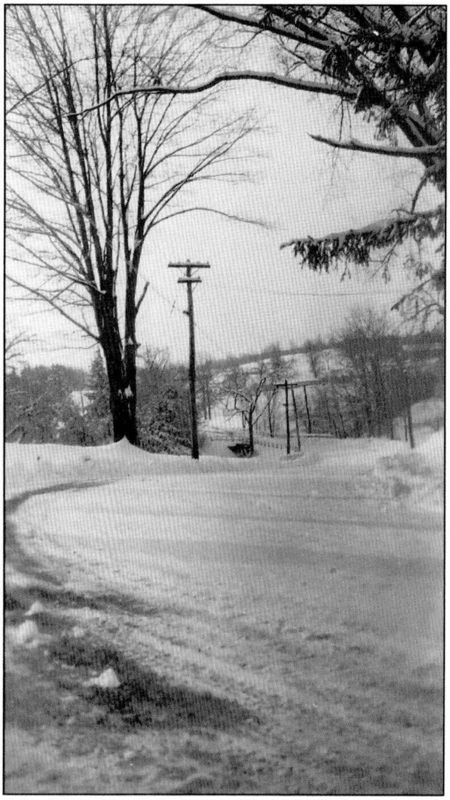

A Winter View South on Sheep Pasture, 1920s. This photograph was taken looking south on Sheep Pasture Road from its intersection with what is now called Depot Street. The bridge over Great Brook is in the background.

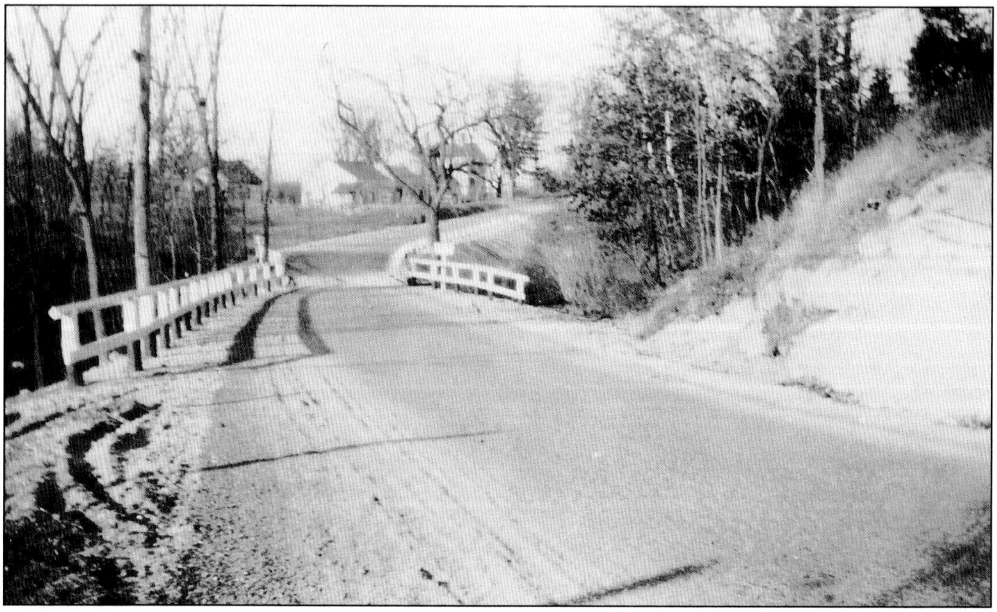

A Winter Scene before 1929. This is a view of the Sheep Pasture Road bridge over Great Brook looking north. The Rockwell-Fletcher home (also seen on p. 10) and out-buildings are visible in the center background; the Center Primary School is also in view.

Chapter Ten

Recreation

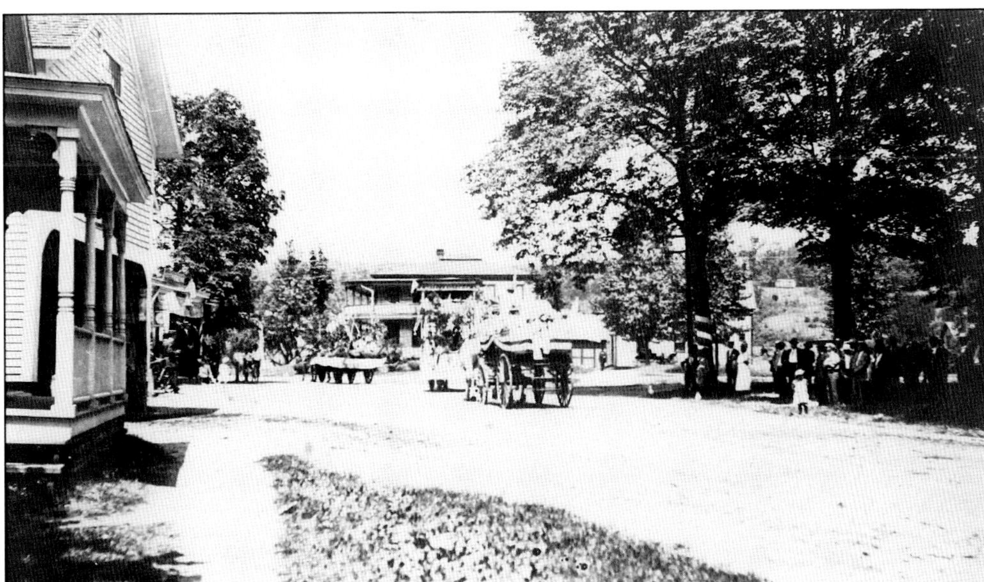

A Fourth of July Parade before 1927. Horse-drawn floats proceed from what is now Depot Street around the corner onto College Highway. The Leblanc house in the foreground, which can also be seen on p. 15, burned in 1927.

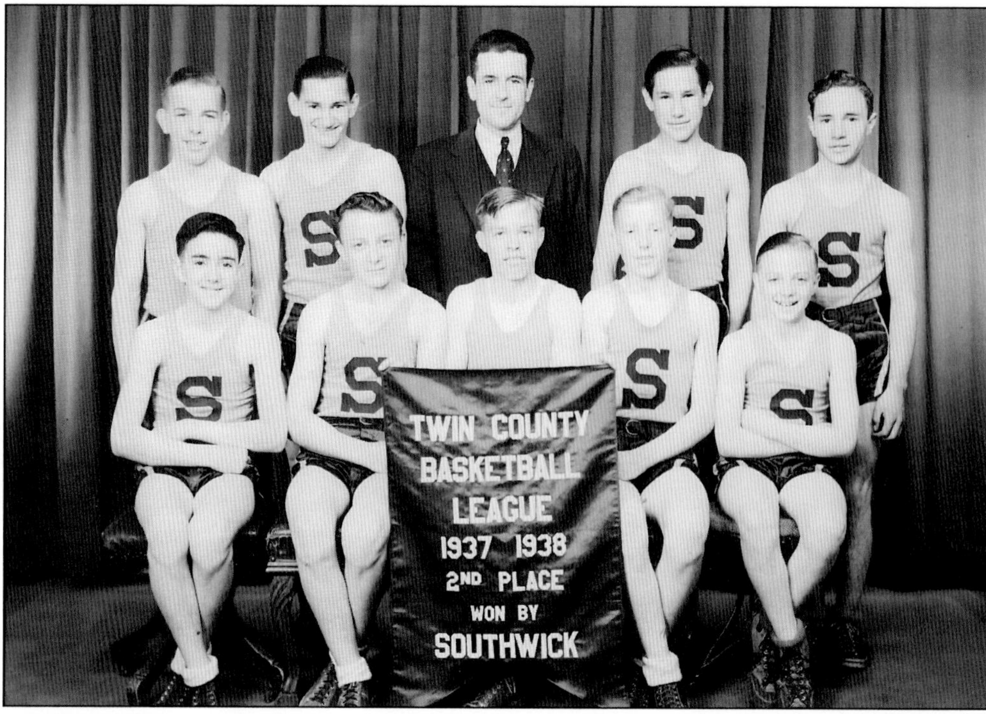

The Boys 1937–1938 Basketball Team. Back Row: Norman Chaffee, Joseph Monczka, Dana Maynard (principal and coach), Joseph Molta, and Joseph Fonsone. Front Row: Theodore Kellogg, Thomas Edwards, Melvin Johnson, Douglas Cass, and Robert Arnold.

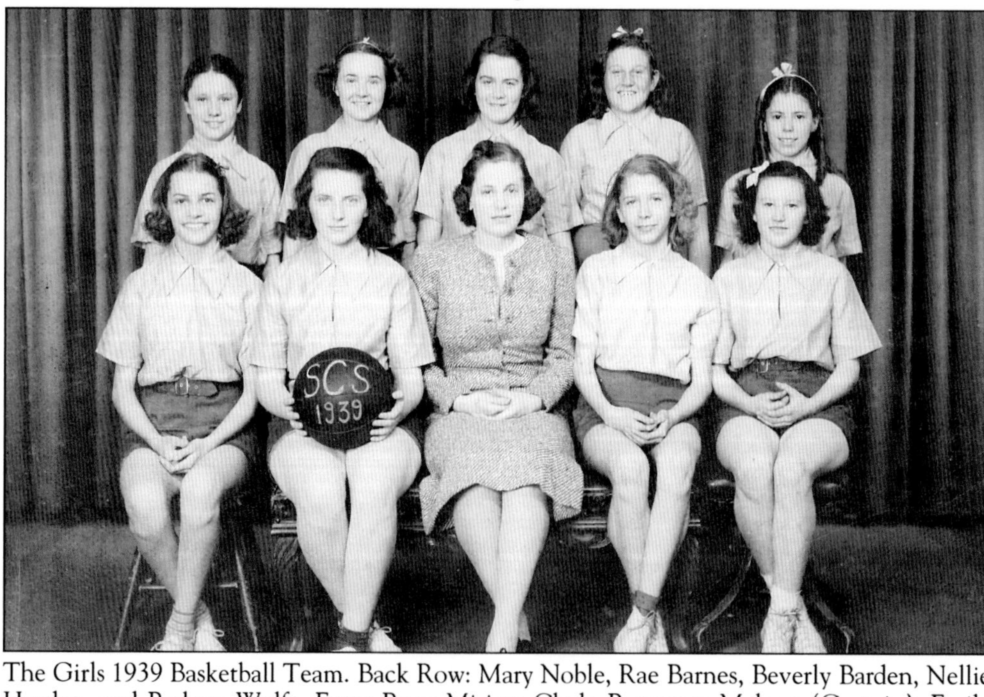

The Girls 1939 Basketball Team. Back Row: Mary Noble, Rae Barnes, Beverly Barden, Nellie Hayden, and Barbara Wolfe. Front Row: Miriam Clark, Rosemary Malone (Captain), Emily Picknelly (teacher), Miriam Anderson, and Helen Pieczarka.

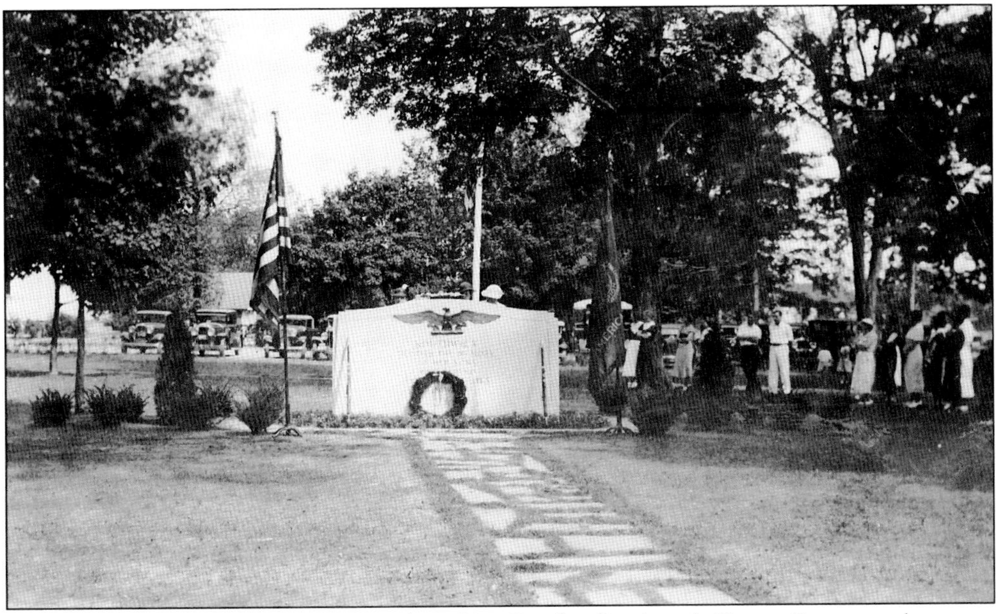

The Dedication of the War Memorial, 1930s. On the Southwick Town Common there was a wooden sign listing only those who had served in World War I until this beautiful stone memorial was dedicated on a Fourth of July in the 1930s. The memorial now includes those Southwick men and women who served in all wars, starting with the American Revolution.

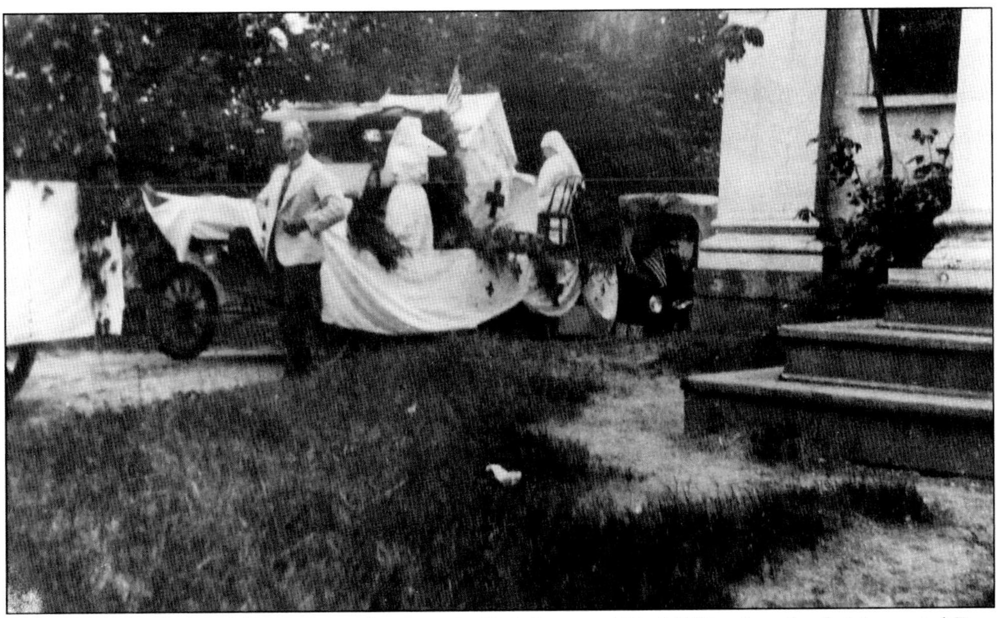

A Red Cross Float. Elaborate parades were held following World War I on both Memorial Day and the Fourth of July. Charles Arnold stands in front of the Red Cross float. Both vehicles are Model T trucks.

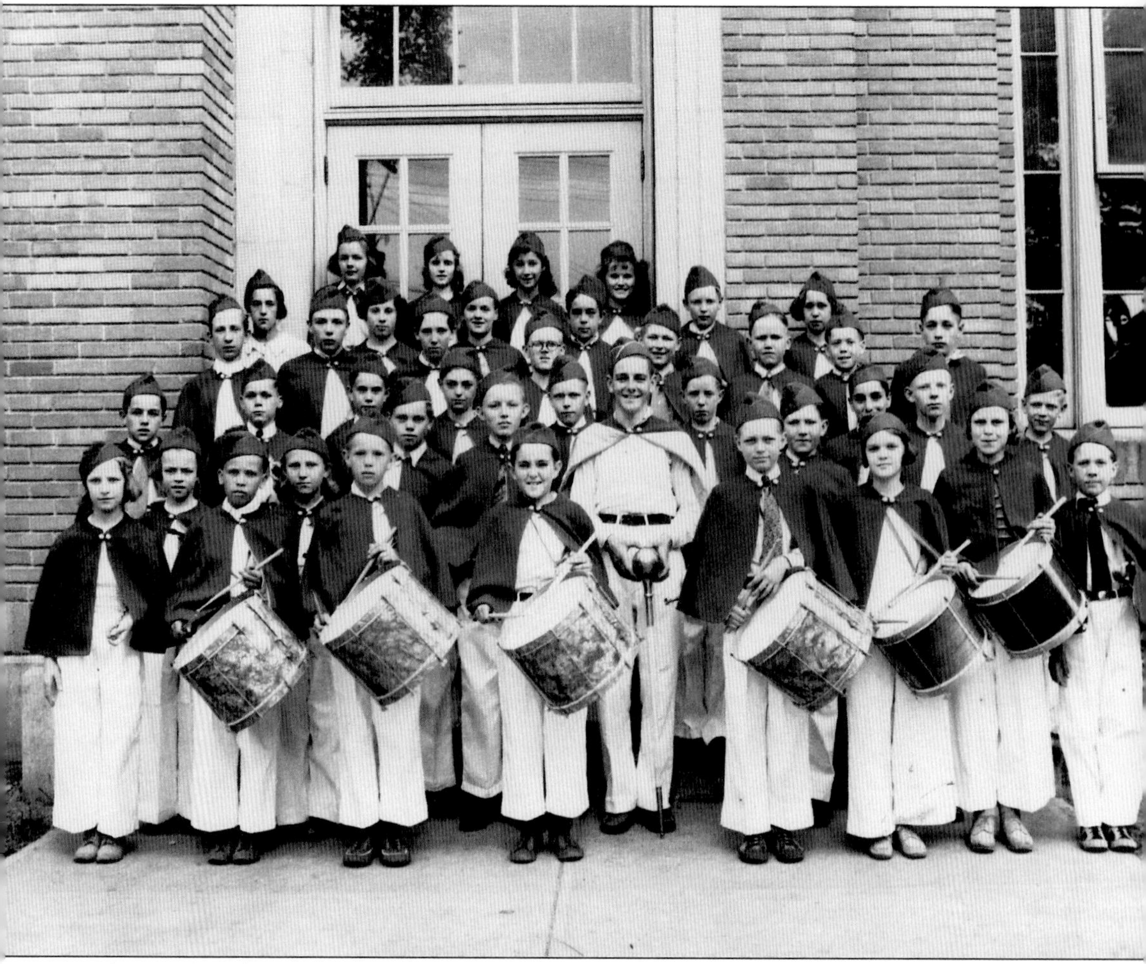

The Southwick Consolidated School Fife and Drum Corps, 1935. Back Row: Regina Brzoska, Laurel Desmond, Julie Horkun, and Bernice Zomek. Fourth Row: Emma Tomasini, Sophie Pieczarka, Patricia Hosley, Ransford Kellogg, Donald Hamberg, and Liz Humason. Third Row: Paul Silan, Frederick M. Arnold, William Maloney, Robert Anderson, Ernest Jasmin, Raymond Mellen, John Greany, and Joseph Rosetti. Second Row: Theodore Pieczarka, Stanley Millot, William Barnes, Charles Gillett (inset), Albert Nutter, John Pihl (inset), Elwood Anderson, William Racine, (drum major—inset), Douglas Cass, Robert Abbott (inset), George Scibelli, Douglas Hamberg, and Eldon Johnson. Front Row: ? Silan, Bernice Pihl, Donald Phillips, Frances Eskerka, Calvin Arnold, Theodore Kellogg, Alfred Fuller, Mary Anderson, Rose Daigle, and William Greany.

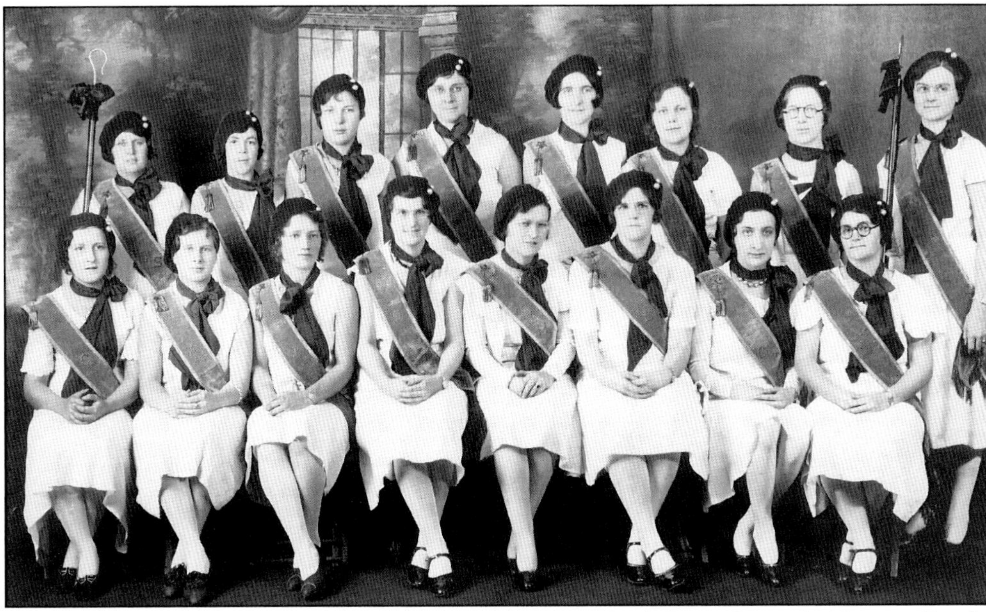

The Southwick Grange #46 Ladies Degree Team, 1931. Back Row: Gertrude Tierney, Bertha Rising Lemon, Helen Lecrenski Pratt, Isabel Root Carr, Irene Bingham Kellogg, Cecila Sponberg Stevenson, Mary Lambson Montovani, and Irene Storey Sponberg. Front Row: Agnes Brzoska Piekarski, May Henry, Bernice Haracz, Mildred Storey Celley, Lillian King Prifti, Marion Barnes Smith, Bertha Rowe Allen, and Lillian Morgan Hardy.

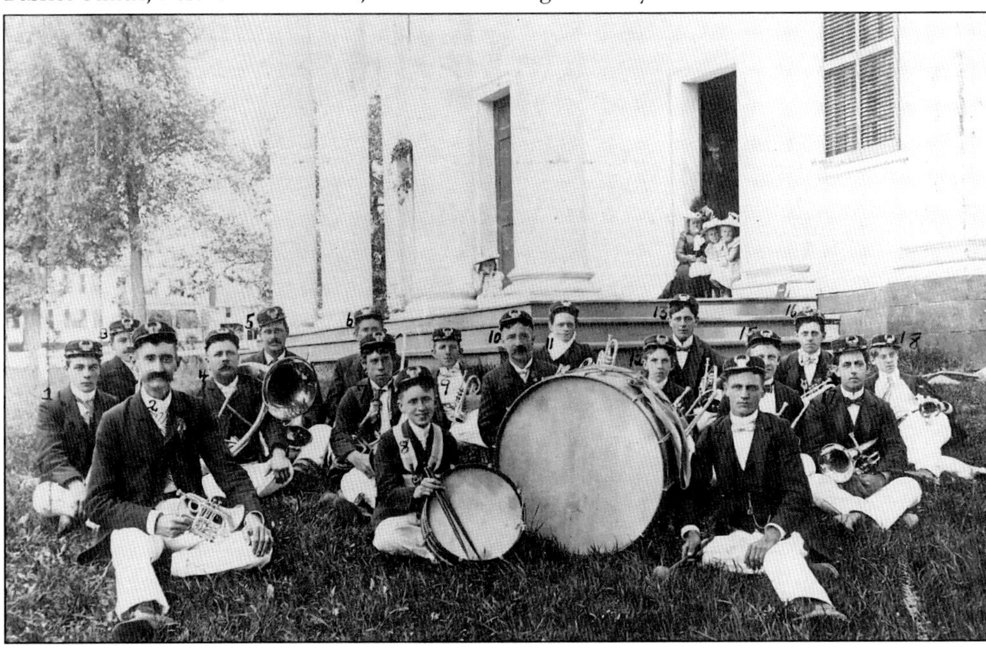

The Southwick Community Band, *c.* 1900. The members are as follows: 1-Joseph Galpin, 2-George Lancaster, 3-William Storey, 4-Chester Galpin, 5-Harry Hudson, 6-Judson Rising, 7-Lawrence Rising, 8-Raymond Fletcher, 9-Harry Warner, 10-Earl Boyle, 11-Kenneth Gillett, 12-a Hosmer (?), 13-James Doherty, 14-unknown, 15-Charles Arnold, 16-Ernest Hollister, 17-Fred Talmadge, and 18-Malcolm Harding.

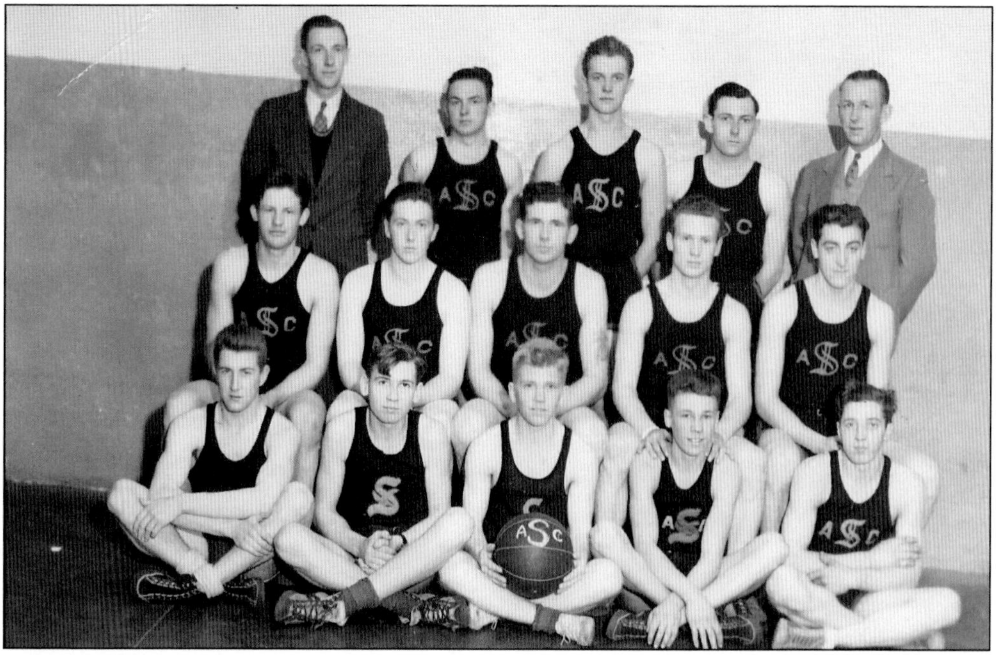

The Southwick Athletic Club. This was a town team composed of the following: (back row) Raymond Griffin (coach), John Brzoska, Malcolm Wilcox, James Phelps, and Jasper Drummond (manager); (middle row) Alfred Ryll, William Malone, Clifford Gibson, Walter Johnson, and Pando Prifti; (front row) James Loundes, Russell Gibson, Elmer Johnson, Alfred Hicks, and Walter Gaido.

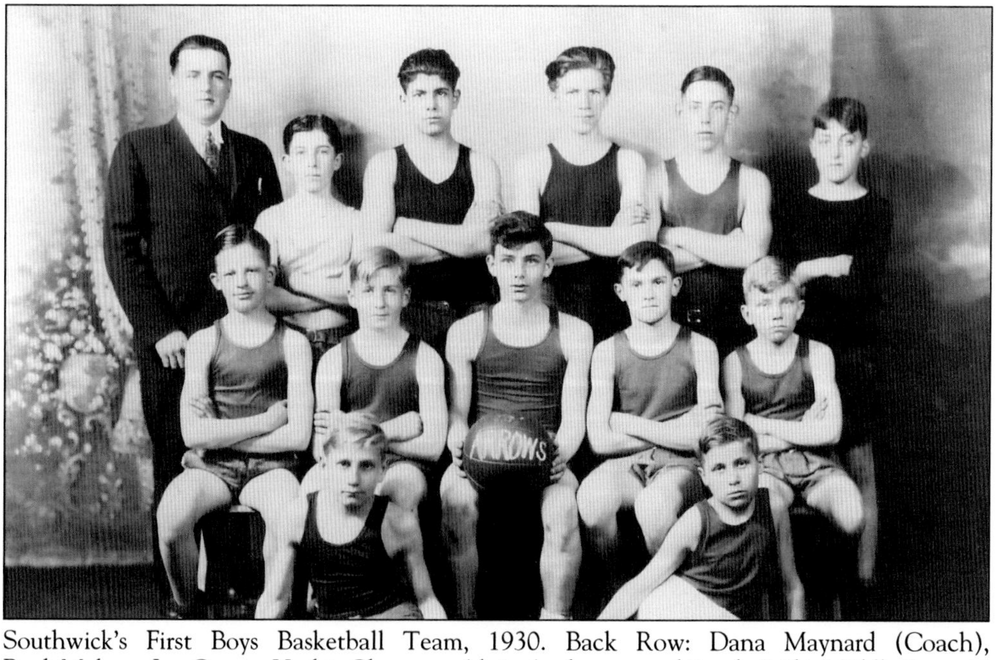

Southwick's First Boys Basketball Team, 1930. Back Row: Dana Maynard (Coach), Buck Malone, Joe Garcia, Herbie Chestnut, Alvin Anderson, and Pando Prifti. Middle Row: Al Ryl, Bud Fletcher, Henry Tierney, Max Holcomb, and Elmer Johnson. Front Row: John Jackson and Walter Wolfe.

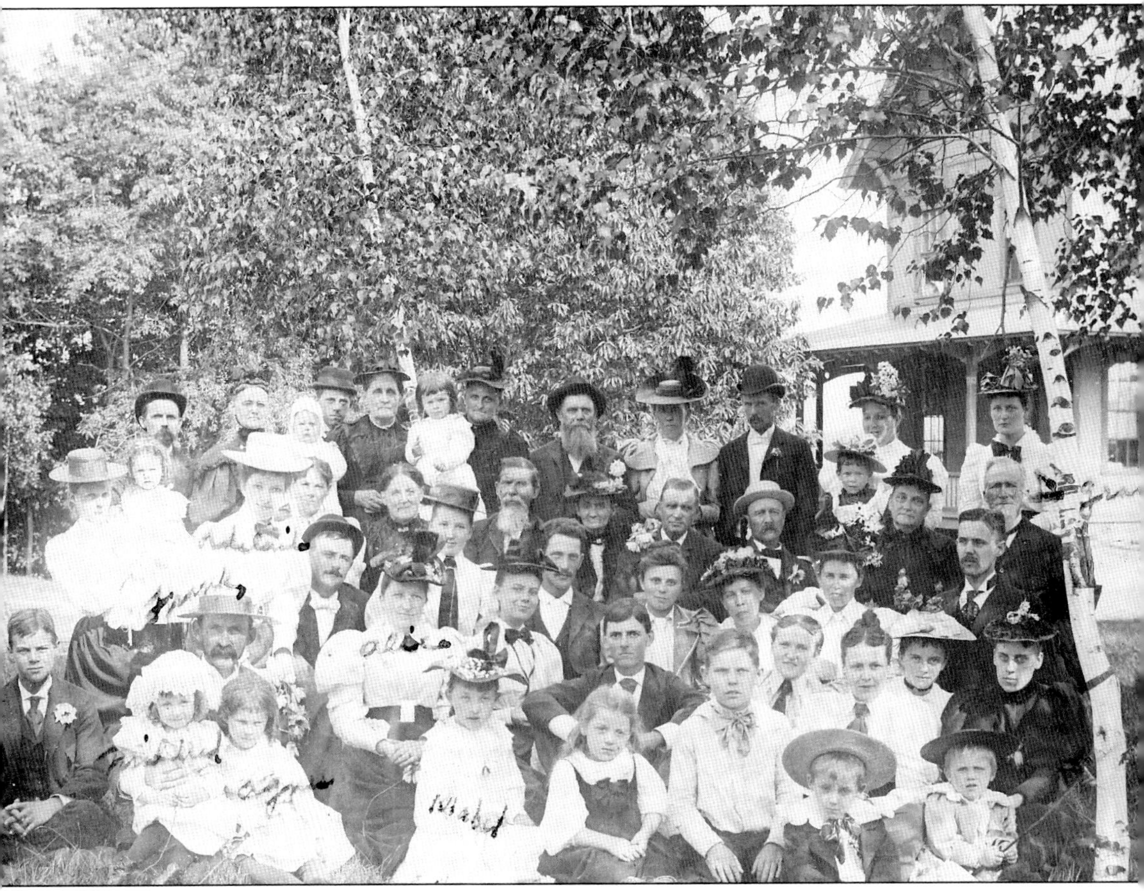

A Hollister Family Picnic at Congamond Lakes, *c*. 1893. Back Row: Uncle Edwin H., Aunt Etta H., Baby, Ernest H., Mrs. Gardiner, Baby Elva H., Aunt Mary H., Uncle Dwight H., Dwight's wife (?), Herbert H., Lizzie H. Case holding her daughter Lena Case, and Maggie Tennant. Fourth Row: Etta Reed (in front of baby), Aunt Etta H., Uncle Julius H., Aunt Abbie H., Uncle Bennett H., Asa Case, Grandmother Jane H. Fowler, and Grandfather Luther Fowler. Third Row: Lennie Bugbee holding her daughter Pearl, Aunt Adelaide Fowler, Albert H., Clara H. (Judson's daughter), Herbert Miller, Jennie Miller, Grace H., Lilla H., and Arthur H. Second Row: Father Frank Noble, Mother Alice Fowler Noble, Greta H., Luther H., Ida H. (Judson's daughter), Gertie H., Edna H., and Mrs. Arthur H. Front Row: Cyrus (Julius' son), Mildred Noble, Agnes Miller, Mabel Noble, Gladys Reed, Edmond H. (Julius' son), Dwight H., and Richard H. (sons of Arthur). Mabel Noble wrote this caption.

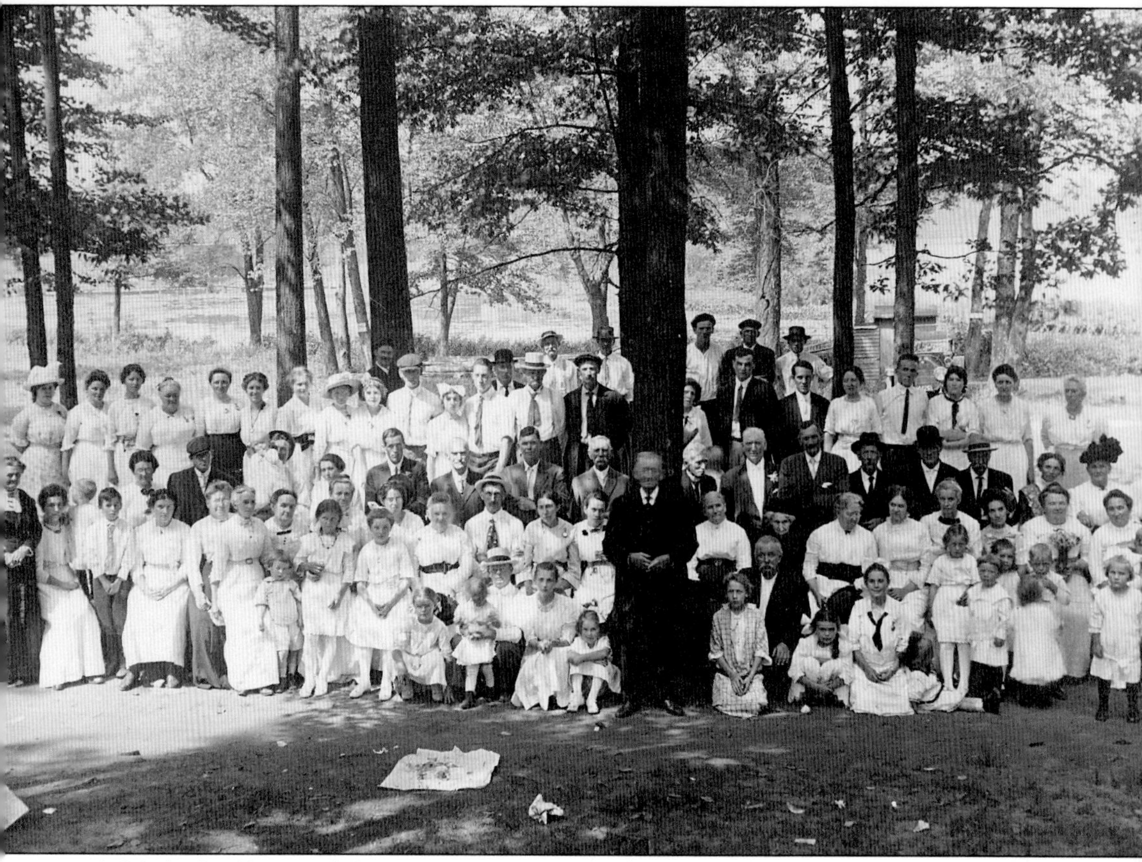

A Methodist Episcopal Society Picnic, 1914. Back Row: William Storey, Eugene Lambson, William Warner, W.S. Steere, Victor Johnson, Walter Saunders, and Frank Gorkey. Fourth Row: Mrs. Wright (from Springfield), Mrs. Eva Storey, Sadie Anderson, Mrs. A. Holcomb, Mrs. W.S. Steere, Mrs. A. Johnson, Lillian Johnson, Mrs. E.W. Jobbins, Myrtle Robinson, Lawrence Johnson, Marion Warner, Ernest Edwards, A. Holcomb, Fred Johnson, Mrs. George Root, George Root, unknown, Minnis Miller, Allie Miller, unknown, Mrs. Arthur Davis, and Mrs. Eugene Lambson. Third Row: Mrs. Charles Skinner, Charles Skinner, Albert Johnson and son Wallace, Mrs. Lowell Mason, Chester Gillett, Birney Holcomb, Frank Skinner, Charles Root, Rev. Miller, Rev. Caton, Elwin Hills, Edward Holcomb, Warren Phelps, John Mason, Mrs. Wright (from Schenectady, N.Y.), Mrs. R. B. Campbell, and Mrs. Frank Lambson. Second Row: Mrs. Lewis Morgan, Mrs. F.O. Holcomb and sons Oliver and Porter, Hazel Skinner, Mrs. M.M. Vining, Mrs. Foster Vining, Mrs. John Mason, Mrs. E.L. Hills, Mrs. C.S. Gillett, Mrs. B.G. Holcomb, Whitney Root, Mrs. W. Root, Mrs. F. Skinner, Benjamin Palmer in front of tree, Mrs. Rev. Miller, Mrs. Farnhum, Mrs. Caton, Lizzie Holcomb, Mrs. Edward Holcomb, Mrs. Warren Phelps, Mrs. W.C. Saunders, Mrs. William Warner, and Mrs. Leroy Lambson. Front Row: Merrill Mason, Margery Storey, Alma Steere, Irene Storey, Rev. Jobbins holding Mildred Storey, Marie Holcomb, Myrtle Storey, Nellie Lambson, Henry Miller, Ethel Curtis, Isabel Root, Doris Holcomb, Kenneth and Doris Phelps, two Davis children, Ruth Warner, another Davis, and Winona Desmond.

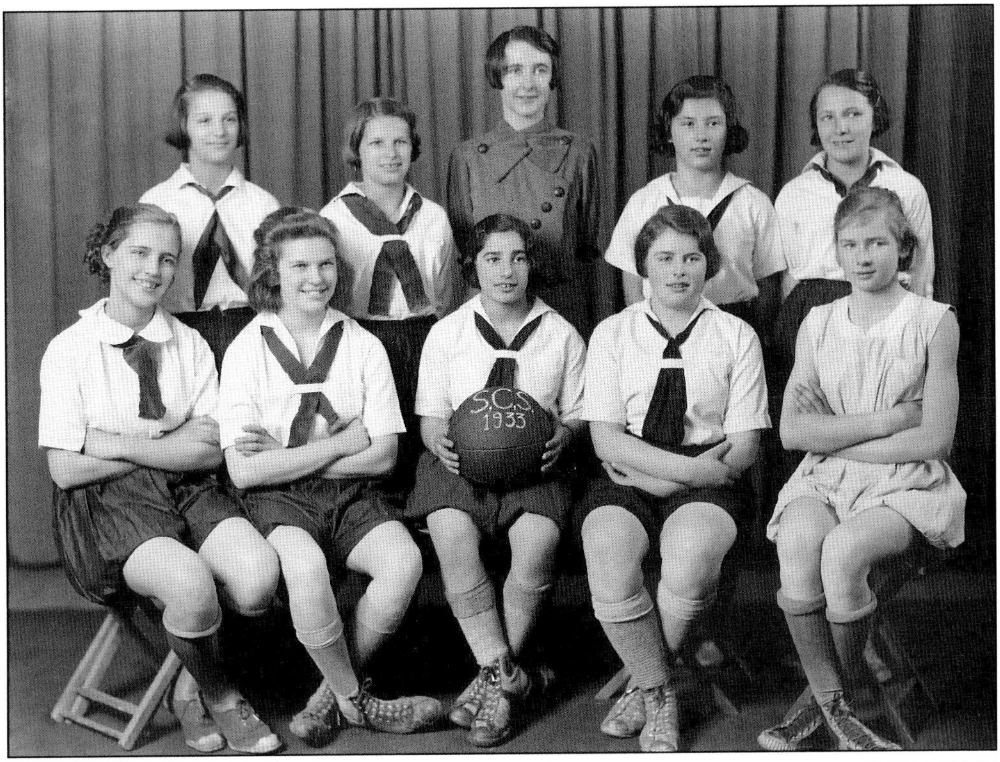

The 1933 Girls Basketball Team. Back Row: Philomena Ruffo, Amelia Backus, Irene Kellogg (coach), Julia Pieczarka, and Violet Davis. Front Row: Blanche Jameski, Nadine Stanley, Mary Scibelli, Eileen Malone, and Shirley Johnson.

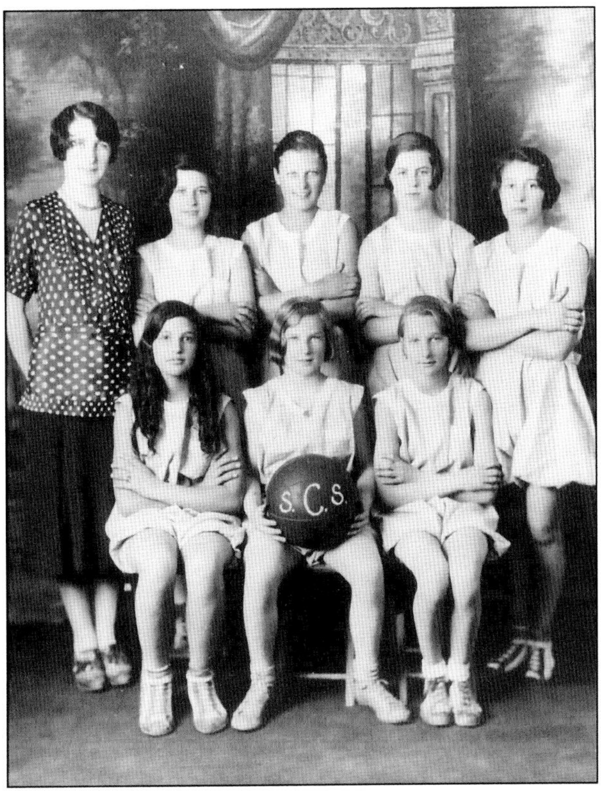

The Girls Basketball Team of 1931. Back Row: Irene Bingham (coach), Marguerite Tierney, Josephine Backus, Helen Brzoska, and Mary Paroli. Front Row: Carmilla Sylvernale, Alberta Johnson, and Anne Jackson.

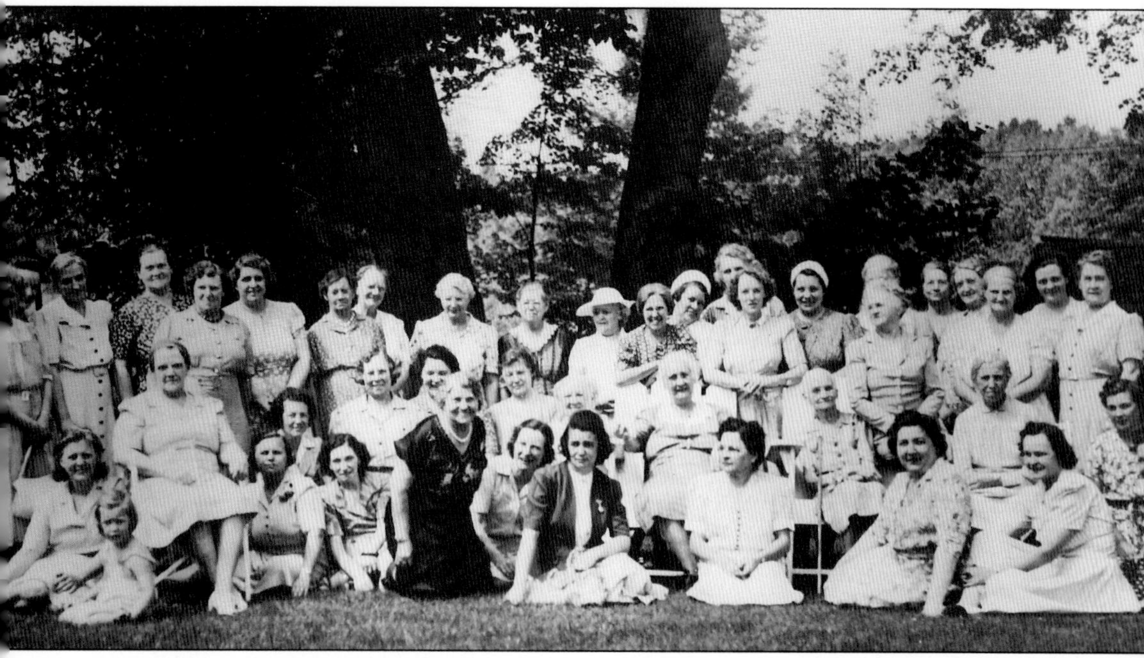

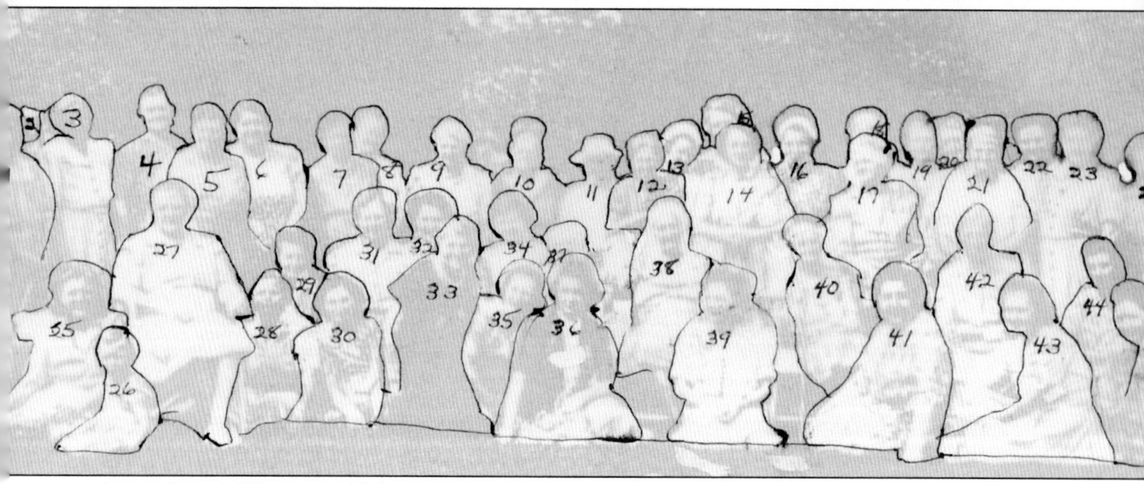

A Southwick Women's Club Picnic, 1939. The following women have been identified: 1-Grace Moore (Millard), 2-Gloria Lambson (Lorenzo), 3-Elizabeth Arnold (Fred), 4-Florence Heiman (Moses), 5-Corabelle Edson, 6-Jane Tuttle (Merwin), 7-Rose Griffin (Robert), 8-Mary Stone (Charles), 9-Ann Galpin (Joseph), 10-Silence Matthews (Charles), 11-Ella Mason (Lowell), 12-Lucy MacDonald, 13-Ellen Johnson Anderson (Walfrid), 14-Frances Hosley, 15-Flora Nelson (Godfrey), 16-Hattie Hawley (Clarence), 17-unknown, 18-Effie Griffin, 19-Lillian Gillett (Arthur), 20-Myrtle Webb, 21-Albertine Mellon (John), 22-Dagma Mason (Harold), 23-Ethel Fletcher (Raymond), 24-Mrs. Harden, 25-Jeanette Galpin, 26-Jeanette Galpin's niece, 27-Agnes Hudson (Clarence), 28-Beatrice Mellon (Guy), 29-Mrs. Stoneback (George), 30-Mary Griffin (Oren), 31-Lena Trench, 32-Sylvia Hamberg (Hendrick), 33-Etta Reed, 34-Lu Lu Johnson, 35-Jean Mason (Merrill), 36-Helena Duris (Joseph), 37-Grace Steere (Ralph), 38-Stella Arnold (Charles), 39-Evelyn Anderson (Enfred), 40-Inez Russell (Ann Galpin's mother), 41-Hattie Noble (Carlyle), 42-Leona Barton (Glover), 43-Peg Griffin (Raymond), 44-Rachael Arnold (Tower), and 45-Doris Roberts (Arthur).

Chapter Eleven

The World War II Scrap Drive

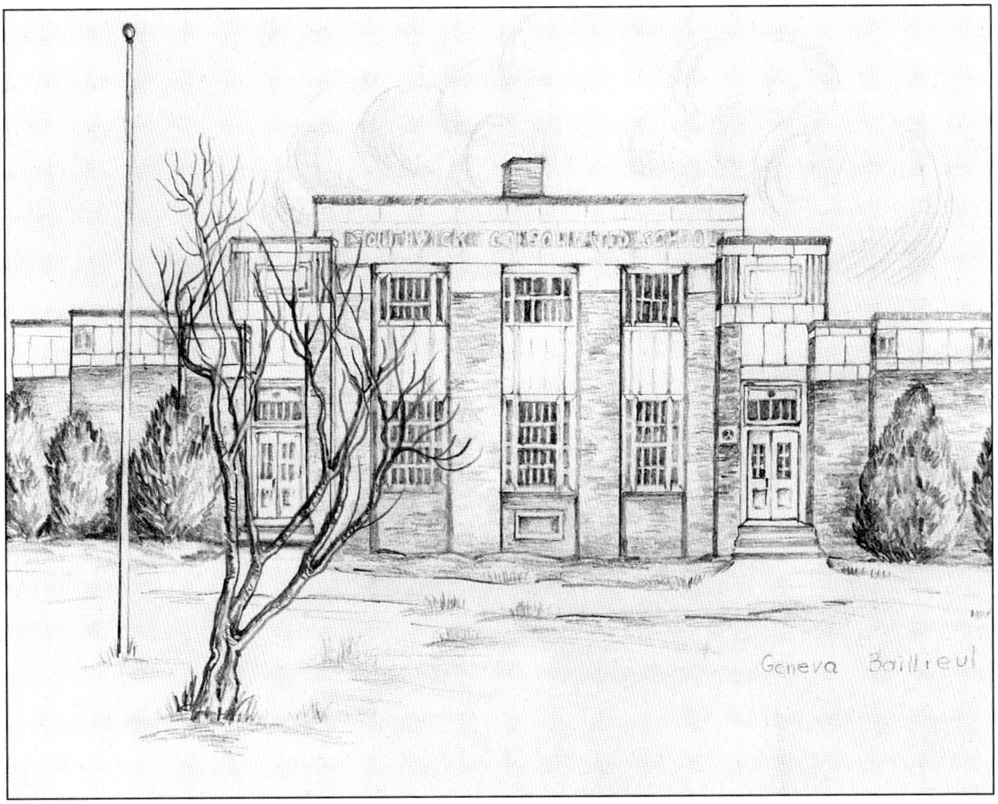

The Southwick Consolidated School. Shown in a pencil sketch by Southwick artist Geneva Baillieul, the Southwick Consolidated School, built in 1928–29, was the first major commission for Malcolm B. Harding, a Southwick-raised architect who lived and worked in neighboring Westfield. Designed in the Art Deco style, the building is constructed of Portland concrete and cream-colored brick. In the 1980s, when it ceased functioning as a school, the building was used by many town organizations. At a town meeting in 1995, the Town of Southwick voted to renovate this structure for use as the town office.

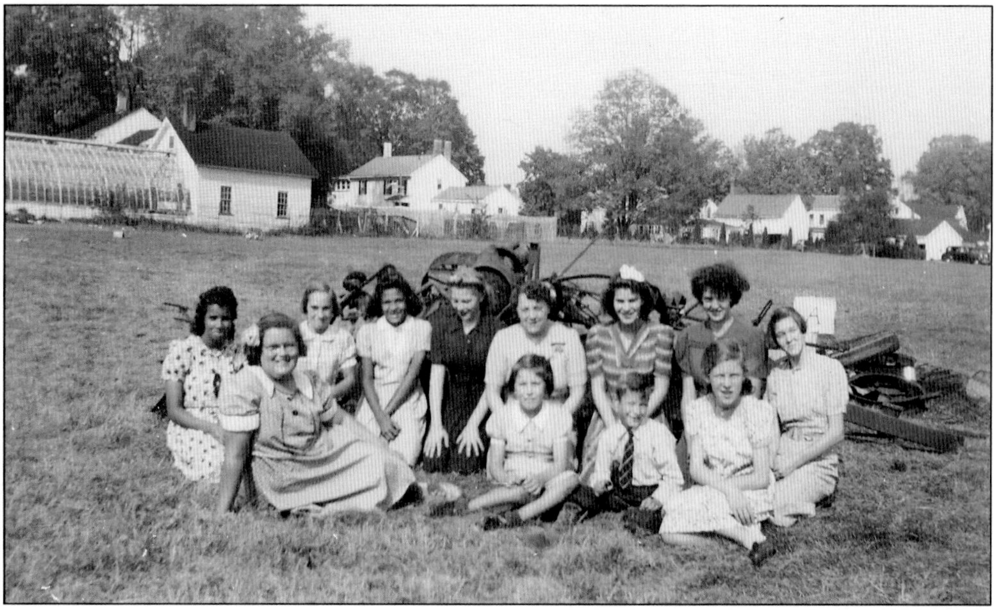

Grade A. In October 1942, the Southwick Consolidated School conducted a drive to collect scrap metal to be melted down for the war effort. The classes competed to see which one would bring in the most, and judges were the school bus drivers Laurence Johnson, Ralph Deming, Clarence Hudson, and William Arnold. Back Row: Leona Phillips, unknown, Catherine Williams(?), Blanche Menard(?), Dorothy Hollister (teacher), unknown, unknown, and unknown. Front Row: Edna Steere, Doris Elander, unknown, and Beverly Johnson.

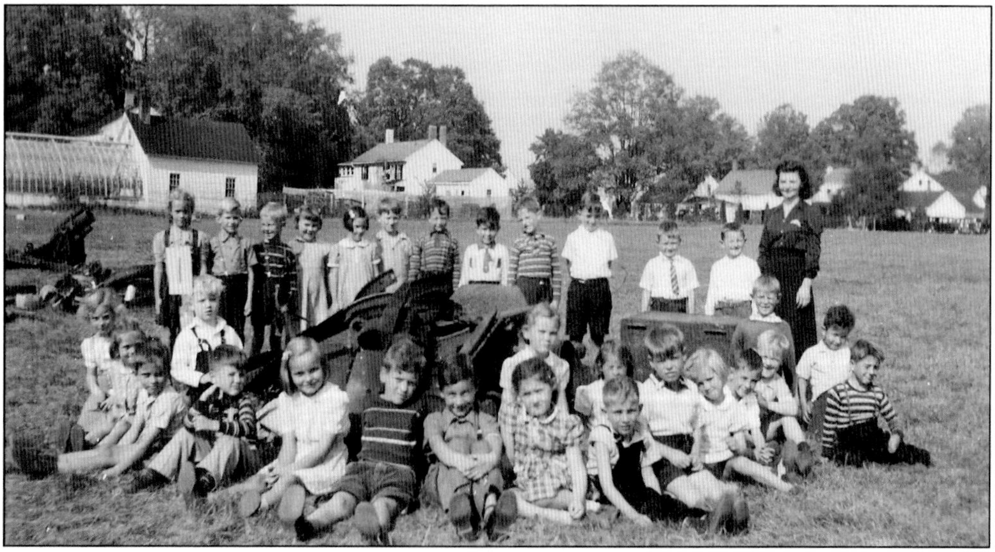

First Grade. Back Row: Judith Ann Anderson, Stanley Zomek, unknown, Ann Keenan, Shirley Ann Rutka , unknown, Zane Davidson, Freddie Kellogg, Robert Pollard, unknown, unknown, Frank Mika, and Grace Lyons (teacher). Front Row: Eleanor Hepburn, Diane White, unknown, Raymond Brzoska, the boy standing is Carl Butler, Alice ?, Robert Van Mater, "Junior" Buynicki, Priscilla Welch, Eva Sponberg behind Priscilla, Barbara Thibeault beside Eva, unknown, Richard Lemon, unknown, Leslie Ellis, unknown, unknown, Russell Phillips, and Savino Gaioni. The boy in front of the teacher is unknown.

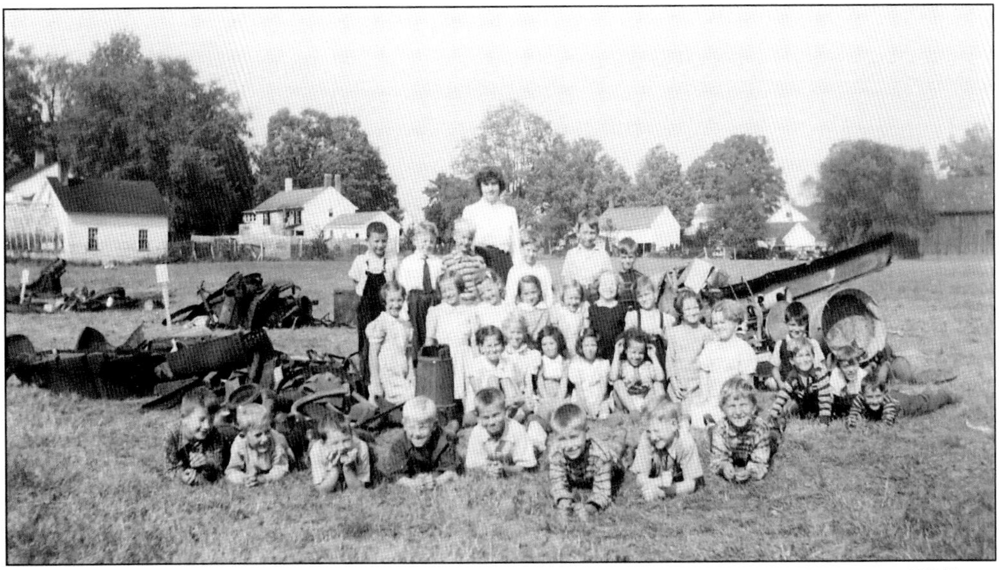

Second Grade. Teacher Helen Rush (Maloney). Back Row: Benjamin Cressotti, William O'Connor, Charles Pratt, Richard Sylvernale, George Davis, and Donald Saunders. Third Row: Priscilla Stewart, Janet Weissmann, Shirley Stromgren, Janet Lee (?), unknown, unknown, and Barbara Chestnut. Second Row: Clara Guertin, Patricia McMullin, Dorothy Molta, Jennie Molta, Lucy Young (?), Betsey Lenore (?), RoseEllen Keenan, Joseph Marini, Jack Karlstrom (on his haunches), Gordon Wolfe, and George Peterson. Front Row: Bruce Kenyon, Henry Gelgut, Robert (?) Pollard, Edward Hepburn, Edward Chekovsky, Samuel Elander, George Holcomb, Walter Monczka.

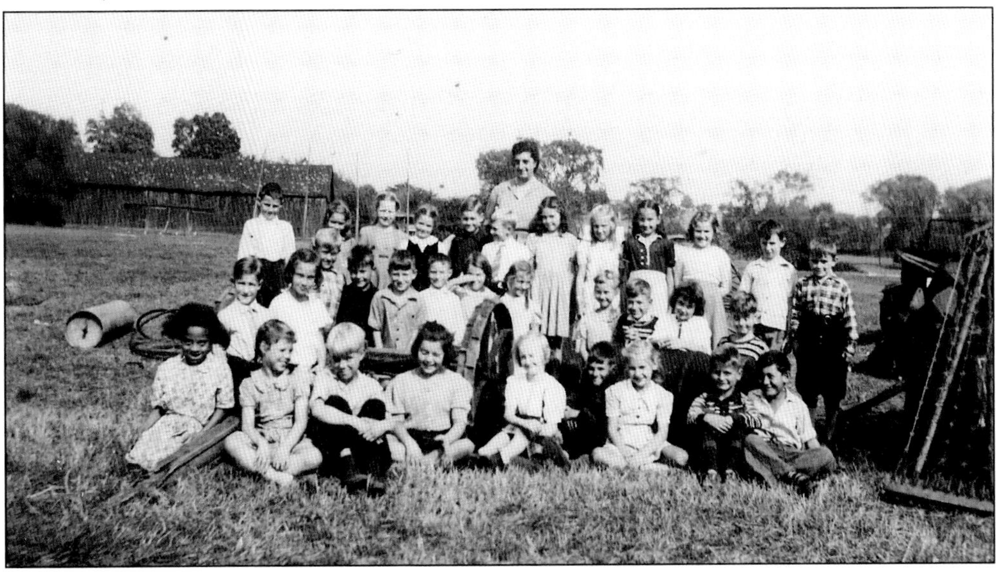

Third Grade. Teacher Araxie Bedrossian. Back Row: Joseph Mika, unknown, Carol Hamberg, Lourde Altobello, Richard Finsen,unknown, Marilyn Kellogg, unknown, Jane Lecrenski, unknown, Donald Maynard, and Daniel Keenan. Middle Row: Ronald Jackson, Penny White, Richard Case (?), unknown, unknown, unknown, unknown, unknown, unknown, Barbara Lent, and unknown. Front Row: Margaret Williams, Anna Lemon, Walter Griffin, unknown, Lois Roberts, unknown, Elizabeth Tysz, Raymond Griffin, Thomas Campagnari.

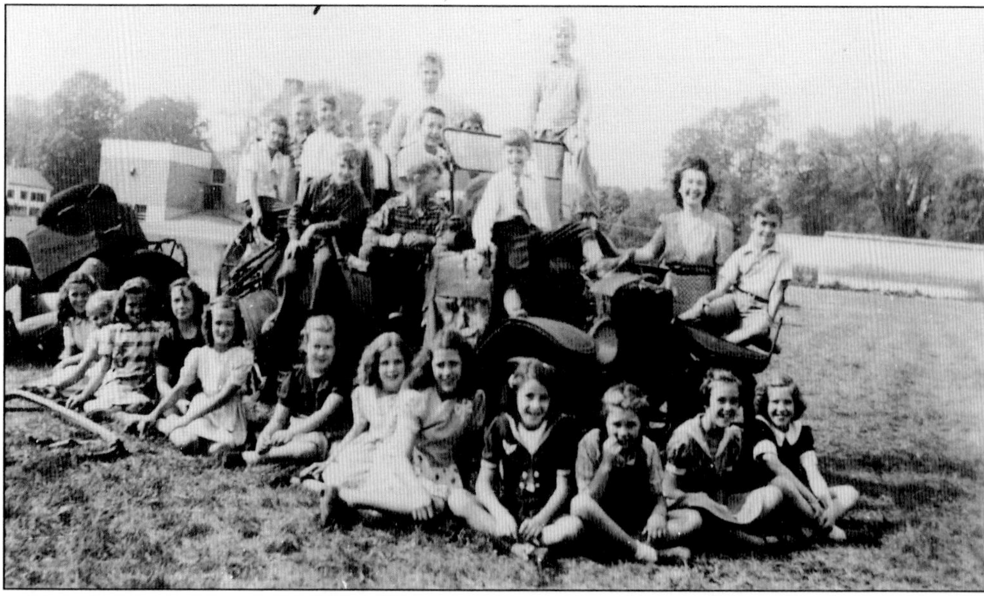

Fourth Grade. Back Row: William Johnson (?), Richard Berry, Donald Chmura (?), Floyd Hayden, and James Cressotti. Behind James is Carl Johnson, and in front of James is Richard Castle. Edward Bonini is in front of Donald and Floyd. The tallest boy in back is Norman Cass with Robert Wilson in front of him; then teacher Priscilla Packard (Deveno) and Richard Wolfe. Front row: Janet Zamparini, Dorothy Van Mater, Julia Tish, unknown, Jane Columbia, Janet Burrows, Rose Peterson (?),unknown, Marion Lamothe, unknown, Dorothy Stewart, and unknown.

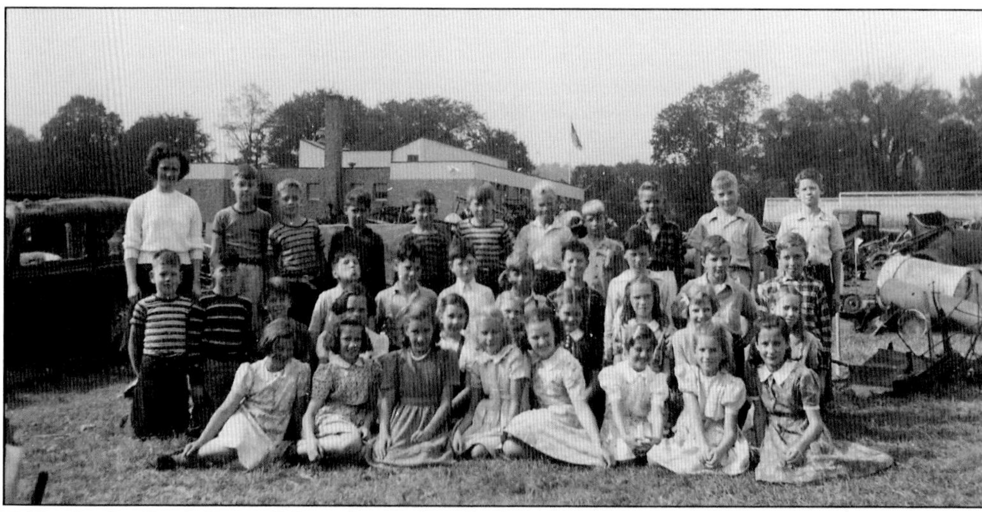

Fifth Grade. Back Row: Eileen Ryan (teacher), Wayne Barnes, unknown, James Avalone, Walter Johnson, Allen Johnson, Fred Williams, Ronald Robbins (?), Philip Bergstrom, Clyde Jones, and Norman Johnson. Third Row: George Chickering, Philip Mason, Richard McMullin, unknown,unknown, Frank Pollard, Arthur Wolfe (?), Lawrence McLaughlin, Walter Maynard, Richard Stromgren, and Fred Tryon. Second Row: Barbara Hawley, Elaine Desmond, Ruth Sampson, Dorothy Wolfe, Barbara Tryon, unknown, and Mary Greany. Front Row: Rose Peterson, Ila Maynard, Lois Murphy, Hazel Anderson, Frances Mika, ? Cressotti (?), Cynthia Karlstrom, and unknown.

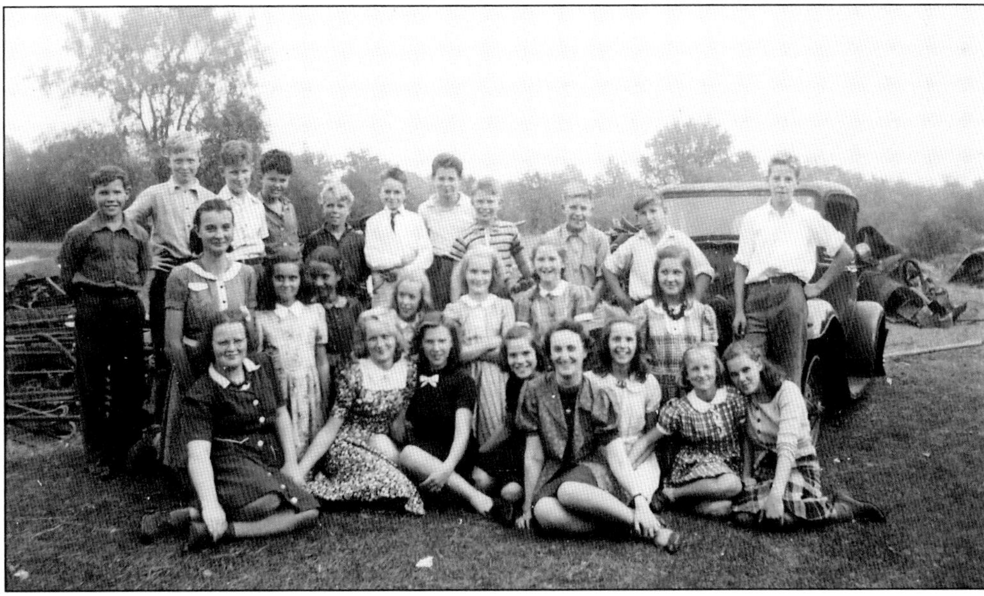

Sixth Grade. Back Row: Thomas Davidson, Melbert Johnson, Philip Hall, unknown, George Griffin (?), Francis Elander, Alfred Laudee (?), Kenneth Johnson, William Muggles, Jack Molta, and Robert Bergstrom. Middle Row: Carolina Cressotti, Winifred Gibbons, Florence Phillips, Jean Anderson, Eleanor Anderson, Grace Carr, and Jean Monczka. Front Row: Betty Barden , Jane Maskill, Betty Wirtz, unknown, Carolyn Clark, Mary Solek, and Henrietta Altobello. Teacher Thelma Wolfson Montovani is seated in front.

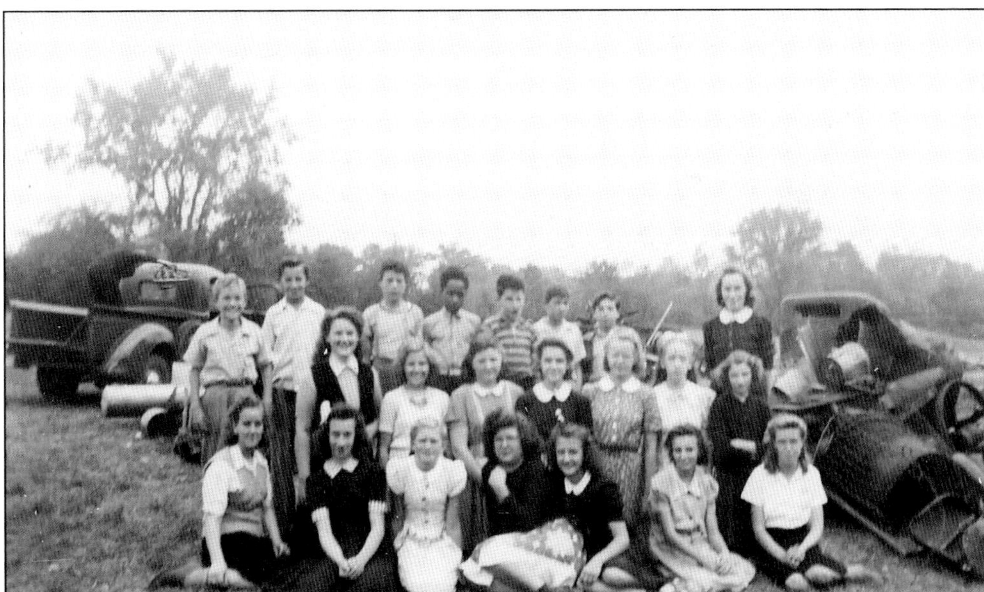

Seventh Grade. Back Row: Robert Burrill, John Horkun, ? McLaughlin (?), Thelon Kemp, David Laudee, unknown, Robert Greany, and Stella Wasik (teacher). Middle Row: unknown, Gwendolyn Saunders, unknown, Annabelle Bovat, Nancy Burrows, Clara Anderson, and Rita Misisca (?). Front Row: Joanne Hosley, Dorothy Knowlton, Tyola Karlstrom, Alma Massai, Helen Moriarty, Helen Godek, and Eleanor Tryon.

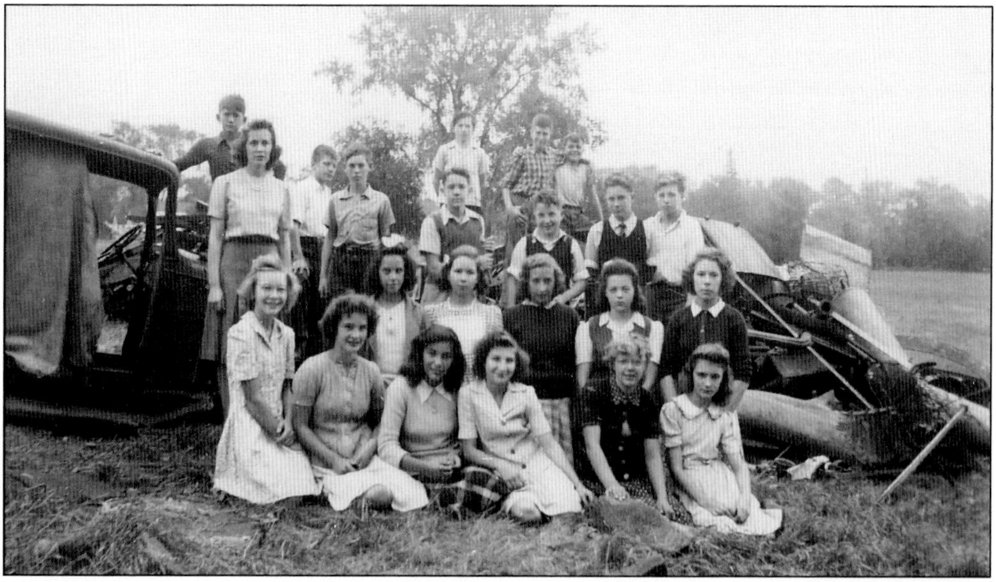

Eighth Grade. Back Row: Robert Saunders, Frank Pieczarka, Paul Mason, and Jim Fuller. Third Row: Emily Picknelly (teacher), John Solek, Roy Johnson, Agusto Lavallee, Robert Maynard, unknown, and Larry ? (?). Second Row: Shirley Gibbons, Jean White, Sally Case, Norma Fuller, and Christine Elander. Front Row: Mary Tysz, Betty Castle, Thelma Lancioni, Shirley Bonini, Beverly Carr, and Martha Johnson.

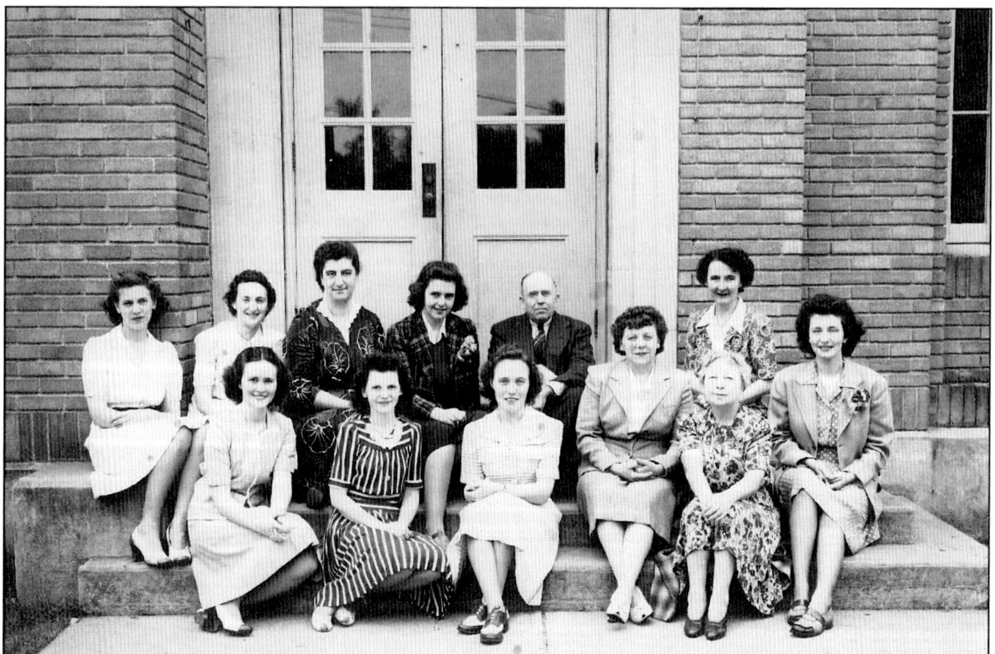

Teachers at the Consolidated School, 1942. Back Row: Emily Picknelly Steere, Thelma Montovani, Roxy Bedrosian, Helen Rush Maloney, M.C. Moore, and Irene Kellogg. Front Row: Eileen Ryan, Grace Lyons, Stella Wasik, Dot Hollister Melberg, Helen Johnson, and Priscilla Deveno. (Caption copied verbatim.) Mr. Moore was the principal; Helen Johnson taught music.

Chapter Twelve

Churches

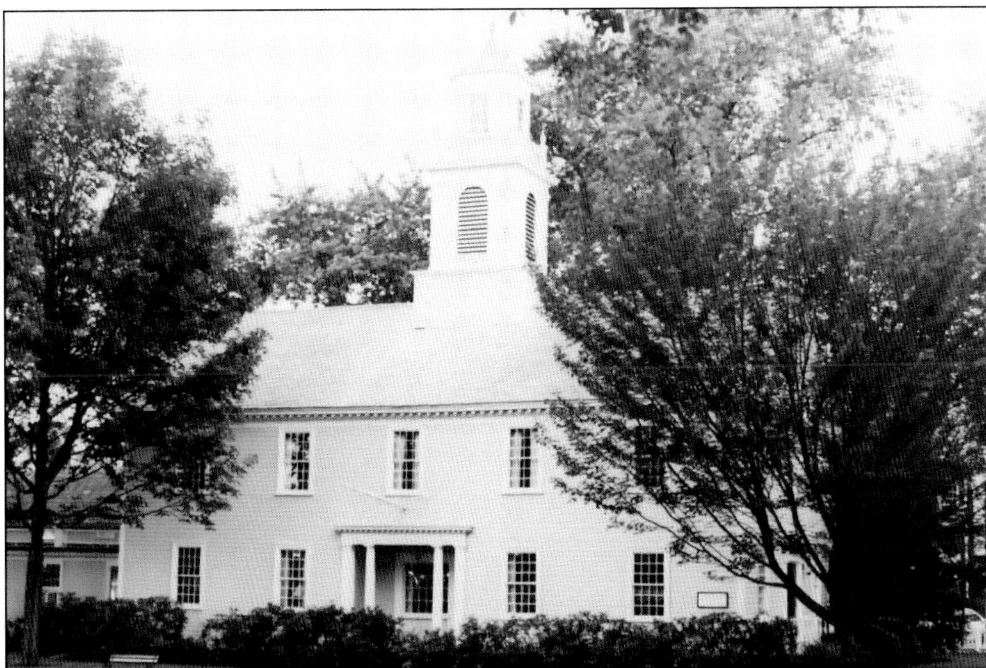

First Baptist Church, 1995. The oldest Southwick church building still in existence, the Baptist Meeting House was built in 1822 where Dunkin' Donuts now stands. Records of the First Baptist Church of Southwick begin in 1806 and end in 1933. In 1930, the building was sold to Mrs. James Storrow, who had the building taken down and re-erected in Storrowton Village on the Eastern States Exposition grounds, where it remains to this day, in somewhat altered form, as an integral part of the Storrowton Tavern, at 1305 Memorial Avenue, West Springfield, Massachusetts.

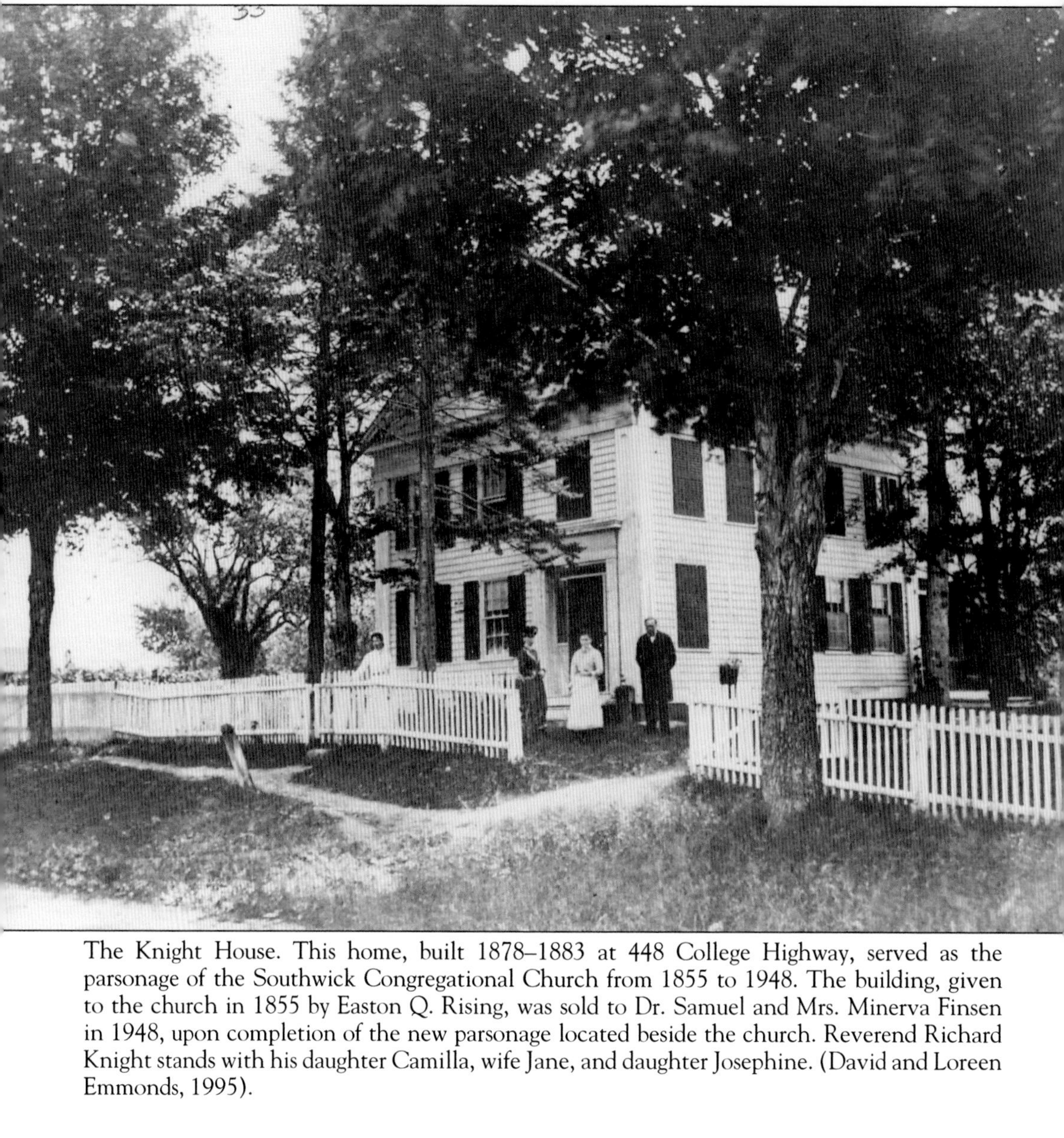

The Knight House. This home, built 1878–1883 at 448 College Highway, served as the parsonage of the Southwick Congregational Church from 1855 to 1948. The building, given to the church in 1855 by Easton Q. Rising, was sold to Dr. Samuel and Mrs. Minerva Finsen in 1948, upon completion of the new parsonage located beside the church. Reverend Richard Knight stands with his daughter Camilla, wife Jane, and daughter Josephine. (David and Loreen Emmonds, 1995).

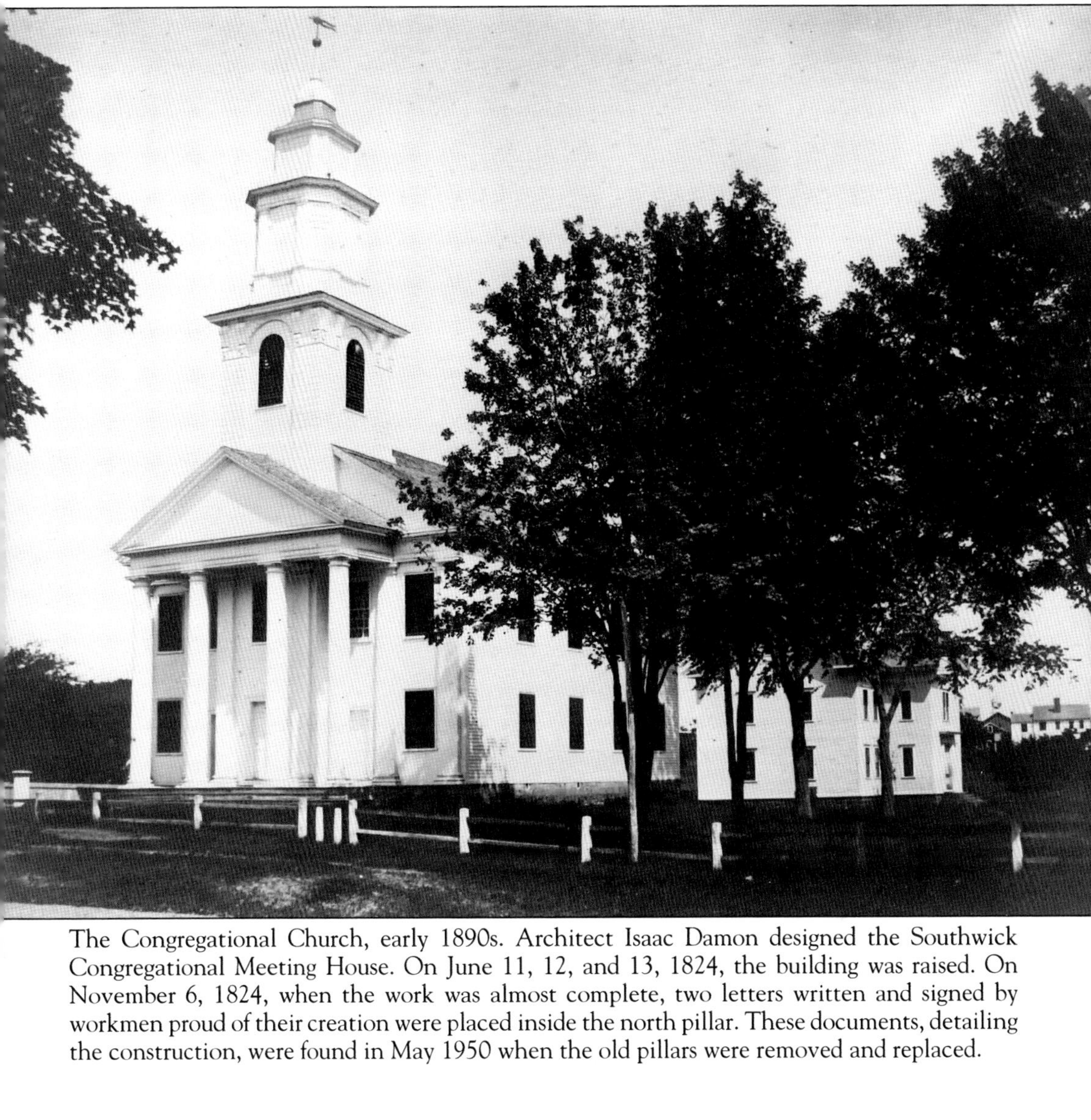

The Congregational Church, early 1890s. Architect Isaac Damon designed the Southwick Congregational Meeting House. On June 11, 12, and 13, 1824, the building was raised. On November 6, 1824, when the work was almost complete, two letters written and signed by workmen proud of their creation were placed inside the north pillar. These documents, detailing the construction, were found in May 1950 when the old pillars were removed and replaced.

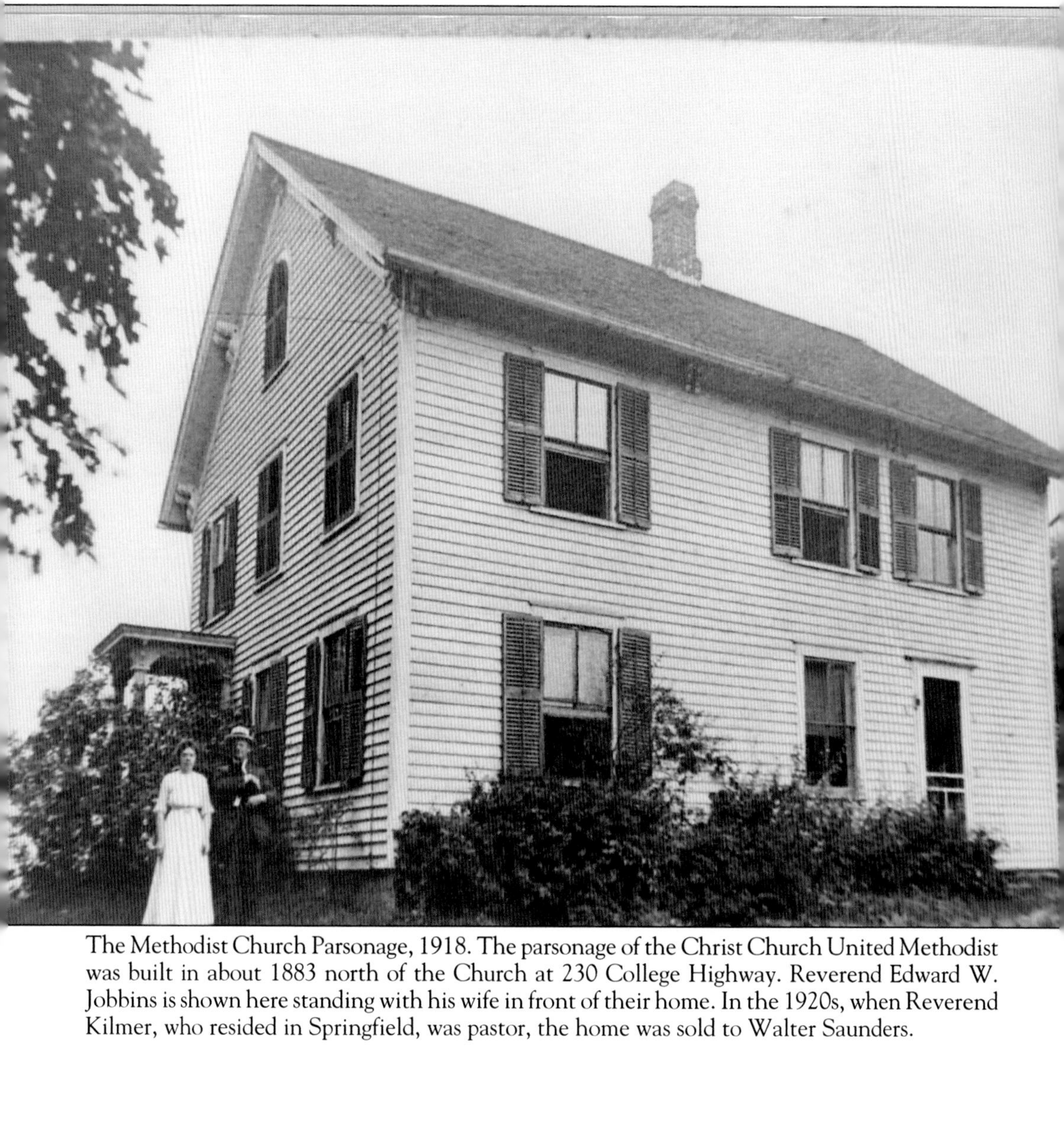

The Methodist Church Parsonage, 1918. The parsonage of the Christ Church United Methodist was built in about 1883 north of the Church at 230 College Highway. Reverend Edward W. Jobbins is shown here standing with his wife in front of their home. In the 1920s, when Reverend Kilmer, who resided in Springfield, was pastor, the home was sold to Walter Saunders.

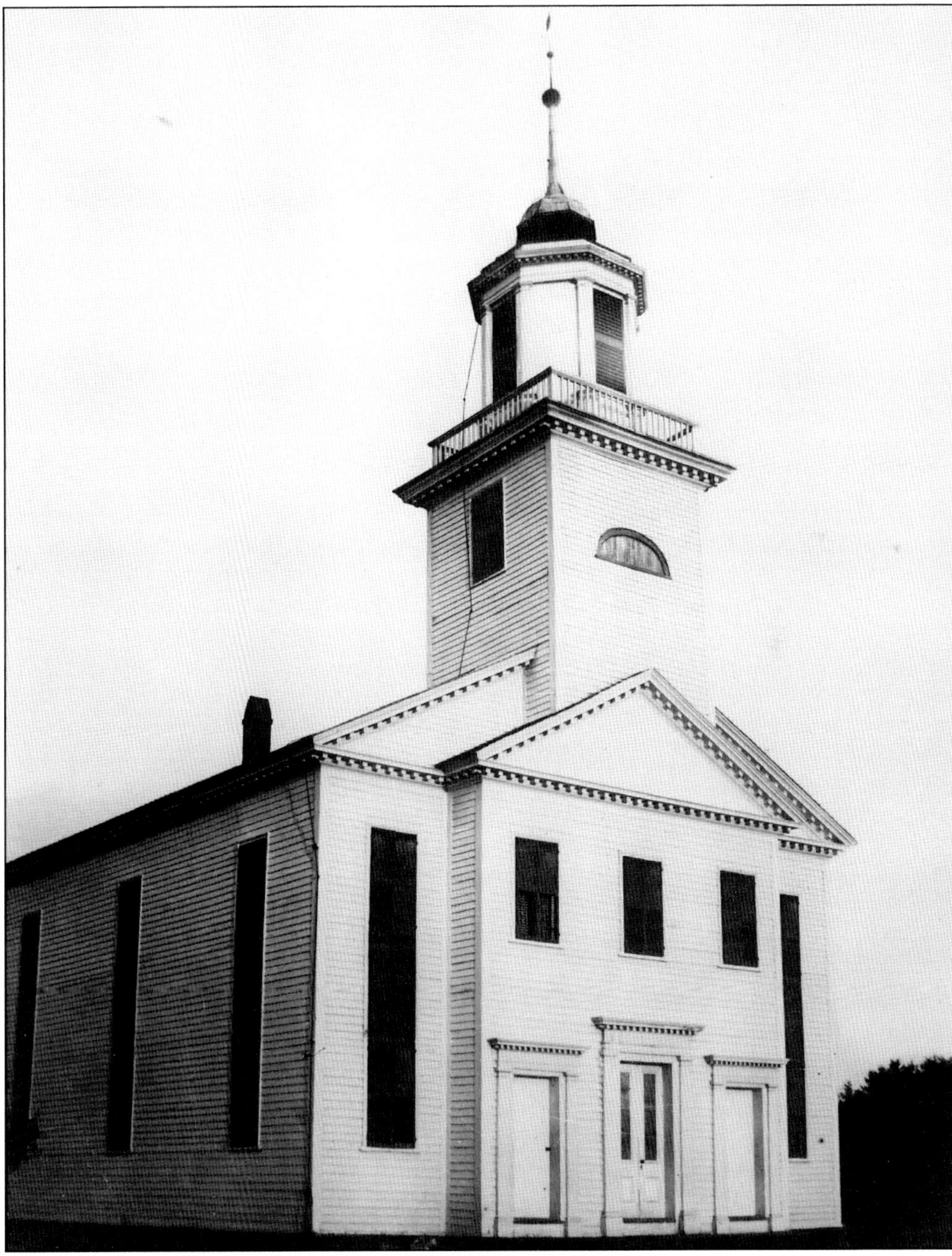

The Christ Church United Methodist. When a new meetinghouse was built in 1824 about a mile north of its former location, the gentry of the south part of town, Almond and Rhodolphus Gillett, Squire Forward, Squire Root, and Captain Moore, were major contributors for the building of a new church nearer to their homes. Built by Mr. Allen and dedicated in 1826, the church was the site of prayer meetings conducted by preachers of the Granville Circuit at the beginning, with the settling of its first minister a later event. In 1923, the church was remodeled: the sanctuary was moved to the newly installed second floor and Sunday school rooms, a kitchen, and a dining room were put in on the ground floor.

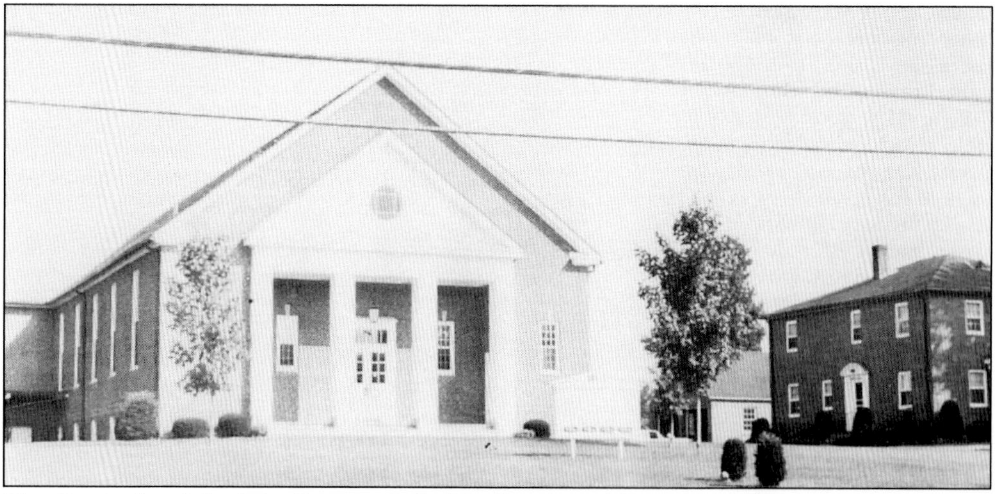

The Our Lady of the Lake Roman Catholic Church and Rectory. Father James Kirby of St. Mary's Church in Westfield announced in 1945 that a committee had been formed to raise money and supervise construction of a Roman Catholic Church in Southwick. Named Our Lady of the Lake by Father Kirby and built on land donated by Daniel Keenan, the church at 222 Sheep Pasture Road was built in stages. From Easter 1948 through Christmas Eve 1961, worship was held in the basement, called the chapel. The blessing of the upper sanctuary was performed by Bishop Christopher Weldon on January 6, 1962.

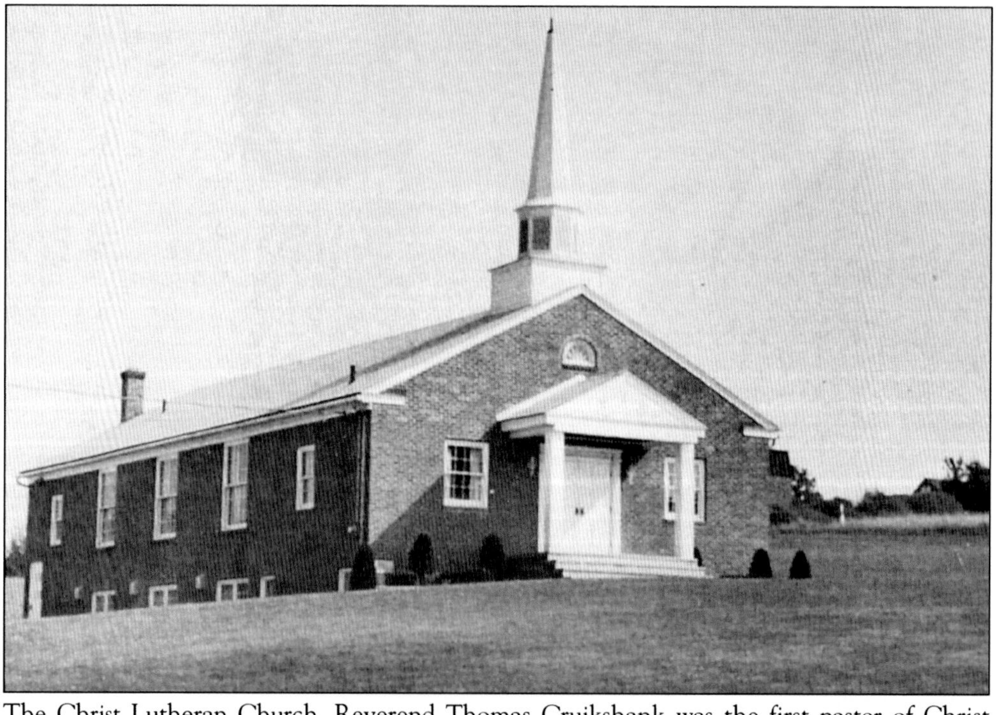

The Christ Lutheran Church. Reverend Thomas Cruikshank was the first pastor of Christ Lutheran Church, founded in 1962. Worship services were conducted at the American Legion Post #338 for three years. In 1965, the church building was constructed with parishioners supplying much of the labor. The current pastor of Christ Lutheran Church at 568 College Highway is Jeffrey King.

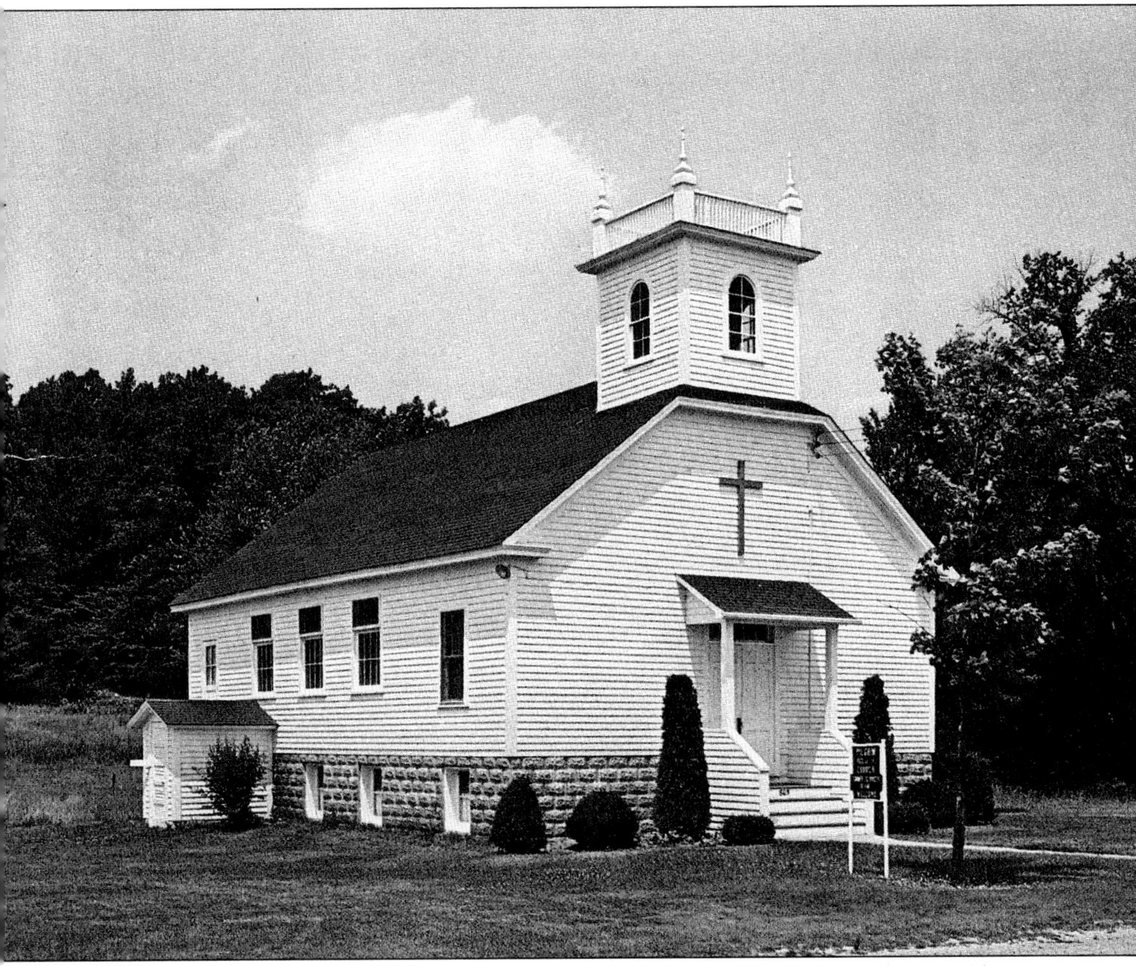

The Pilgrim Covenant Church. Founded by people of Swedish lineage in 1902, the Free Christian Society of North Granby, Connecticut, built its first meeting house on West Street, now Loomis Street, in North Granby. In 1926, when a new church was to be built, the technicalities involved in moving the church organization from Connecticut into Massachusetts were too difficult to surmount. Using materials from the old church, the new building was erected just over the state line at 605 College Highway in Connecticut. All services were conducted in Swedish until the 1930s, when some English was introduced. In 1946, the "Swedish," which had been in the organization's legal name from 1904 until then, was dropped.

Acknowledgments

Southwick Historical Society, Inc. Life Member Lee Hamberg, who has collected Southwick postcards for many years, allowed us to use his neatly organized album for this project. He suggested that working with the original images, rather than with copies, would enhance the finished work. We offer our thanks to him, and to all those people who, over the years, have collected so many of the photographs and captions in this book. Gilbert Arnold and his cousin Towar come to mind as examples. Many people, including Warren Hastings, Leon Barnes, Orlo Jackson, and Ida Skelly, shared images from their personal collections with Gib and Towar. We have tried to retain as many of the original captions as possible. If this practice has resulted in a misspelling of anyone's name, we apologize heartily. Please let us know if this has occurred, so that we can correct our records.

Some of the images in *Around Southwick* were obtained from the Society archives, donated by many individuals over the years. For the photographs of people whose names were not known, Frederick M. Arnold's identification of the local people of bygone days has been invaluable. For captions for the 1942 Scrap Drive photographs, we are indebted to Cynthia (Karlstrom) Seibert, who made many identifications and then contacted others to obtain many more. Many others, students at that time, also contributed to the final result.

When the Society requested photographs and/or postcards on loan for possible inclusion in the book, the response was very gratifying. Alice Baiardi, James Beck, Dorothy Coward, Henry Englehardt III, Carol Garrant, Anna Jackson, Jean Mason, Philip Mason, Mary Saunders, Patricia Savoy, George Scibelli, Marion Vecchio, and Norma Yourous each trusted us with treasured mementos.

Historical Facts and Stories about Southwick by Maud Gillett Davis has been a valuable reference. *Southwick Bicentennial Book 1770–1970* has also been helpful.

If you have any questions about this publication or if you would like to obtain a copy of any specific image, please write to the Society at P.O. Box 323, Southwick, MA 01077.

Thanks are given to all the members of the Southwick Historical Society, Inc. for their encouragement and support for this and other worthwhile projects. With Ethel Fraser as our hostess, Marion Guild spent many hours on the mechanics of the production. Lynn DeChesser and Myrtle Elton provided assistance. Ann Young served as contact person for potential donors and lenders of photographs and for pre-orders of this volume. Gilbert Arnold and Jeannette Burdick, both Southwick-born, were proofreaders of the captions.These seven members merit an extra thank you. My young friend, Valerie Kuzmeskus, did research on and wrote about the ice harvesting operations on the Congamond Lakes. Kudos to her, and to my friend Audrey Sherman, who helped with the final proofreading. My gratitude is immense to my family, especially my husband Harold, for their support and love, and to God who gives us life and so many other blessings each day.

Patricia L. Odiorne, Editor